IMAGES
of America

FOREST CITY

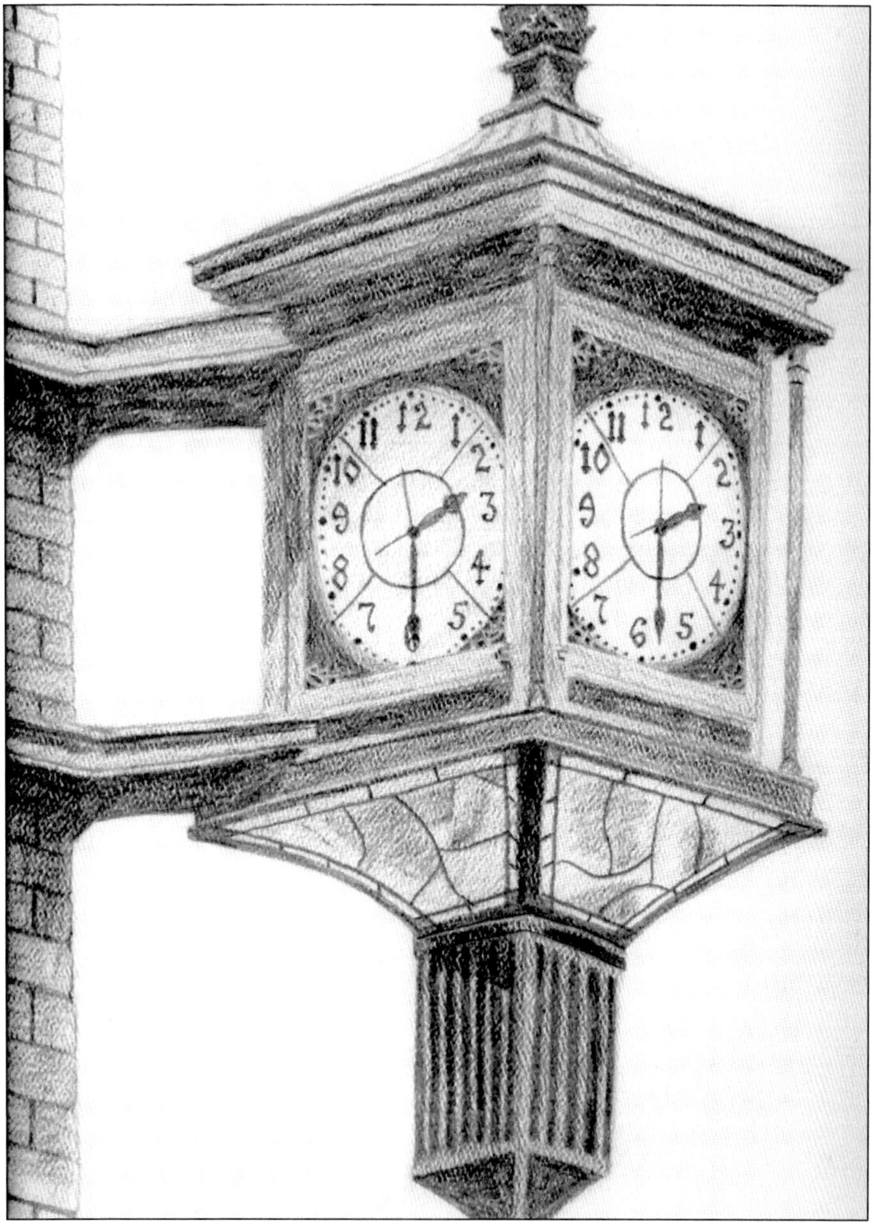

Mary Curtis shared her drawing of the functional town clock, originally on the Farmers Bank and Trust Company at Depot and Main. Worth Morgan (later vice president and manager of the Union Trust in Forest City) set the clock daily. Worth's brother Hicks Morgan, station master at the Forest City Southern Railway Depot, had Railroad Standard Time telegraphed to him daily; he shared the time with Worth at lunch. Worth's son, Bob, began changing the town clock's batteries monthly when he was only 10 years old.

On the Cover: The cover photo shows Albert Mauney and acquaintances in front of his car at Horn's Store. Albert had served in France with Willis Towery, for whom the American Legion Post #74 was named. (Courtesy of William Brown.)

IMAGES
of America

FOREST CITY

Anita Price Davis and
James M. Walker

ARCADIA
PUBLISHING

ISBN 978-0-7385-4218-8

Published by Arcadia Publishing
Charleston, South Carolina

Library of Congress Catalog Card Number: 2005932751

For all general information contact Arcadia Publishing at:
Telephone 843-853-2070
Fax 843-853-0044
E-mail sales@arcadiapublishing.com
For customer service and orders:
Toll-Free 1-888-313-2665

Visit us on the Internet at www.arcadiapublishing.com

This book is to honor Forest City, North Carolina: its people (past and present), its organizations, its milestones, and its prevailing positive presence in the county, the state, and the nation.

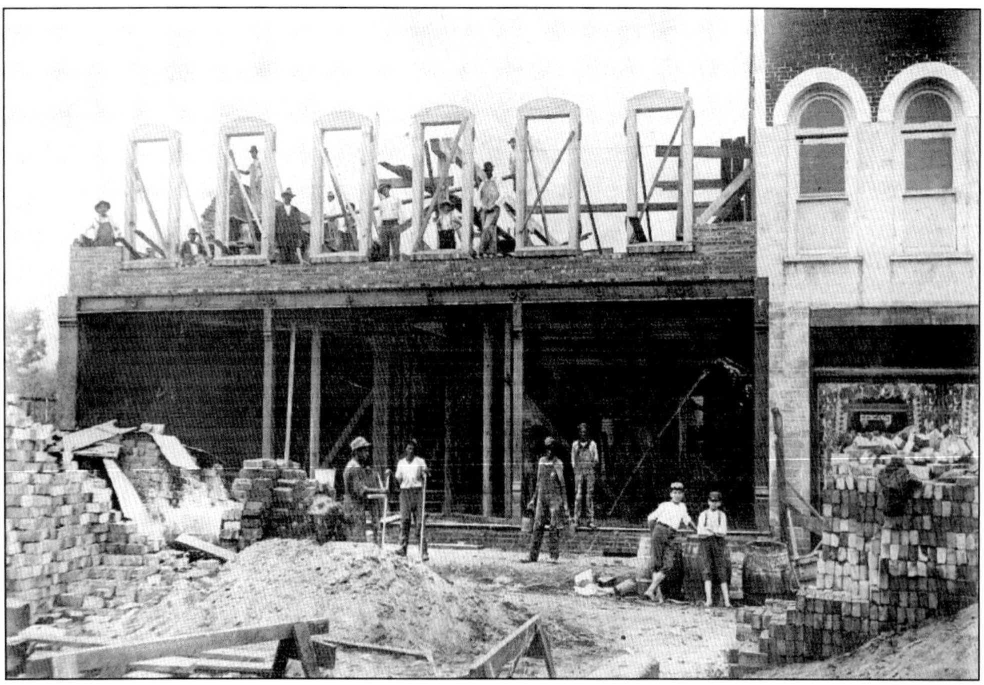

The construction of the earliest storefronts in Burnt Chimney/Forest City is something that no one today can remember. Images on film, however, remind the general public that Forest City should not be taken for granted. (Courtesy of Beth and Daniel King.)

Contents

Acknowledgments

The people of Forest City have generously shared their photographs and their information with each other and with us. Interestingly, several different sources would sometimes share the same image—evidence of the generosity of the people with one another and with us.

The help in publicizing our endeavors, the aid in conducting the interviews, the emotional support, the sharing of treasured materials, and the encouragement of others have aided in the production of Images of America: *Forest City*. The media and certain individuals have greatly facilitated the production of this work. These people include especially Virginia Rucker, Betty Jo Carpenter, and A. D. ("Al") Lancaster. Carolyn Barbee spent hours researching and sharing what she gleaned. Jeanne Price, Annette Martin, and Dan Martin worked untiringly—or at least without fail. Robert M. Watkins made his archives available to the authors. Others who generously helped were Louise Smith Blanton, Bill Brown (World War II Navy veteran and banker for 32 years), Betty Jo Carpenter, Martha Grace Estes, Maimy Thompson Gumbs, Louise Hunt, Geneva Jenkins, Sara Johnston, Sara Jolley, Hollis Owens Jr., Charlie Vess, Robert and Caroline Jones, Beth and Daniel King, Blaine Logan Jr., Martha Davis, Helen and Milton Higdon, Bill and Mary McArthur, Bob Morgan, and Clarence Griffin (through his works). Danielle Withrow, Jean Gordon, Jerrell Bedford, David Brown, Greg Hils, Jane Thompson Gurley, Frances Pilgrim, and Paul Tim Jones Jr. were generous and gracious. The Mooneyham Public Library and its staff (Mary Sandra Costner, Sue Toms, and Rita Womack), Jim Bishop and WCAB, Jim Brown and the *Courier*, Mary Curtis, and WAGY freely gave us their help. To all of you who volunteered information, thank you. In addition, our appreciation goes to the entire community, our families, and friends for continued confidence and interest.

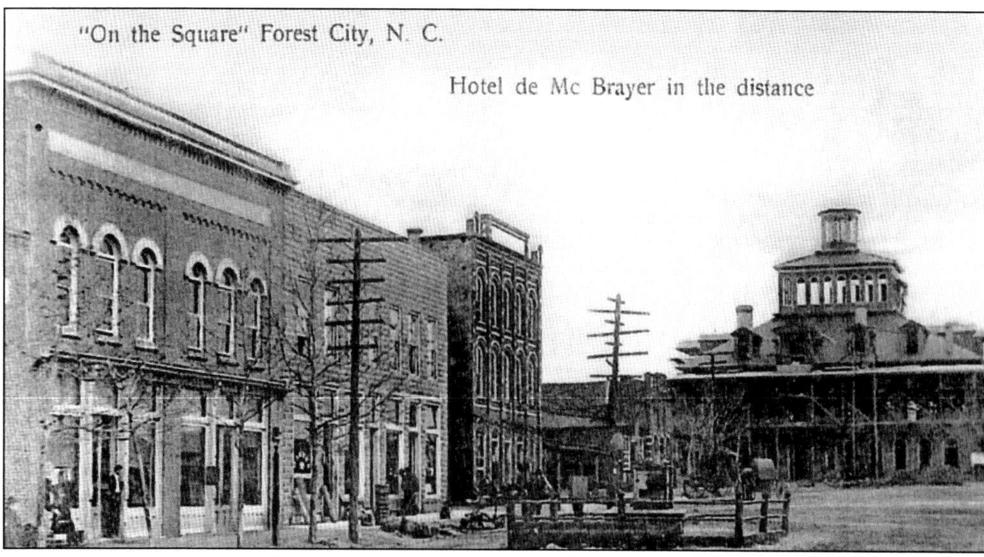

Dr. T. C. McBrayer owned both a local sanitarium for tuberculosis victims and the Mabree Hotel (also called the Mabry Hotel and the McBrayer Hotel). The Mabree was an important part of Forest City's landscape. "Will" McArthur's photograph shows the hotel under construction. The watering trough in the center of the square indicates the year is c. 1904. (Courtesy of Beth and Daniel King.)

INTRODUCTION

Prior to 1749, the area now known as Rutherford County was the frontier and, according to Clarence Griffin, was "almost indefinable. . . .[The county] covered a large territory, the major portion of it uninhabited by the white man, and claimed [by the Cherokee tribe of Native Americans]" (Griffin, *History of Old Tryon and Rutherford County*, Asheville: Miller Pringin, 1937, 4–7; hereafter referred to as Griffin).

In 1768, the Colonial lawmakers created Tryon County from the western portions of Mecklenburg County. Within that area were 13 townships; it would, however, be 1778 before the North Carolina Assembly would vote to separate Tryon County into Rutherford County and Lincoln County.

The region now known as Rutherford County probably had the most organized militia of any county in the state (Griffin, 4-5, 7, 42). The people within that region were divided in their loyalties during the Revolutionary War. Some called themselves Patriots; others called themselves Tories or Loyalists. Men from the county participated in the Battle of Kings Mountain (1780) and the Battle of Cowpens (1781). When the hostilities ceased, the residents tried to resume their daily lives:

> Rutherford County after the war had a very simple social structure. The county had no villages. The only manufacturing was in the home; commerce—interrupted by the War—had not revived. There were no newspapers in the county, currency had depreciated, religious instruction was skimpy, markets were poor, and highways were bad. The fields of activity were on the farm, in the home, and in the forests only (Griffin, 119).

The 1790 Census reported Rutherford County with 1,136 "Heads of families" and 164 families, with 611 slaves. The total population was about 7,775. The population increased rapidly; by 1810, it had grown to about 13,202. (Griffin, 123, 125, 149.)

Rutherfordton, the oldest town in the county, became the county seat. Smaller, unorganized communities began to spring up, particularly at crossroads. Rich, fertile soil surrounded one particular county crossroads: that at the juncture of the Shelby-Rutherfordton Road and the Spartanburg-Lincolnton Road. The level terrain made the locality a favorite agricultural community. A well-known landmark near this crossroads was the home that James McArthur built in 1830 (Historical Subcommittee of the Rutherford County Bicentennial Committee, *Rutherford County 1979: A People's Bicentennial History*, 467, Rutherfordton: Liberty Press). The neighboring community acquired the name Burnt Chimney after the James McArthur House burned in the 1850s. Burnt Chimney became the official name of the village in 1861, when the first post office was located in the John Bostick house, built in 1825.

By the time North Carolina had seceded from the federal union in 1861, public opinion in Rutherford County generally favored the Confederacy. Competition to prepare an entire militia company for active duty arose particularly between two communities: Rutherfordton (the county seat) and Burnt Chimney. The Burnt Chimney Volunteers drilled and paraded near the charred grounds of the James McArthur house. What is now the central square of Forest City encompassed the muster site.

On Monday, June 3, 1861, a huge crowd gathered at the Burnt Chimney Muster Ground, which is now marked with a memorial from the United Daughters of the Confederacy. After several citizens gave patriotic speeches, Rev. T. Butler Justice preached a sermon as the Volunteers stood in company formation. At the end of the program, the soldiers bade their families and friends farewell and departed on foot for camp in Raleigh. The Burnt Chimney Volunteers became

Company D of the North Carolina 16th Infantry Regiment. The next day, the Rutherfordton Volunteers (Rutherfordton Riflemen) departed for Raleigh to become Company G of the 16th North Carolina Regiment (Griffin, 249–250).

In 1877, the General Assembly incorporated the town of Burnt Chimney with its 110 residents. Burnt Chimney became Forest City on March 7, 1887, when the General Assembly ratified the act amending the town's charter. The name came from a prominent citizen: Forest Davis, the husband of Molly Harrill, the father of J. W. Davis, and the grandfather of Toliver Davis, Tom Davis, and Jack Davis (Griffin, 341, 353).

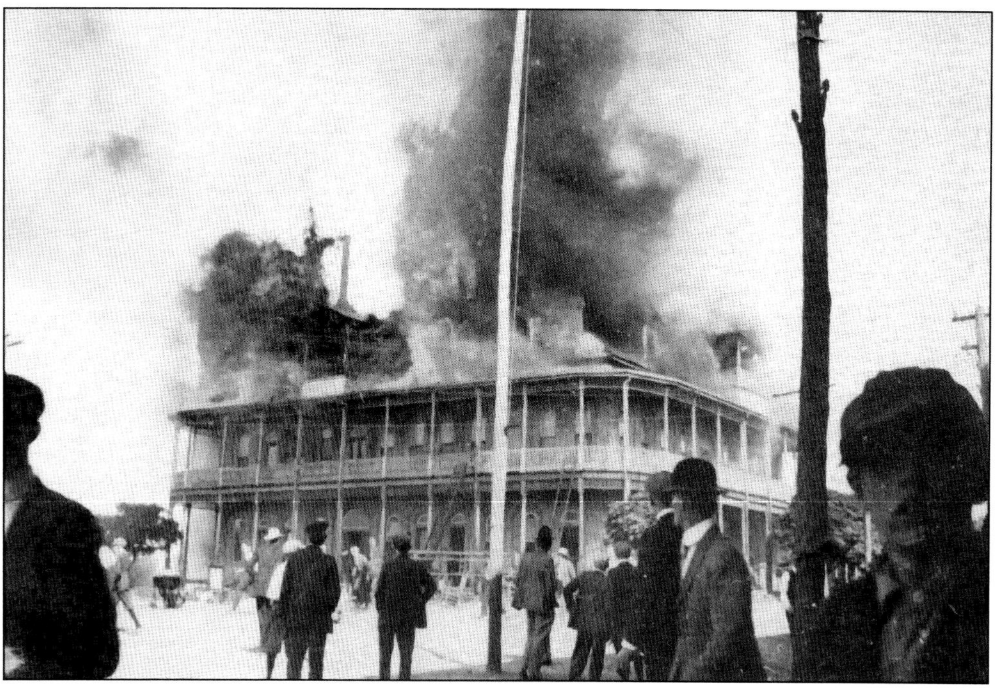

The fire at the McArthur home that gave the Burnt Chimney its name was not the first or the last to sear the town. When the Mabree Hotel (also called the Mabry and the McBrayer) burned in September 1918, Will McArthur was there to preserve images. Second from right and wearing the bowler hat and white collar is J. F. Alexander. (Courtesy of Bill Brown.)

One

Churches in the Community
Meeting Spiritual Needs

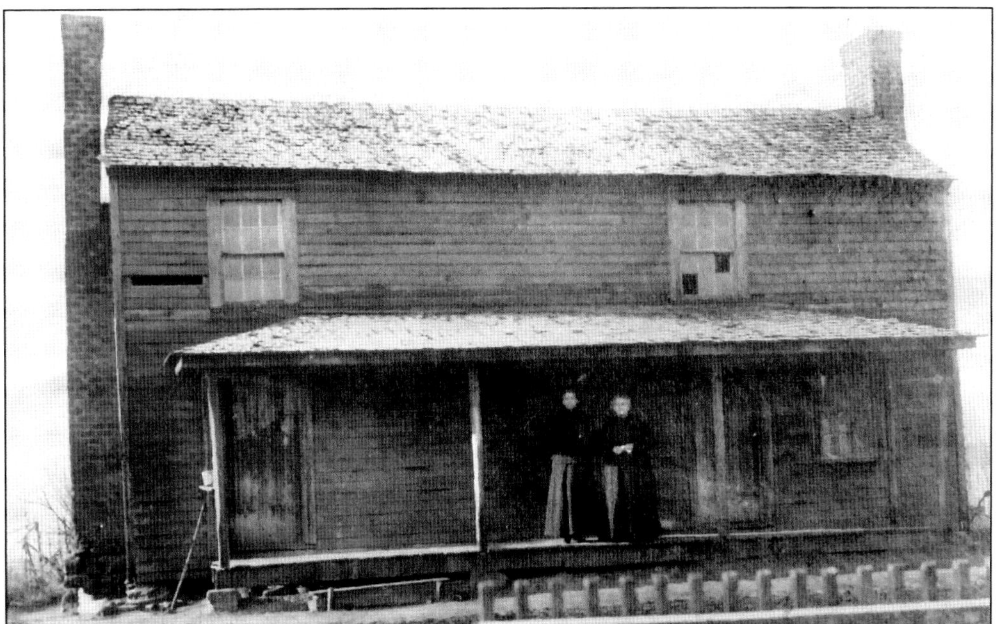

"It is impossible to separate the history of Forest City from its churches," notes Betty Jo Carpenter, First Baptist Church historian. With more than 40 churches in Forest City in 2005, this book could not spotlight all the churches and denominations; it uses a historical perspective and begins with the John Bostick (later "Bostic") home, built in 1825. The house near 300 West Main was the site where 17 interested individuals organized, in December 1848, the first Burnt Chimney/Forest City church: Cool Springs Baptist. Parishioners used the Bostick House for seven years. In 1861, the Bostick House served as the Burnt Chimney post office. (Courtesy of First Baptist Church.)

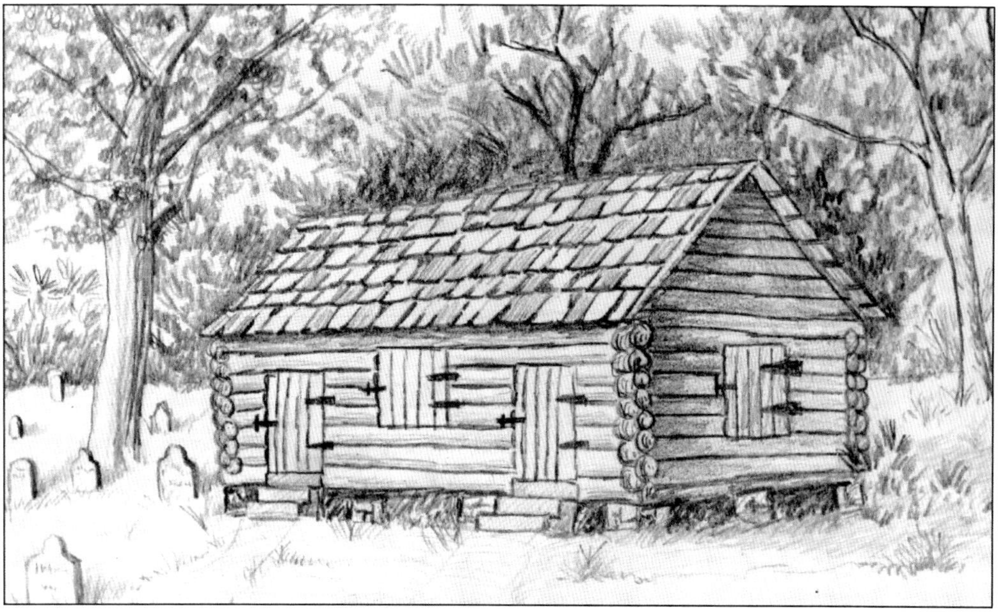

Cool Springs Baptist Church met in the Bostick house until 1855. The congregation constructed the first church building in the Burnt Chimney area. Built of logs, the meetinghouse stood on 3.3 acres of land on present-day Vance Street. The first deacon was John Bostick, and the first pastor was Elder William Harrill. The sketch is by Louis Wessier. (Courtesy of First Baptist.)

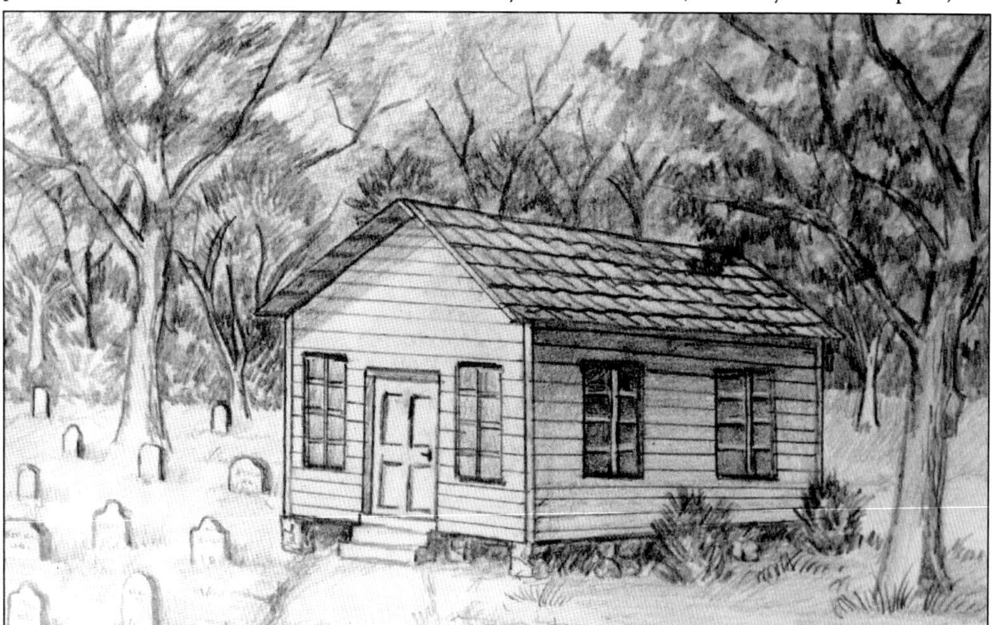

A clapboard frame church—near the present-day Cool Springs Cemetery—replaced the log structure from 1867 to 1889. Louis Wessier's sketch is courtesy of the First Baptist Church and church historian Betty Jo Carpenter. Betty Jo (Mrs. R. E. Carpenter Jr.), a graduate of Converse College as a music major, has taught in public schools, churches, and colleges; she was minister of music at First Baptist Church and county president of the Little Symphony. She received the Converse 1999 Career Achievement Award.

In 1889, a new brick structure at the corner of West Main and Church Streets replaced the clapboard building. Phate Hardin fired the bricks for this first brick building in Forest City. On February 22, 1889, 131 members entered their new church—Forest City Baptist Church. In 1913, construction of the present-day facility at 211 West Main began. The old brick structure served as a school from 1915 to 1922. (Courtesy of Sara Jolley.)

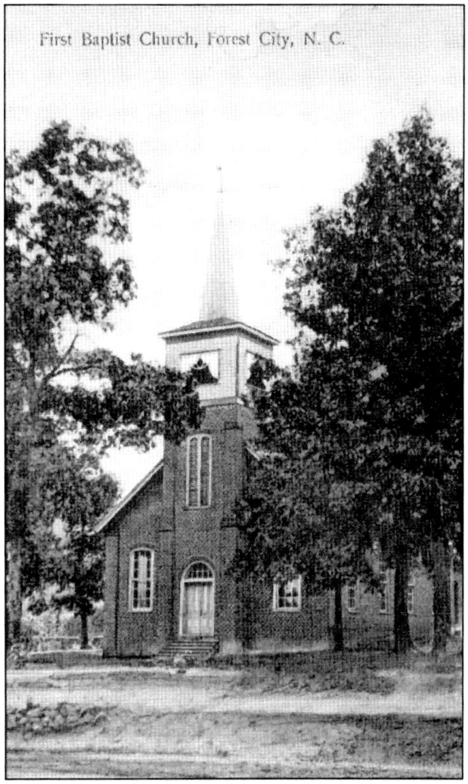

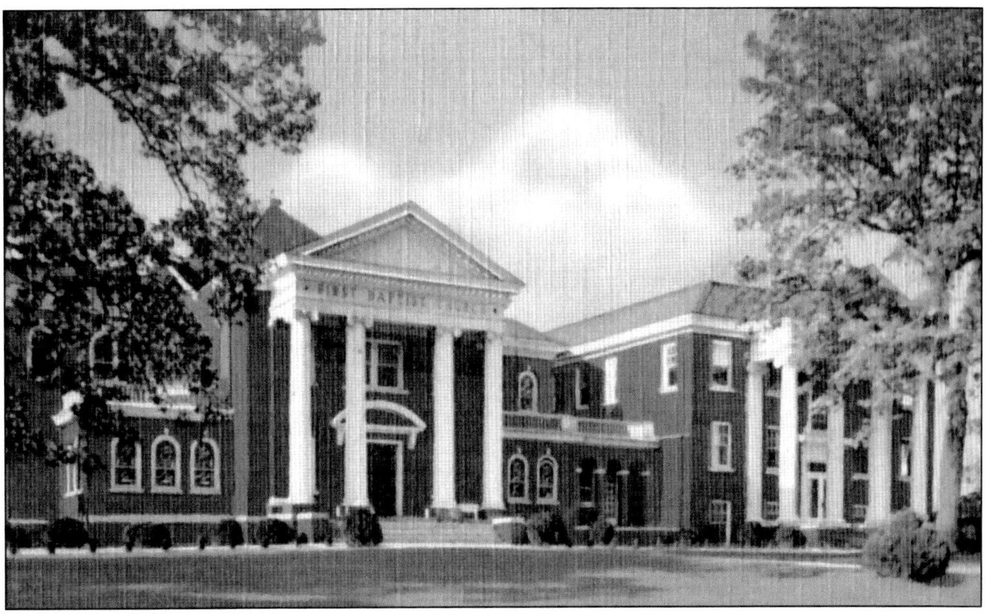

The Forest City Baptist Church congregation moved to 211 West Main in 1915 and—with the organization of Florence Baptist Church—changed its name to First Baptist in 1922. In 1925, the congregation voted to erect its education building (the J. F. Alexander Memorial Building). Both buildings reflect James M. McMichael's Classical Revival style of architecture and have been on the National Registry of Historic Places since 1989. (Photograph by Will McArthur.)

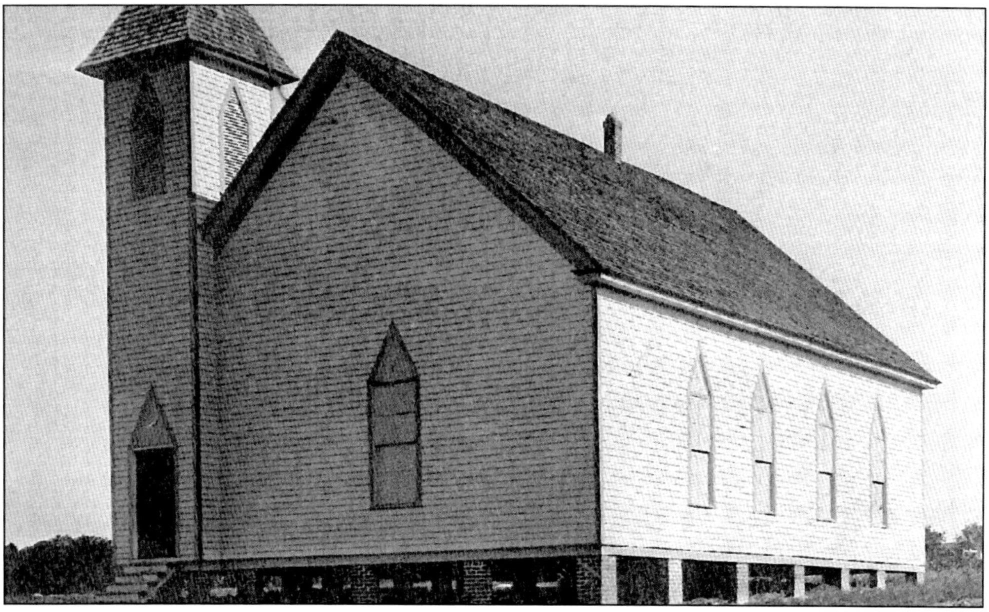

"Forest City and the . . . Methodist Church have grown up together," said the *Courier* on September 21, 1939. Dr. Phillip Grose established Pleasant Grove Methodist Church in 1838. The present-day Pleasant Grove United Methodist Church (outside the Burnt Chimney community) was the "mother" of the First United Methodist Church at 341 East Main (*Rutherford County 1979*, 333). The first church was made of logs; the second (on this postcard), from 1875, was framed. (Courtesy of Beth and Daniel King.)

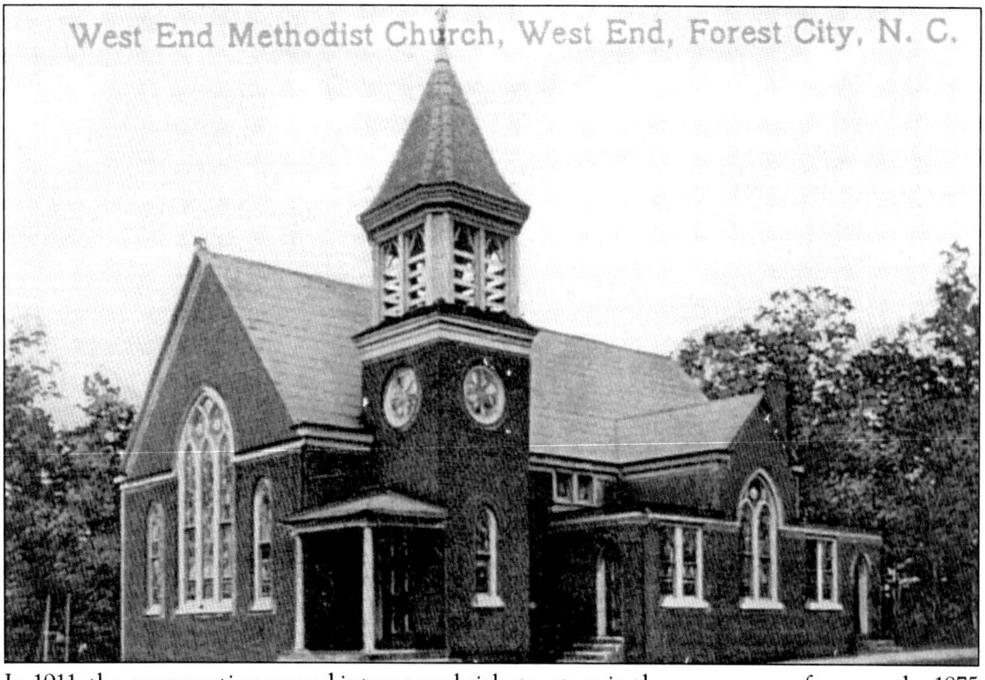

In 1911, the congregation moved into a new, brick structure in the same grove of trees as the 1875 building. Pleasant Grove United Methodist Church still uses the 250 Hudlow Road structure. (Courtesy of Beth and Daniel King.)

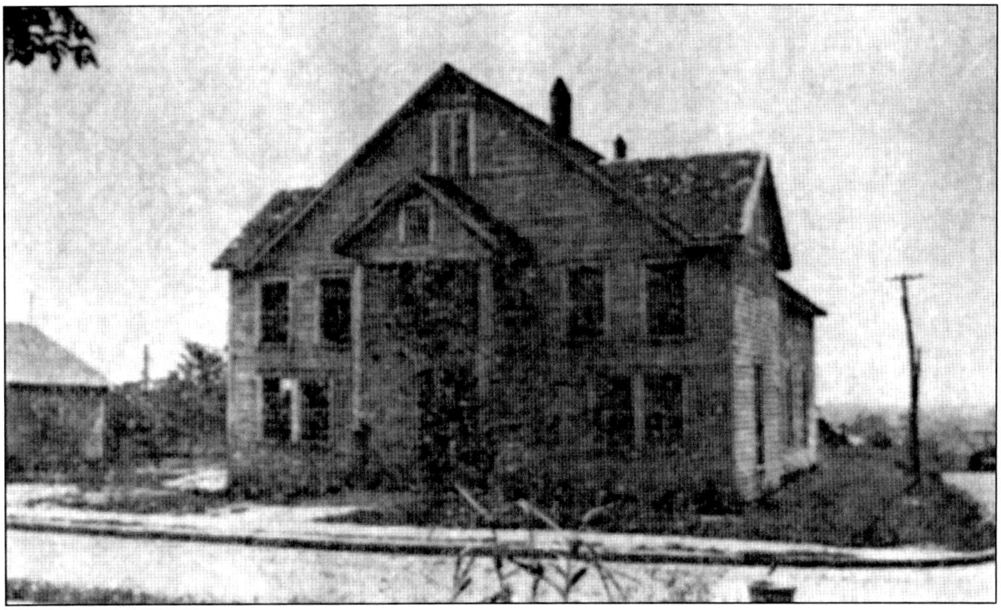

A centrally located structure for Methodists was important as the population of Forest City increased. In 1889, the congregation met in the upstairs of a store building on the south side of Main Street. In 1891, construction of a frame, two-story structure began. This building was later moved to the corner of Oak and Church Streets and used by the Missionary Methodist congregation. (Courtesy of Frances Pilgrim.)

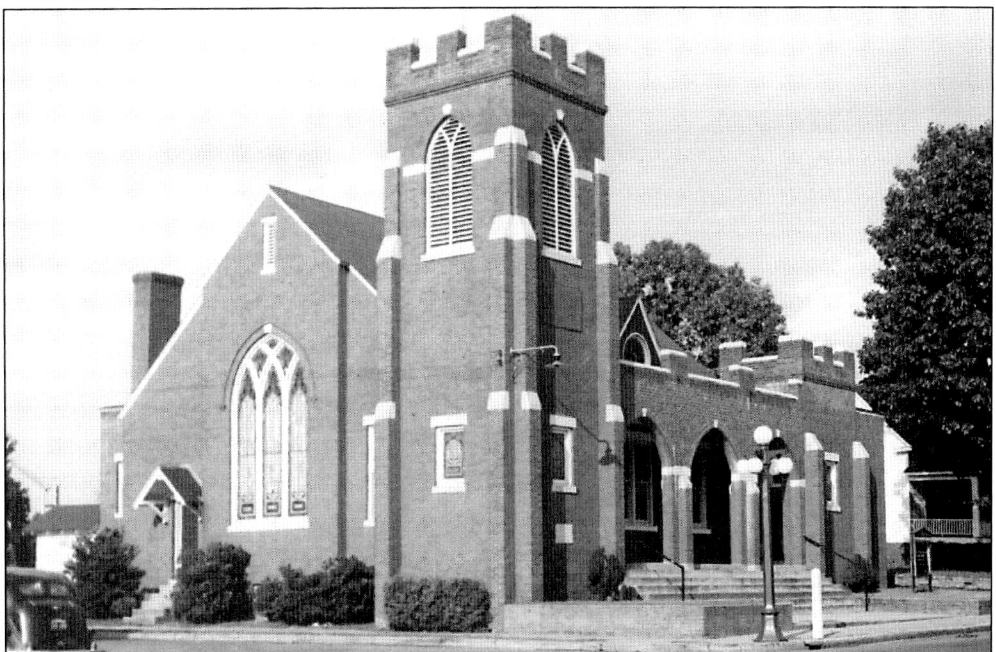

In 1914, the Methodists built (at a cost of $7,000) a brick church at East Main and North Broadway Streets. The cornerstone contained a Bible, church papers, the church discipline, a hymnbook, minutes of the last conference, a copy of the *Forest City Free Press*, and a silver offering. (Courtesy of Beth and Daniel King.)

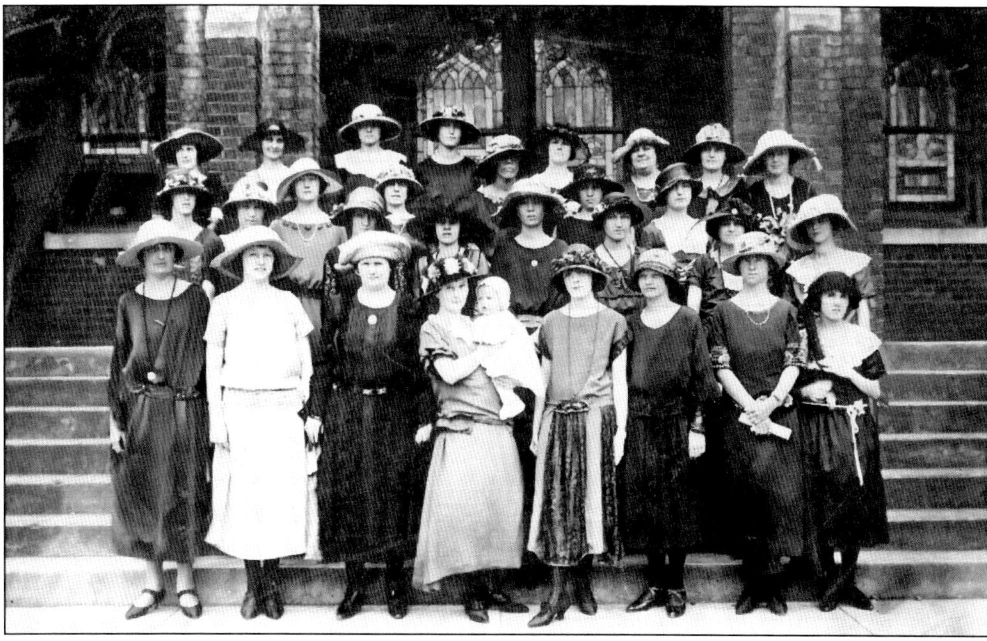

Mrs. J. F. Alexander's Women's Sunday School Class of 1920–1921, Forest City Methodist Church, included, from left to right, (first row) Virginia Holmes McDaniel, Myrtle Tate Higgins, Eunice Tate McDaniel, Mrs. Ben Smith and Ben Jr., Emaline Goforth Whisnant, Maybelle Jones, Minnie Smith, and Ellie Credle; (second row) Mildred Hardin Lee, Lois Davis, Clara Reid Myers, two unidentified, Inez Doggett Roberson, Oveta Sherlin Dobbins, unidentified, Ruth Dorsey Roberson, Frances Holmes McCausland, and two unidentified; (third row) Amelia Stephenson, Mattie Lytle, Kathleen Dorsey Smart, Vera Whisnant, Grace McKeithan Moore, Kathleen Young Alexander, Sudie Young Harris, and Oeland Moore Dorsey. (Courtesy of Beth and Daniel King.)

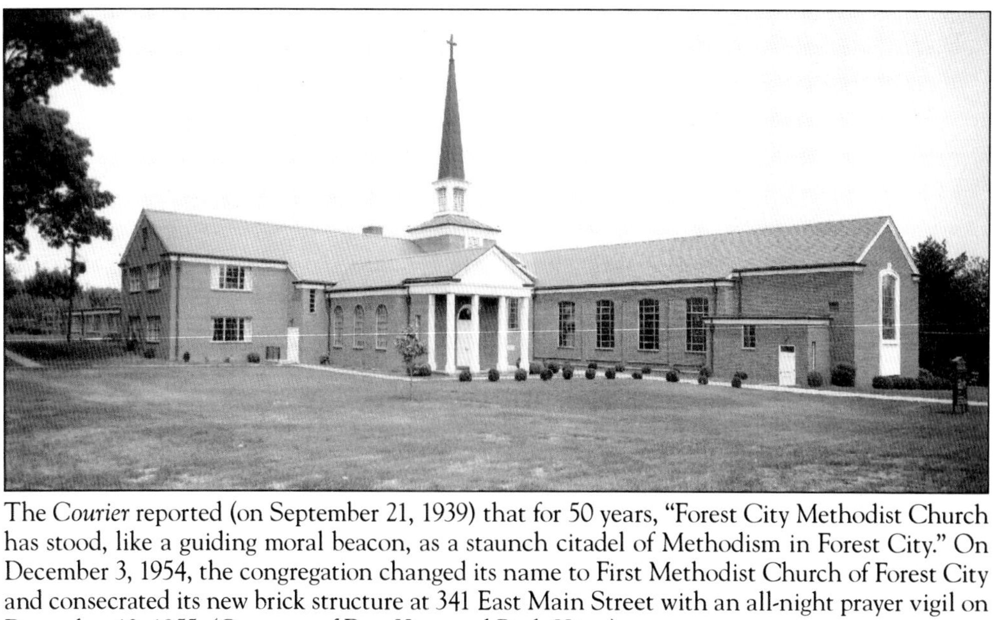

The *Courier* reported (on September 21, 1939) that for 50 years, "Forest City Methodist Church has stood, like a guiding moral beacon, as a staunch citadel of Methodism in Forest City." On December 3, 1954, the congregation changed its name to First Methodist Church of Forest City and consecrated its new brick structure at 341 East Main Street with an all-night prayer vigil on December 10, 1955. (Courtesy of Dan King and Beth King.)

By 1905, Forest City had four congregations: Baptists, Methodists, Wesleyans, and Presbyterians. Rev. Oliver H. Campbell organized its Wesleyan Methodist Church on November 2, 1902. Twelve members met in a rented, Liberty Street dwelling for four years. In 1907, they moved into their Liberty Street Church. T. C. McBrayer donated funds for the 1922 Wesleyan Church on Mill Street. (Courtesy of James M. Walker.)

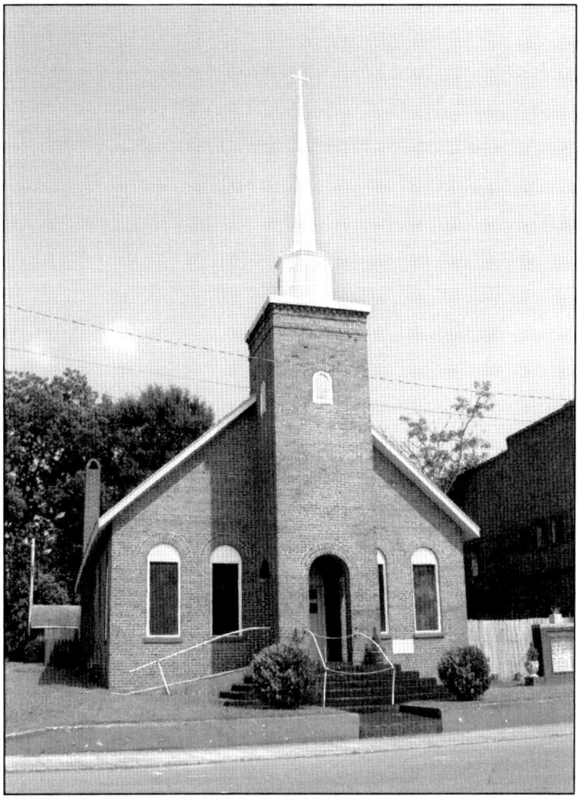

The First Wesleyan Church of Forest City—one of 1,700 Wesleyan congregations in the United States—currently worships at 1102 Church Street, in a building completed in 1966. (Courtesy of James M. Walker.)

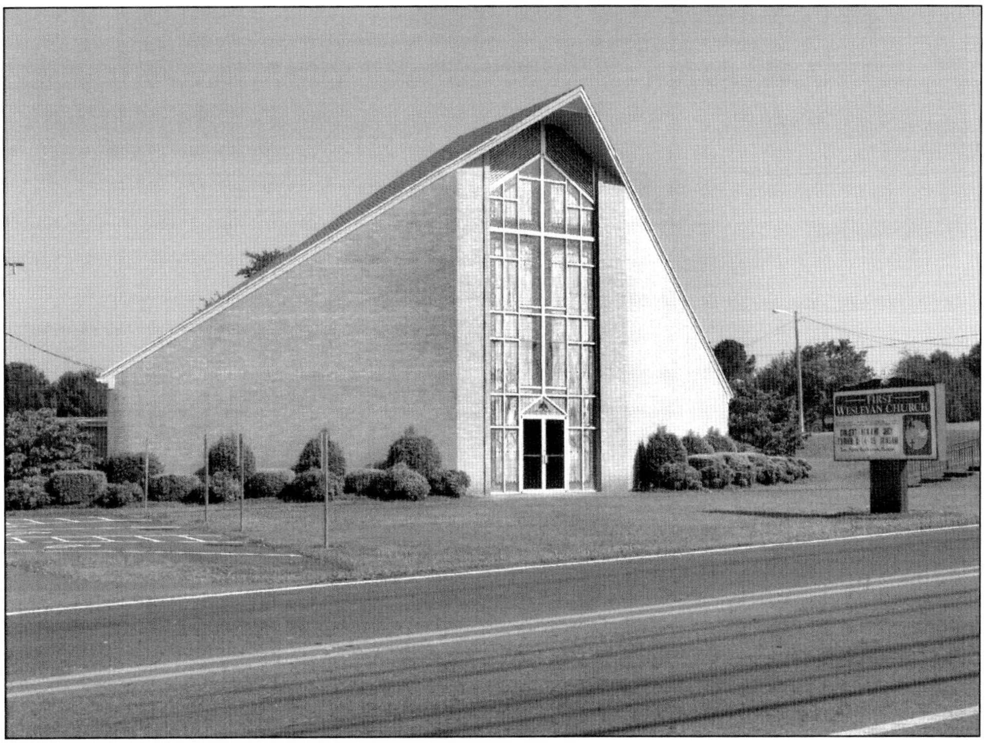

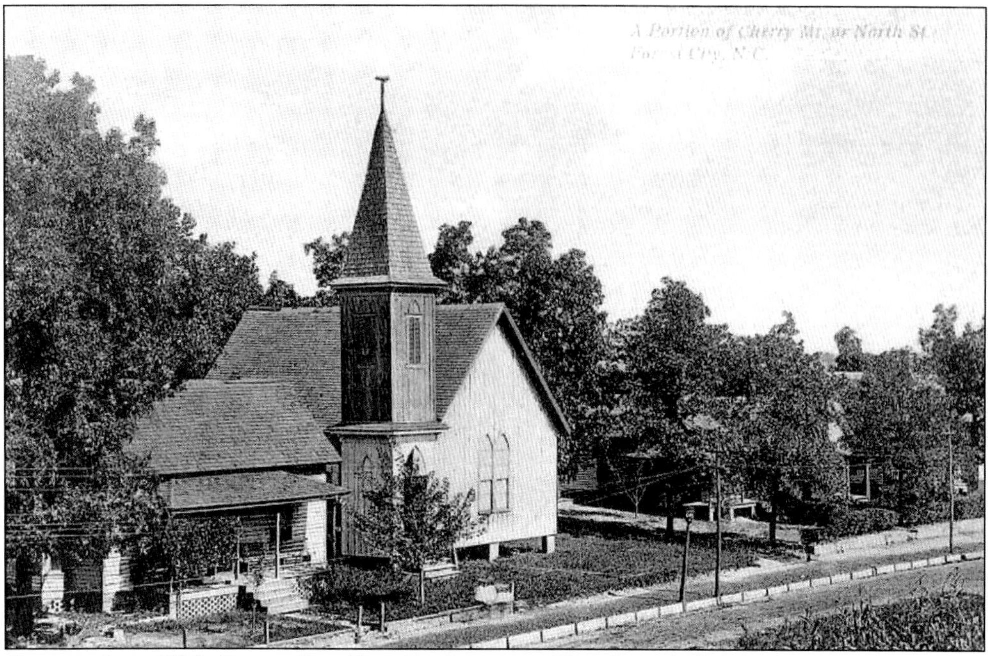

Organized in 1895, Forest City First Presbyterian Church included James E. and Margaret McFarland, Mr. and Mrs. Dorman, and W. P. McCorkle (part-time pastor). Members met monthly in the Methodist church, the old schoolhouse, and the Baptist church. In 1896, members bought land on Cherry Mountain Street and budgeted $392 for construction (*A History of 100 Years*, First Presbyterian Church, Forest City, 1995).

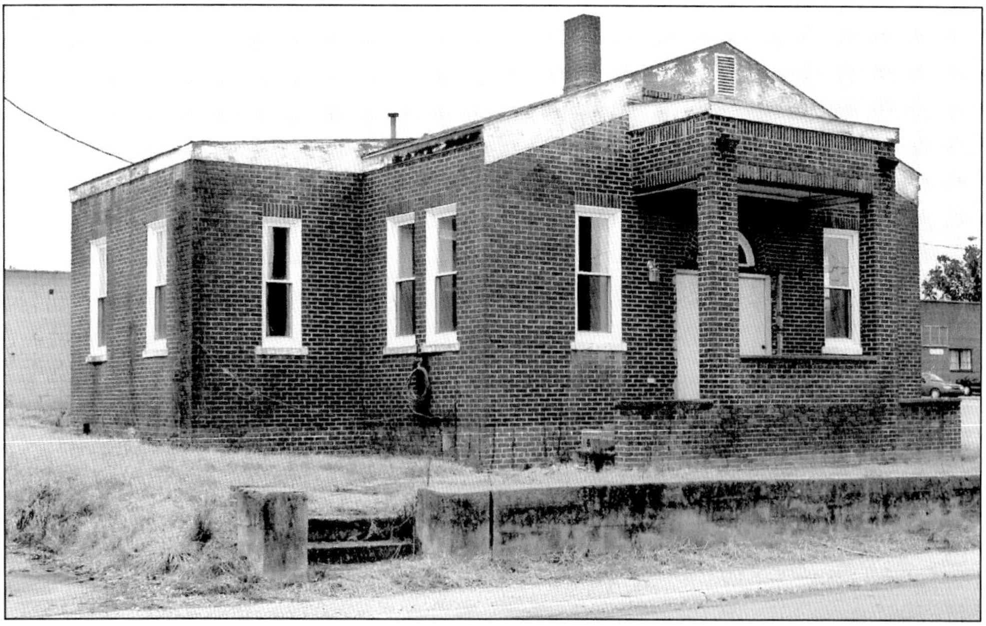

By 1911, the First Presbyterian Church had 20 members. When the wooden Cherry Mountain Street church burned by April 1925 the 46 members had built a red brick building. The new brick building was debt-free because of the untiring efforts of Elder McFarland. The church depended on 10 part-time pastors (*A History of 100 Years*). (Courtesy of James M. Walker.)

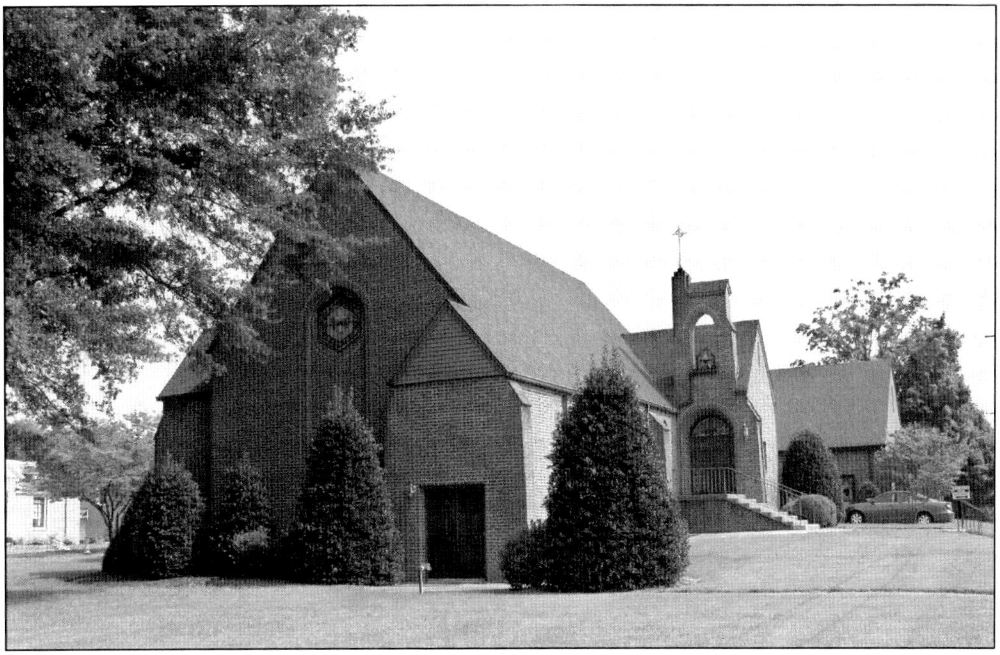

Dr. Oliver G. Jones became the first full-time minister of the First Presbyterian Church in 1938. The 20 members shared him with Ellenboro Presbyterian Church. On July 28, 1940, 67 members dedicated their West Main Street structure; their next pastor, Dr. Allen McSween, was drafted for World War II. In 1995, the 186 First Presbyterian Church members celebrated the centennial. (Courtesy of James M. Walker.)

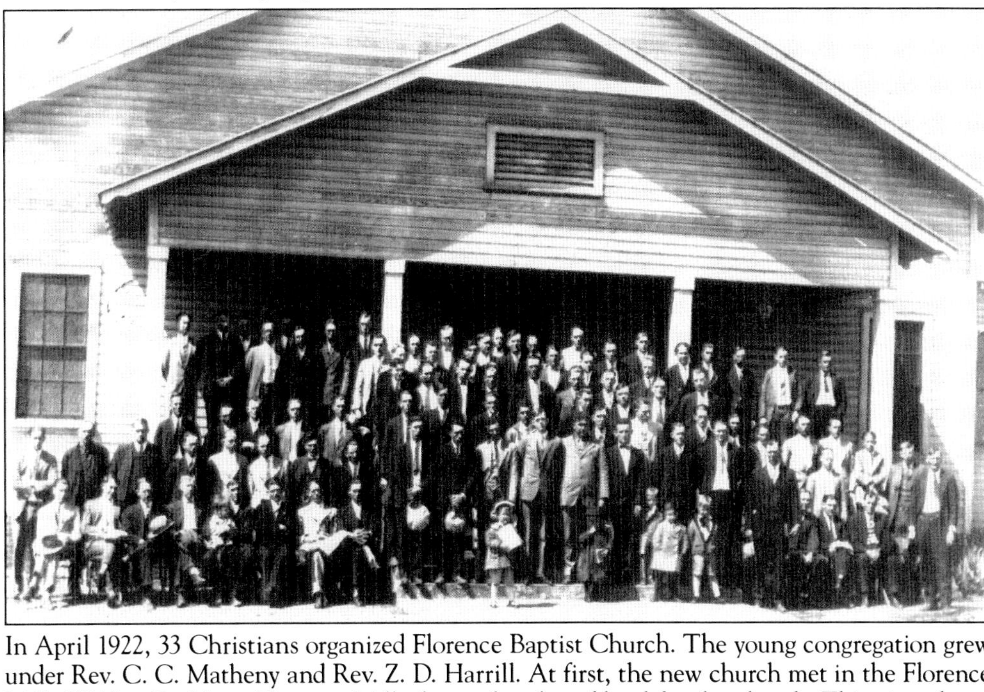

In April 1922, 33 Christians organized Florence Baptist Church. The young congregation grew under Rev. C. C. Matheny and Rev. Z. D. Harrill. At first, the new church met in the Florence Mills Welfare Building. Florence Mills donated a plot of land for the church. This view shows some members in front of the wooden structure. (Courtesy of Paul Tim Jones Jr.)

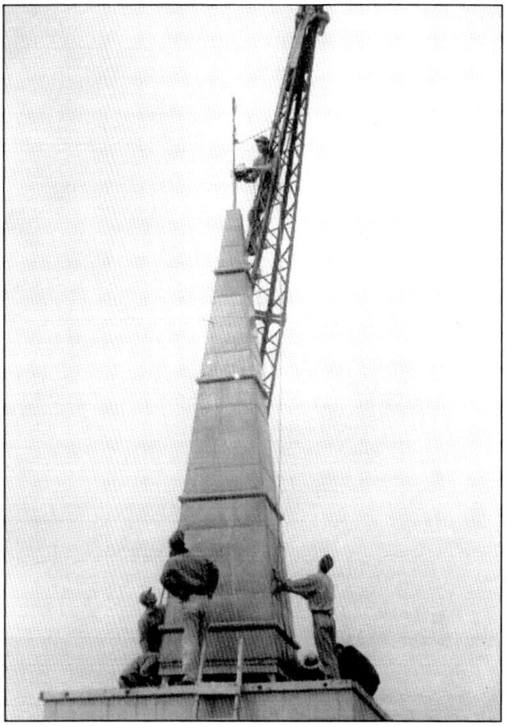

This view shows the setting of the steeple at the Florence Baptist Church. A crane (in the background) hoisted the spire, made by McArthur's Tin Shop. (Courtesy of William H. McArthur.)

The present Florence Baptist Church at 201 South Broadway opened for worship on June 23, 1991. In 2005, the pastor was Dr. Bobby D. Gantt, who had served the congregation since 1985. In 1996, the church boasted more than 800 members. (Courtesy of James M. Walker.)

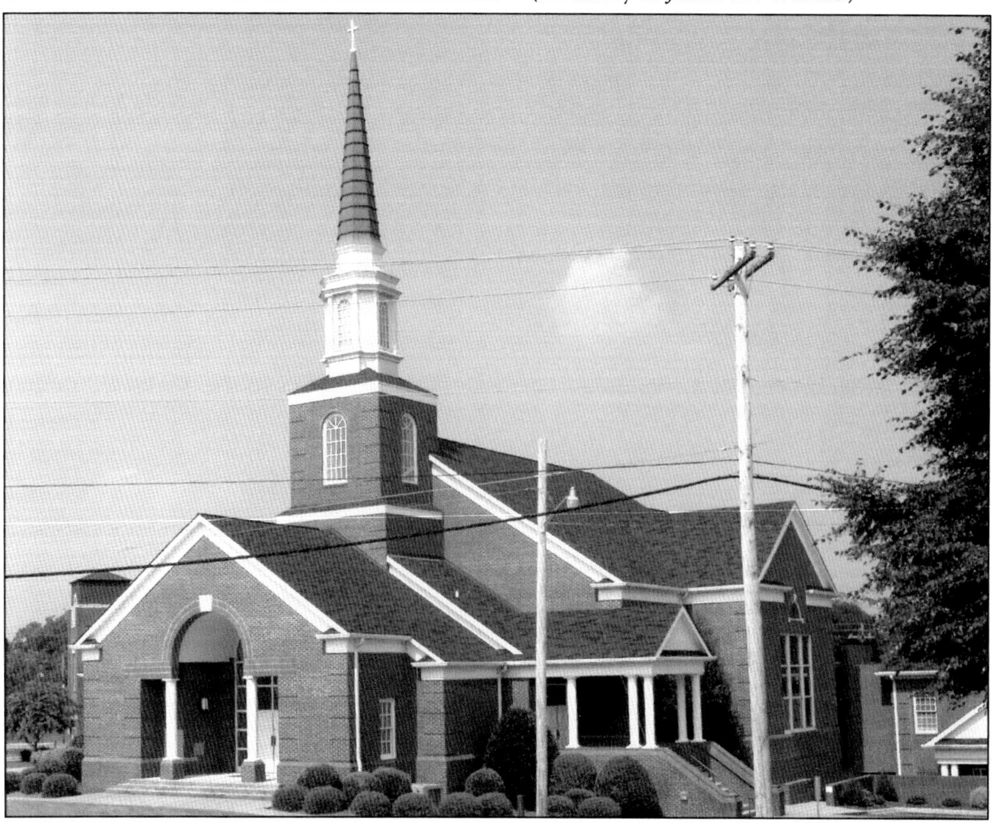

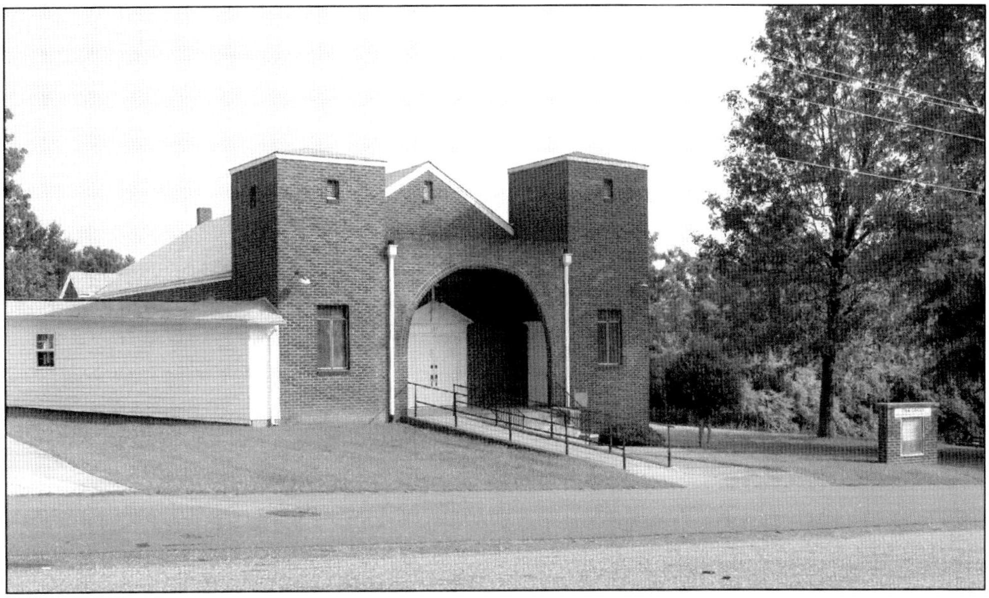

Separate facilities met spiritual and social needs during segregation. Important in the early 1900s was Oak Grove Baptist Church (now Oak Grove Missionary Baptist Church, Inc.). Rev. Howard Taft Dodd noted, "a few pious souls in an effort to satisfy their spiritual hunger formed a small prayer band, which met in several different homes or other places that they could secure." This continued until the members completed their church in 1924; they rebuilt in 1943, but wartime shortages made a quality building difficult. In 1954, they completed the present building (*Rutherford County 1979*, 293–300). (Courtesy of James M. Walker.)

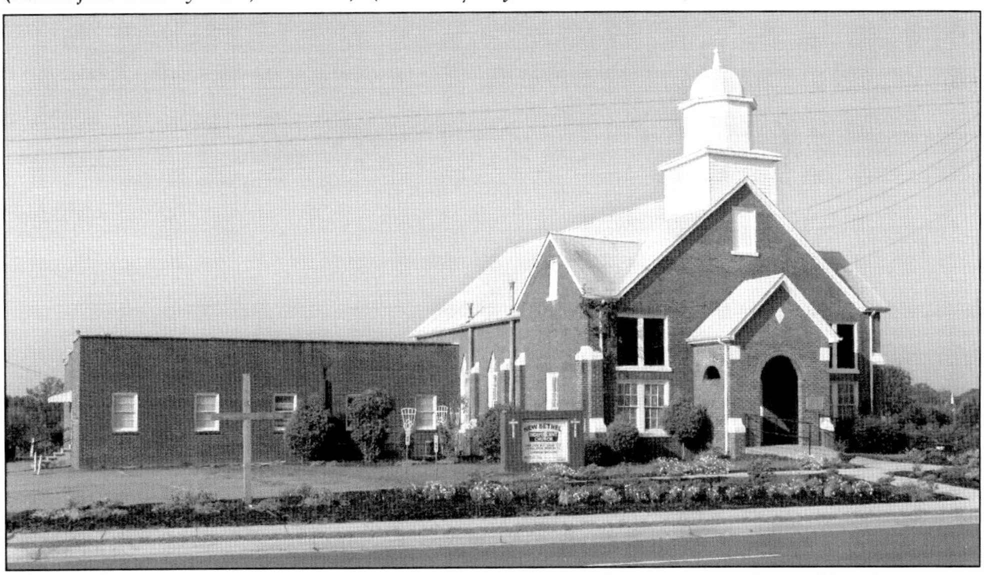

Pastors for the New Bethel Independent Church include Legusta Jackson (the first pastor in 1974), Billy Casey, and (2005) Wallace Gregory. Originally meeting in 1974 at 102 Mills Street, the congregation purchased the Oak and Church Streets building from the Missionary Methodists, who succeeded the Forest City Methodist Church. The church has occupied two separate locations and has housed three congregations. (Information courtesy of Anita Patterson; photograph courtesy of James M. Walker.)

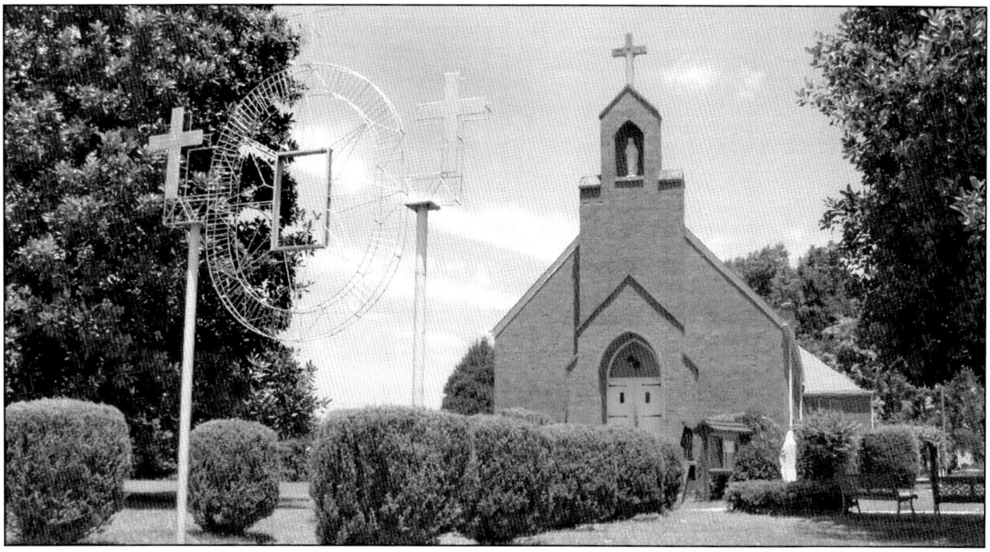

In 1940, Rutherford County had Catholics but no Catholic church. Catholics drove to St. Mary's Church in Shelby for mass. In the 1940s, local Catholics purchased land at 1024 West Main Street and dedicated the Immaculate Conception Catholic Church on September 15, 1950. By 2001, the church had 300 families and had purchased 7.5 acres for a new facility in 2005. (Information courtesy of Immaculate Conception Catholic Church; photograph courtesy of James M. Walker.)

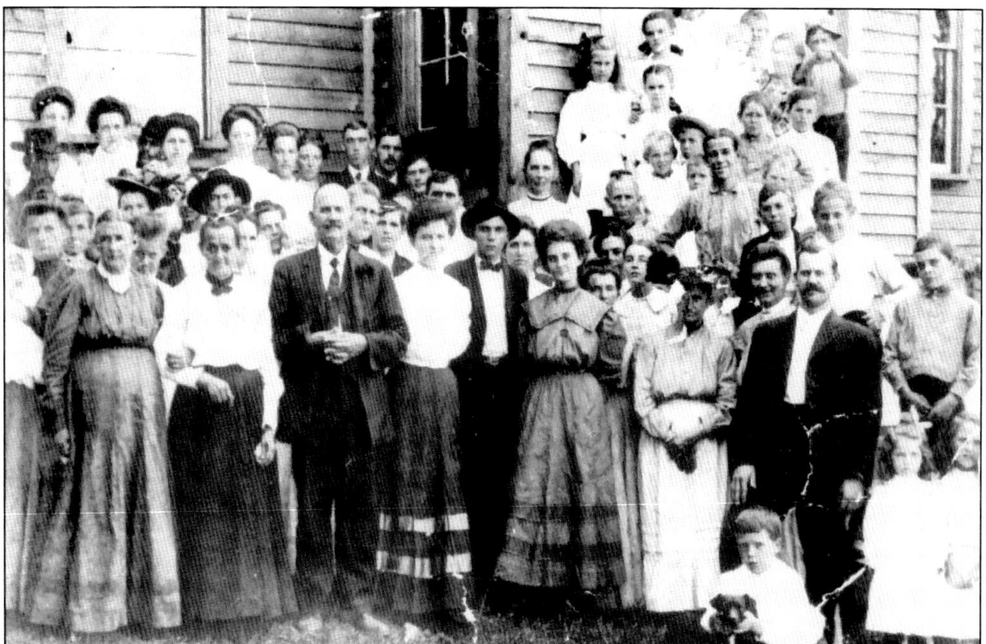

The Missionary Methodist Church purchased in 1913 the Methodist church building at Trade and North Broadway; they moved it to Oak and Church, a lot leased from Florence Mills. Third from left is Pastor "Uncle" Henry Clay Sisk (founder of the Forest City Missionary Methodist Church) with some of his members. (Courtesy of Mrs. Frances Goforth Pilgrim and *My Life Story*, by Rev. H. C. Sisk.)

Two

Markers, Memorials, and Monuments
Remembering

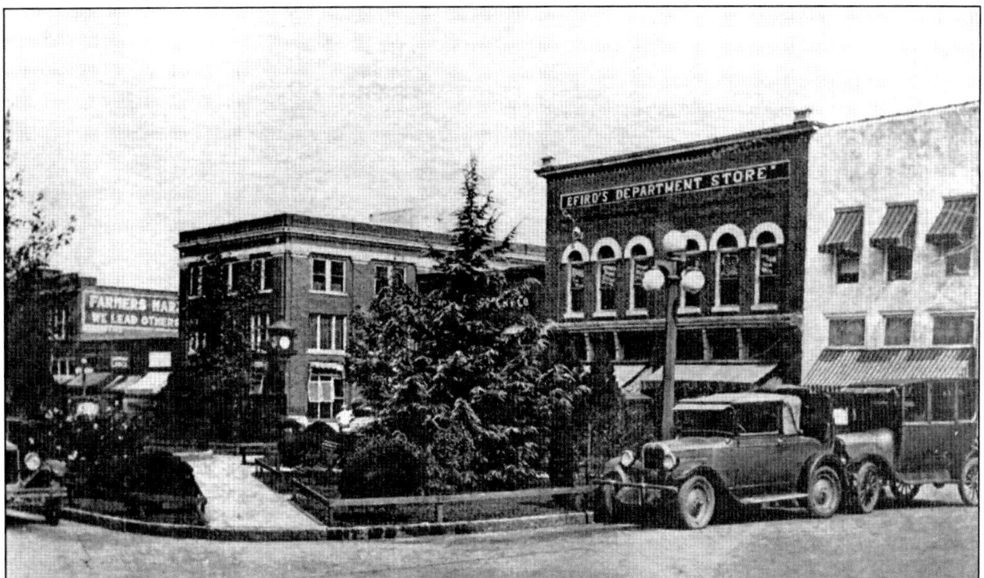

Forest City acknowledges its past and its people. Markers and monuments serve as reminders. Even the central square of Forest City helps citizens remember. In 1914, the town's Betterment Club determined to beautify Main Street. Officers for the club were Mrs. T. R. Padgett, president; Mrs. A. V. Falvey, secretary; and Mrs. G. P. Reid, treasurer. The postcard view is called "A Bit of the Square." (Courtesy of Charles Vess and Danielle Withrow.)

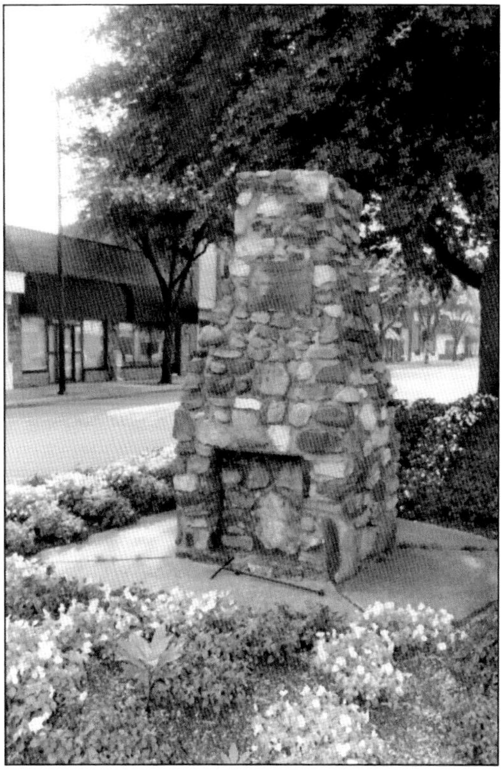

On February 26, 1977—the day before Burnt Chimney's centennial—townspeople brought stones at the request of Gene Blanton, Kiwanis Club chair. The marker on the resulting chimney (six feet high and two feet thick) reads: "The town of Burnt Chimney, 1877–1887. Changed to Forest City, 1887." The name came from Forest Davis, merchant and father of J. W. Davis. (Information courtesy of *Courier, One-Hundredth Anniversary Edition, 1977*; photo courtesy of James M. Walker.)

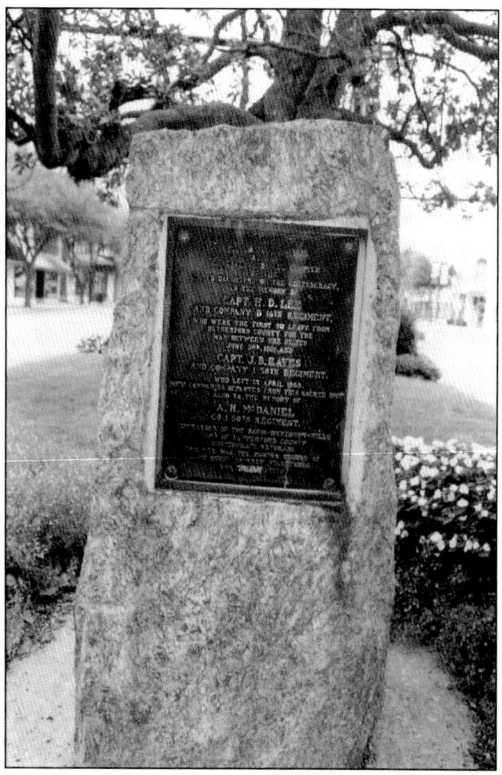

On the west plaza of the Public Square in Forest City is a monument that marks the site of the old Burnt Chimney Muster Ground, used from 1861 to 1865. The monument was a gift from the Lee-Eaves-McDaniel Chapter of the United Daughters of the Confederacy (organized on March 14, 1931). (Courtesy of James M. Walker.)

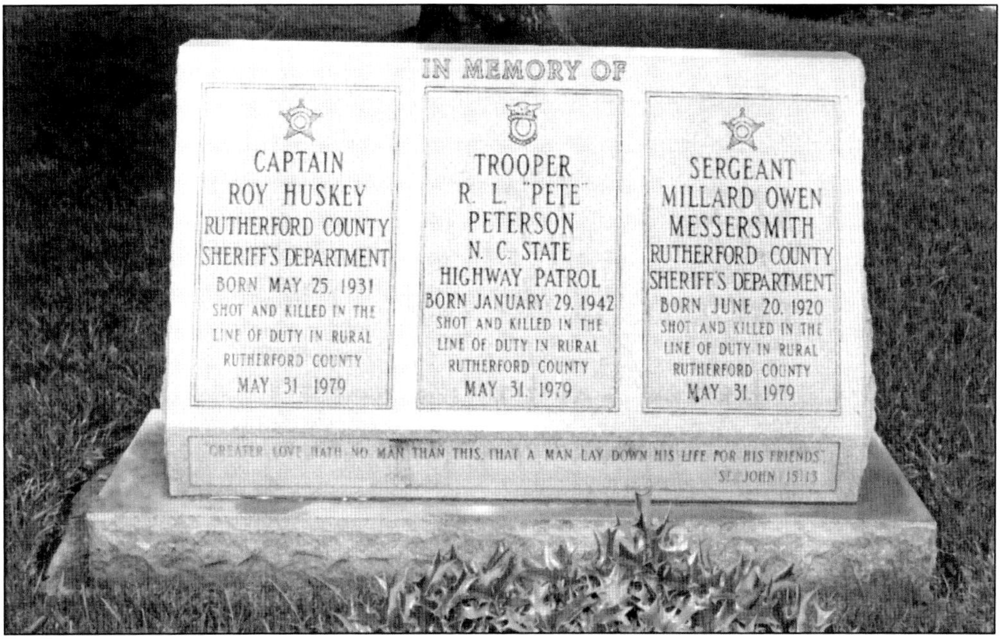

The Public Square on Main Street in Forest City, North Carolina, has one marker in honor of Capt. Roy Huskey (May 25, 1931–May 31, 1979) of the Rutherford County Sheriff's Department, Trooper R. L. Peterson (January 29, 1947–May 31, 1979), and Sgt. Millard Owen Messersmith (June 20, 1920–May 31, 1979). All three men died in the line of duty. (Courtesy of James M. Walker.)

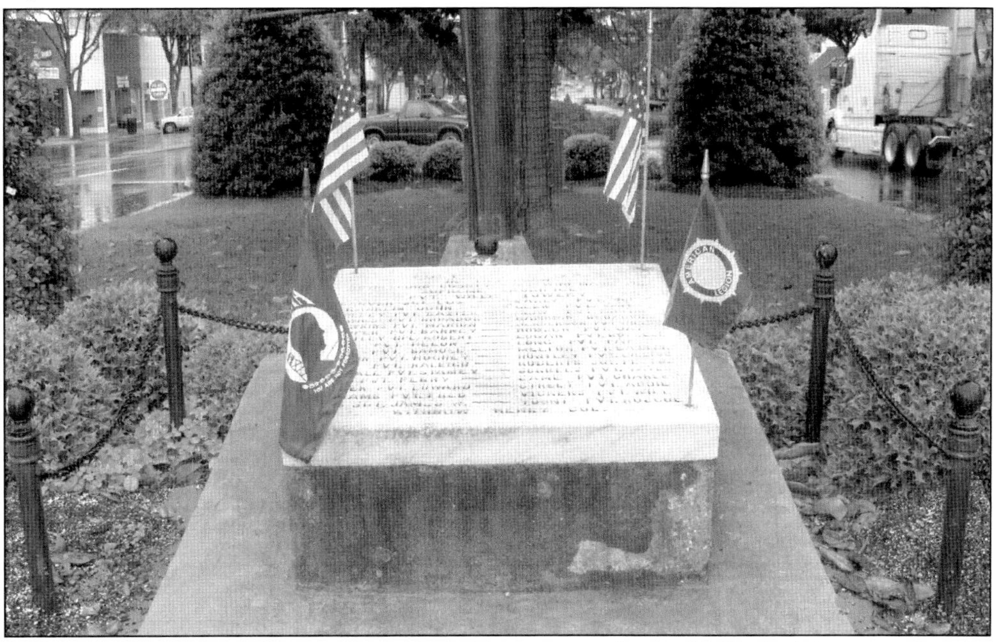

On the Public Square of Main Street is a monument to the 38 Rutherford County men who made the supreme sacrifice during World War I. The Willis Towery Post #74 of the American Legion unveiled the granite marker on November 11, 1924. About 5,000 people attended the dedication. (Courtesy of James M. Walker.)

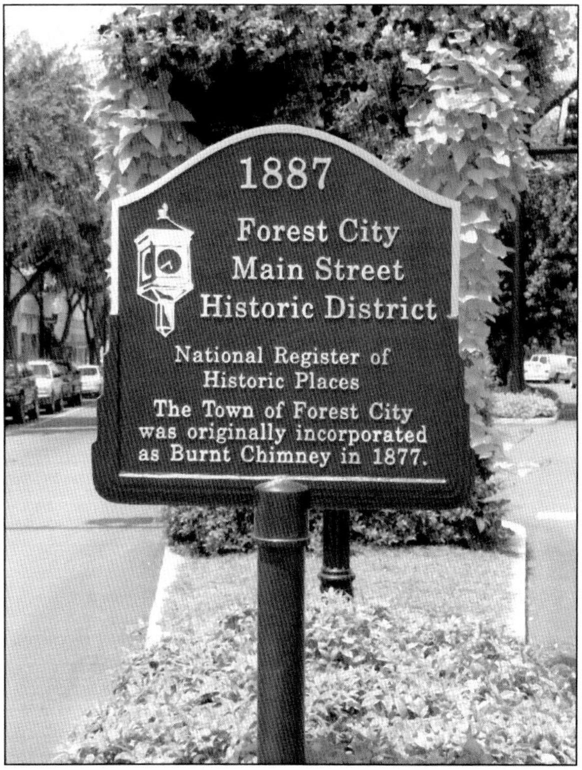

At the intersection of Powell Street and East Main Street is a marker noting the Historic Downtown Forest City District. The marker reads: "1887. Forest City Main Street Historic District. National Register of Historic Places. The Town of Forest City was originally incorporated as Burnt Chimney in 1877." (Courtesy of James M. Walker.)

The Elisha Baxter marker at East Main Street and South Broadway denotes the birthplace of Elisha Baxter. Placed by the Archives and Highway Departments in 1956, the marker reads: "Elisha Baxter. Governor of Arkansas, 1873–74. Union colonel in the Civil War; elected to the U. S. Senate, 1864, but not seated. Birthplace stood 4 1/2 miles S. E." (Courtesy of James M. Walker.)

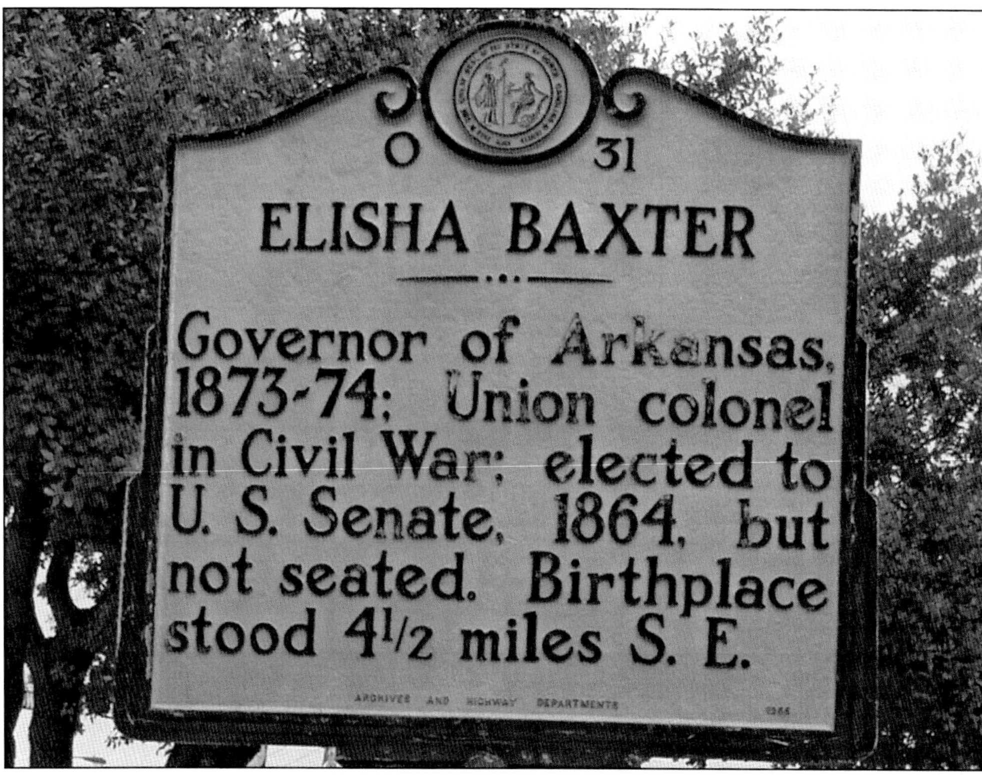

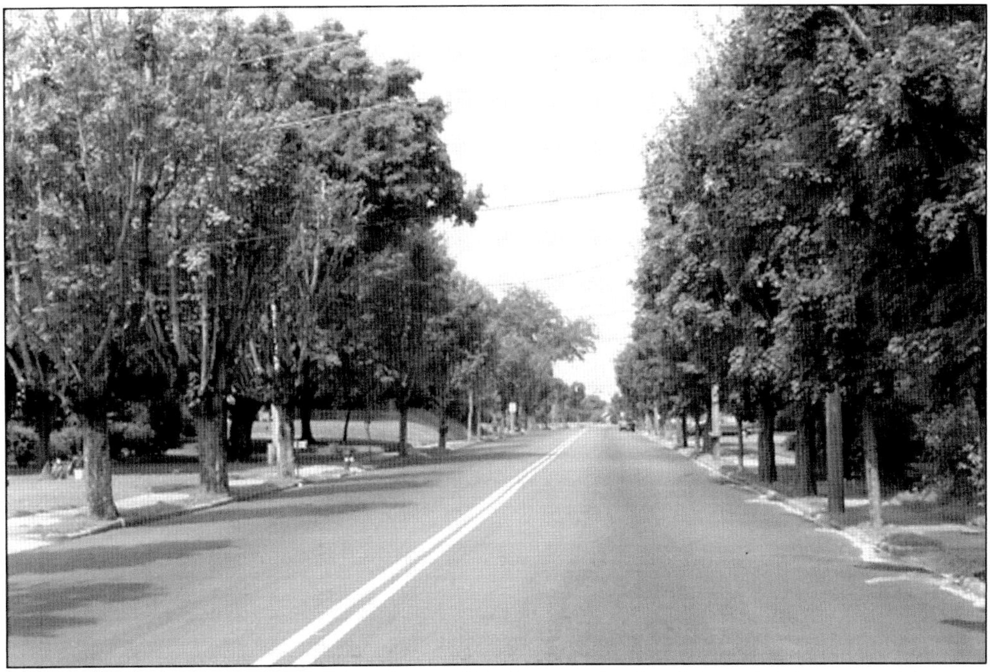

In December 1944, the Forest City Lions Club began planting Memorial Avenue with more than 140 trees for those who died in World War II. A metal sign at Mooneyham Public Library recognizes those county men with a maple tree and cement/brass marker. The second tree on the left is that for Cpl. Arthur Fred Price. (Courtesy of James M. Walker.)

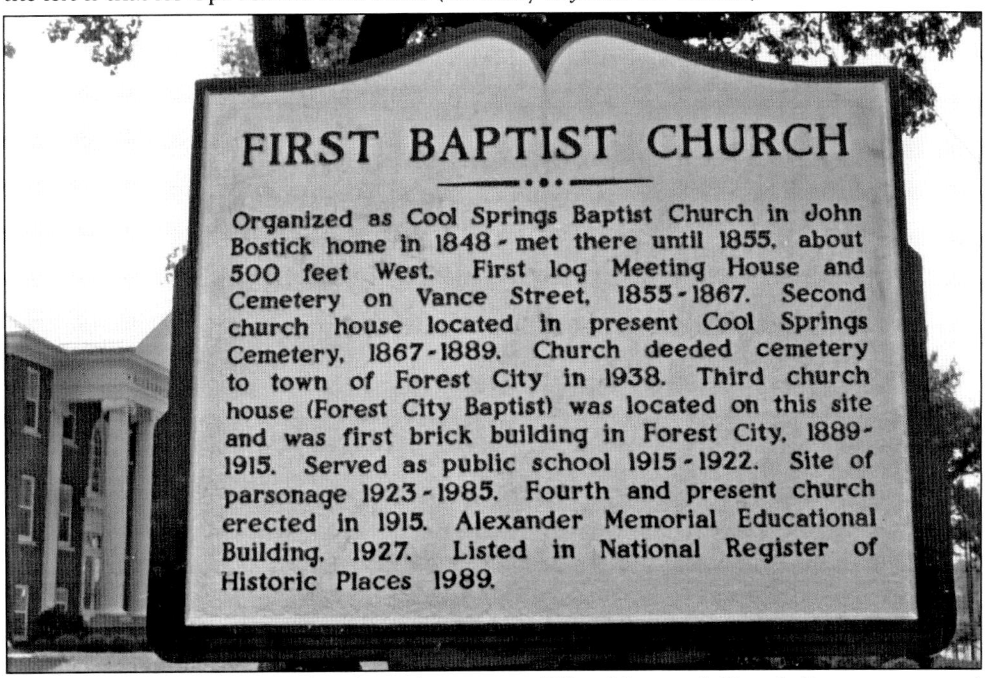

In front of the First Baptist Church, at the corner of West Main and Church Streets, is a metal sign indicating the historical significance of the Cool Springs/Forest City/First Baptist Church. Evelyn Carswell took this photograph. (Courtesy of First Baptist Church.)

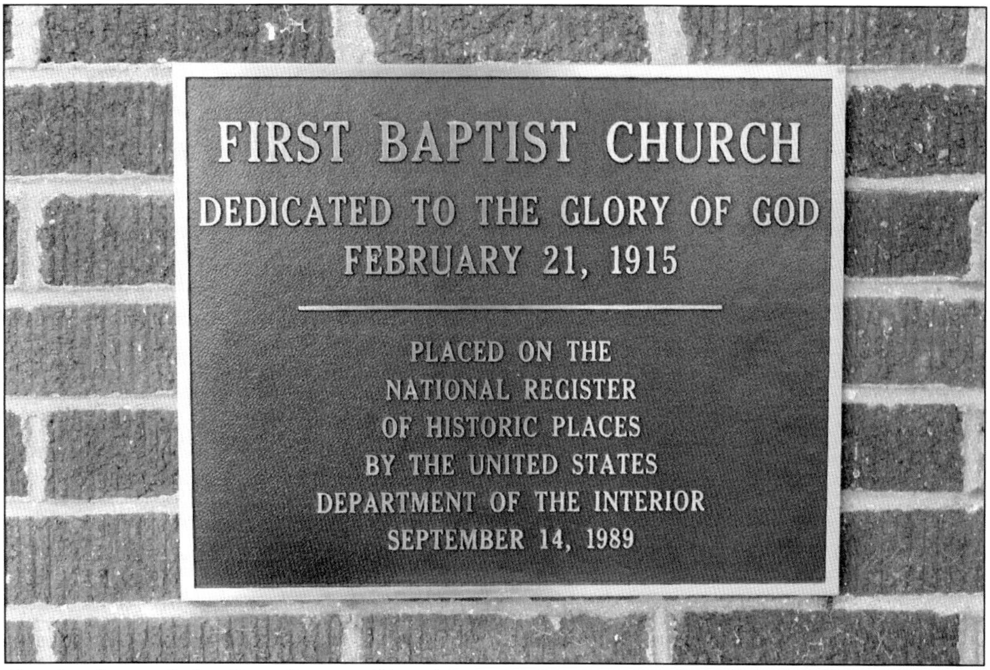

On the front of the First Baptist Church are markers noting that the church and the J. F. Alexander Memorial Building became a part of the National Registry of Historic Places in 1989. James M. McMichael designed the church that is in the Classical Revival style. Built in 1915 and 1927, the brick are still used. (Courtesy of James M. Walker.)

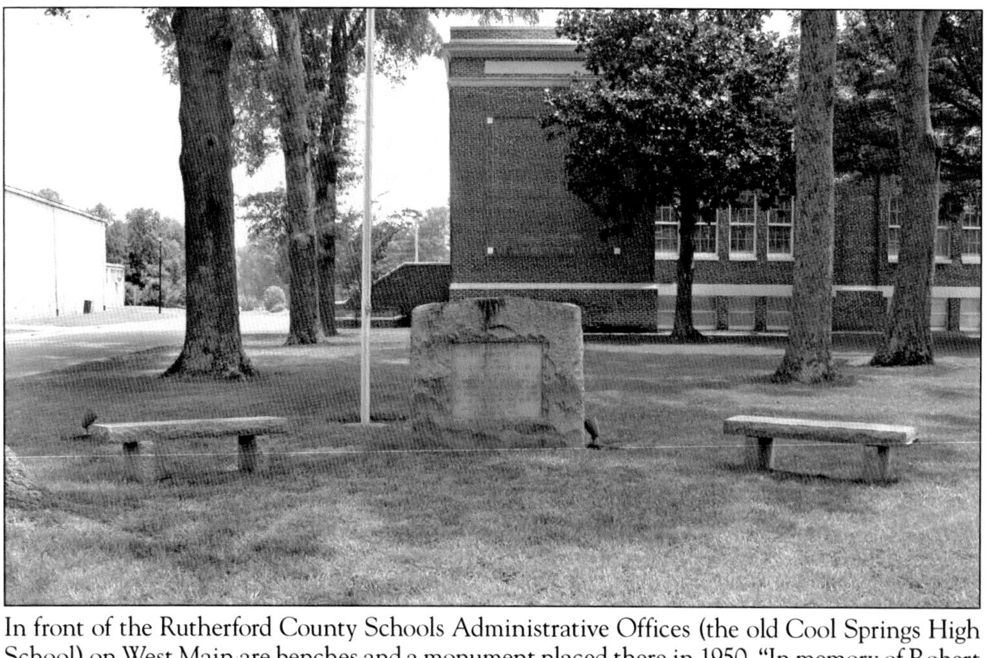

In front of the Rutherford County Schools Administrative Offices (the old Cool Springs High School) on West Main are benches and a monument placed there in 1950. "In memory of Robert McBrayer Harrill and Catherine Suttle Harrill, who gave (in 1865) this property to the trustees of Burnt Chimney Academy for the erection of a public school on the sixth day of January" in 1965. (Courtesy of James M. Walker.)

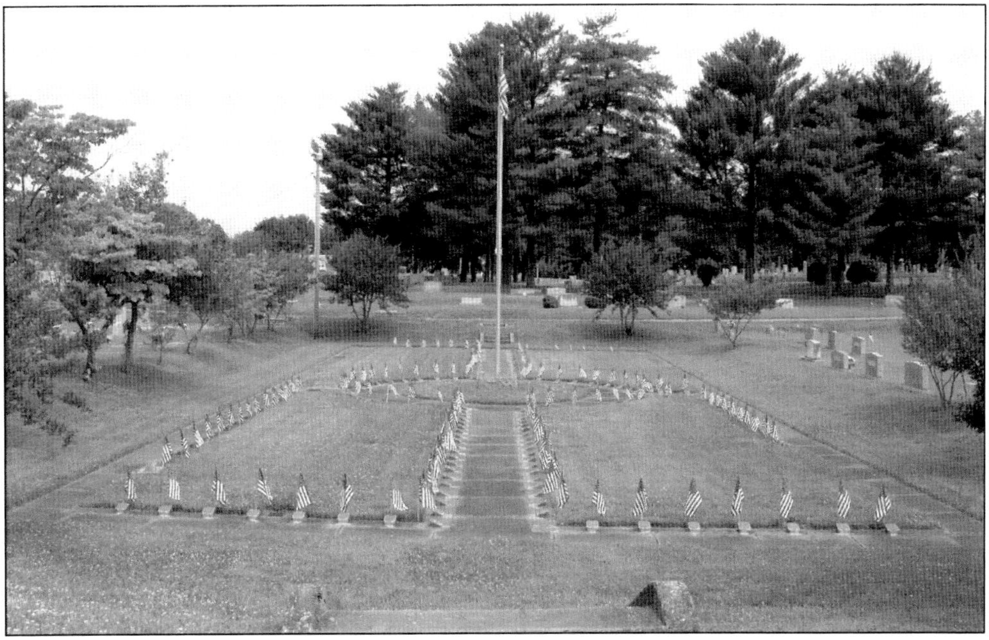

Located behind the Rutherford County Schools Administrative Offices is the Cool Springs Cemetery. On the east side of the cemetery is the Memorial Garden for the Rutherford County men who died in the World War II, the Korean War, and Vietnam. The bronze/concrete plaques there were originally beside the trees on Memorial Avenue. Identical plaques identify those who lost their lives in other wars. (Courtesy of James M. Walker.)

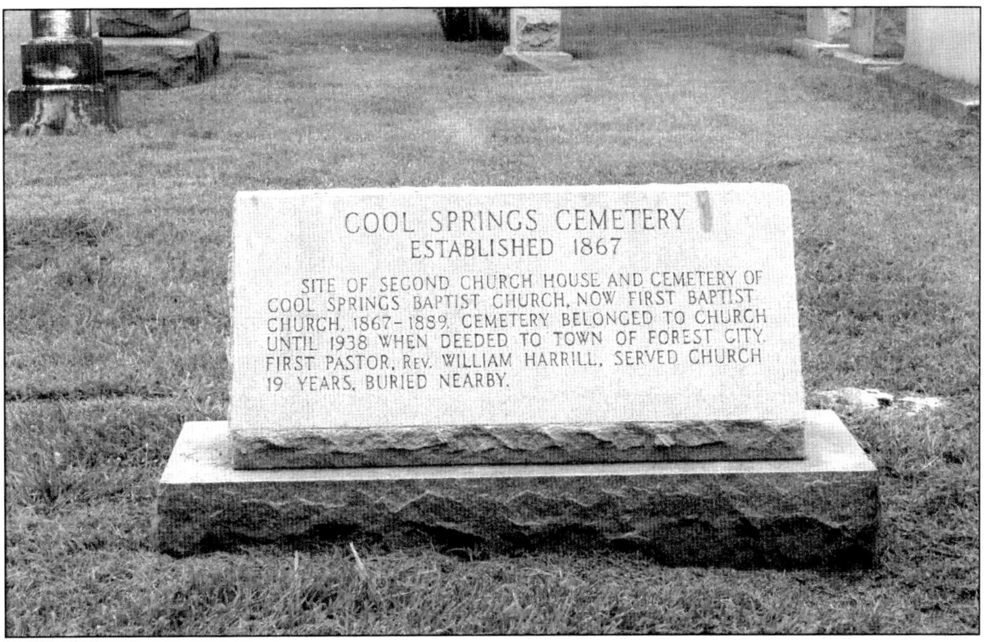

Within walking distance of the Memorial Gardens is a stone marker denoting the site of the second Cool Springs Baptist Church. (The first Cool Springs Baptist Church was on Vance Street.) Chapter one includes a sketch of the old clapboard building erected at this site. (Courtesy of James M. Walker.)

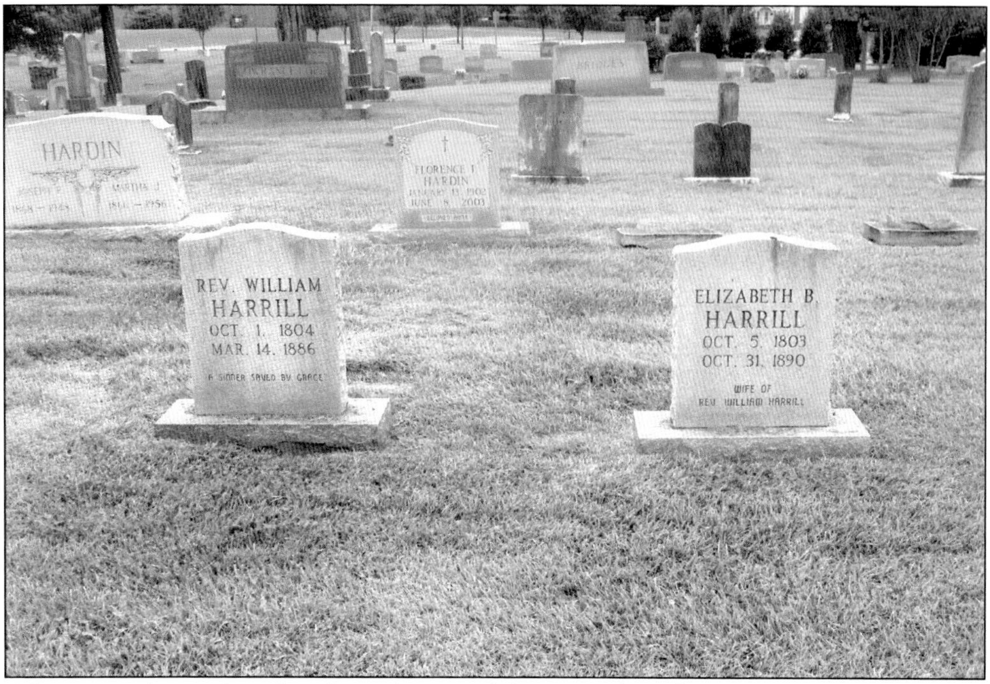

Adjacent to the marker identifying the site of the Second Cool Springs Baptist Church is a marker honoring Elder William Harrill (1804–1886), the first pastor of the Cool Springs Baptist Church. Elizabeth B. Harrill (1803–1890) is beside him. (Courtesy of James M. Walker.)

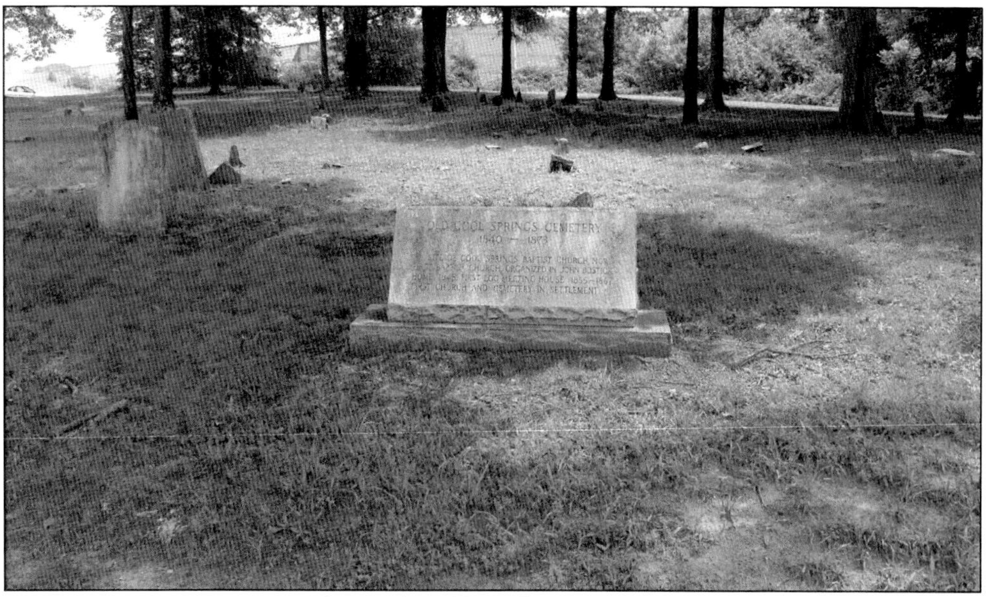

On Vance Street is a stone marker in the Old Cool Springs Cemetery (1840–1973). The marker notes the site of the Cool Springs Baptist Church, now the First Baptist Church: "Organized in John Bostick Home, 1848. First Log Meeting House 1855–1867. First church and cemetery in settlement." A drawing in chapter one gives an artist's conception of the original log structure. (Courtesy of James M. Walker.)

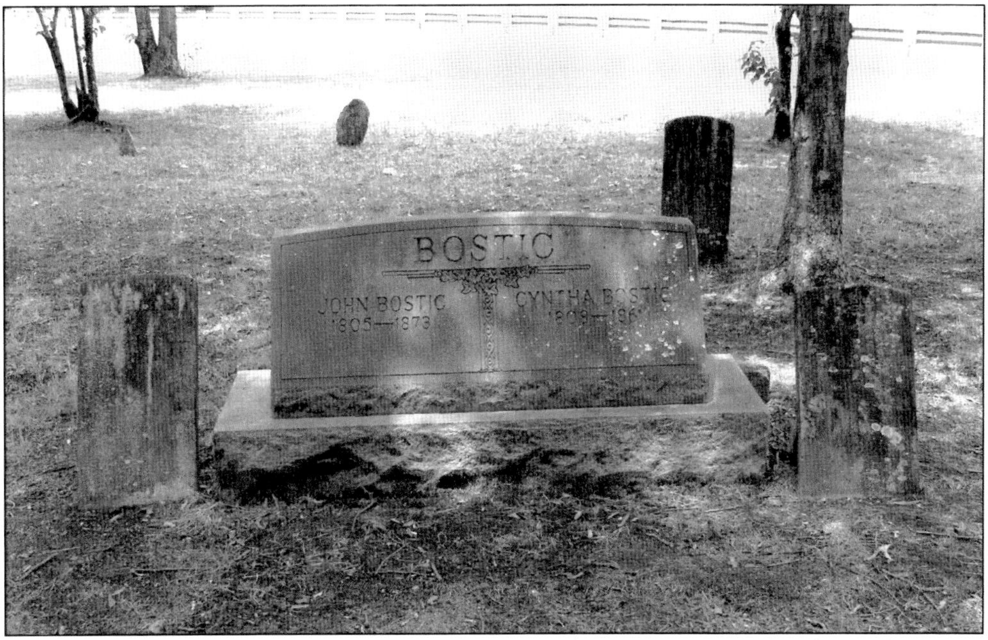

The memorial for John Bostic (at whose home the Cool Springs Baptist Church met from 1848 to 1855) is in the Old Cool Springs Cemetery. Buried beside him is his wife, Cynthia Harrill Bostic. (Courtesy of James M. Walker.)

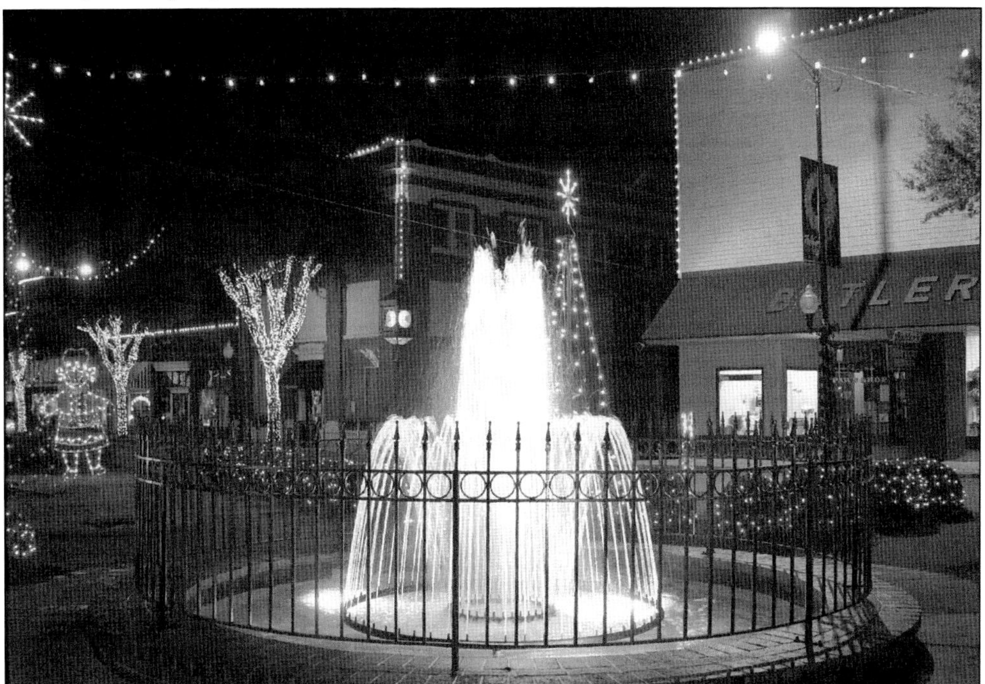

The central square is still a prominent feature of the downtown area. In 1927, the U.S. Department of Agriculture selected Forest City as one of the 10 most beautiful and best-planned towns in the United States. Today the original landscaped median and fountain still exist. (Courtesy of Bob Morgan.)

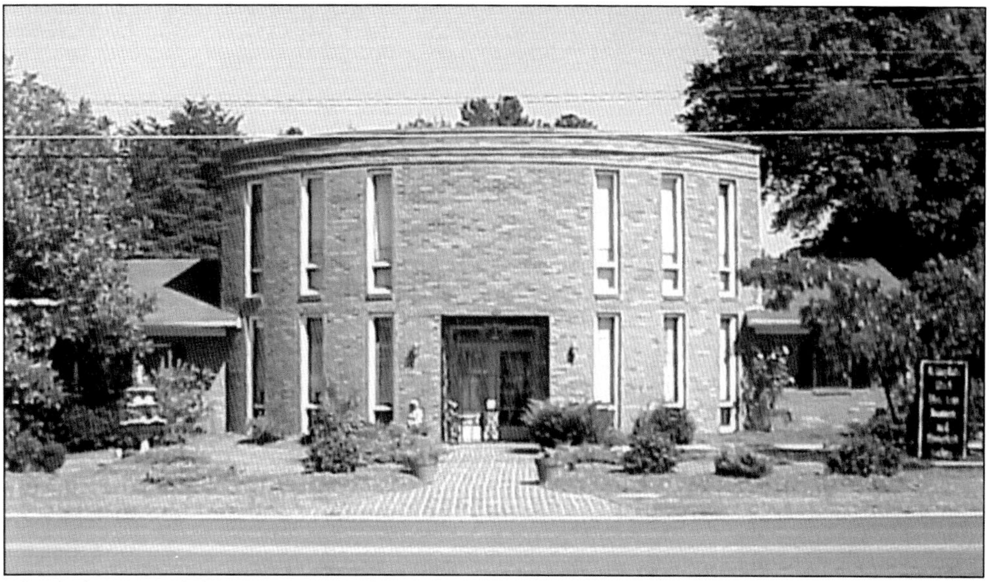

The dedication of the Maimy Etta Black Fine Arts Museum and Historical Society at 404 Hardin Road took place on May 28, 1995. Maimy Thompson Gumbs intended the establishment to do three things: 1) collect, document, preserve, and interpret the art and artifacts of Afro-American and Global Black Art; 2) document and preserve materials of black families and the Thompson family; and 3) help people "encounter the real." (Information courtesy of Maimy Thompson Gumbs; photograph courtesy of Bob Morgan.)

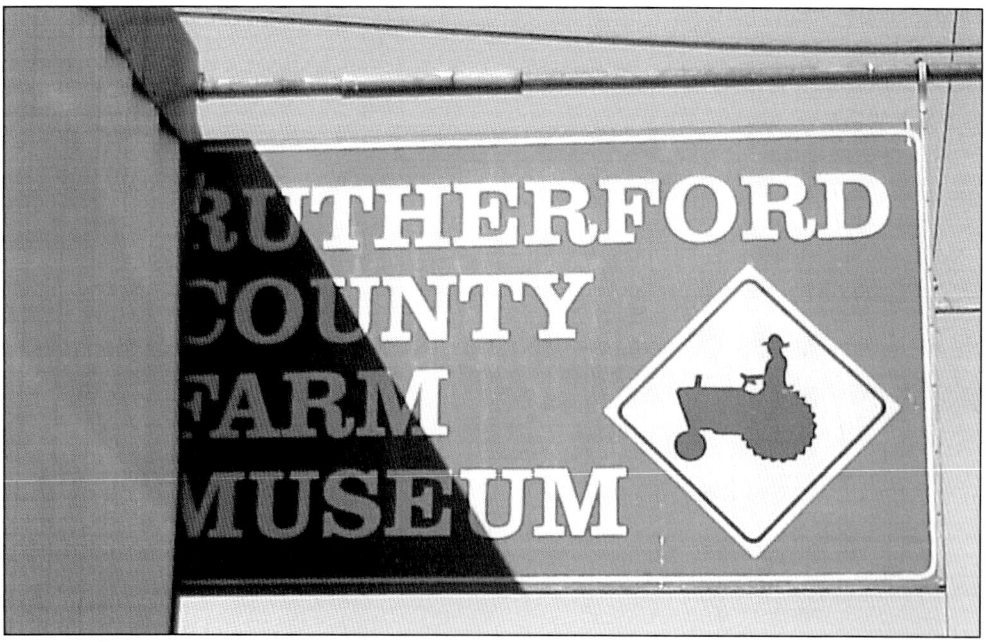

Capt. Wilbur J. Burgin (U.S. Navy retired) helped open the Rutherford County Farm Museum in July 1994 at 240 Depot Street in the J. W. Davis Building. Jim Womack and board members staff the state-incorporated museum, which allows deductions for donated items. Other businesses that have used the J. W. Davis facilities include Toliver Davis's Law Office and the health department clinics. (Courtesy of Bob Morgan.)

On Wednesdays during the 1950s, Dr. William M. Elliott, Mrs. Louise Smith Blanton (shown here), and health department staff helped meet local needs upstairs at 240 Depot Street; they held health clinics there. J. W. Davis Plumbing and Electrical Supplies occupied the lower level of the building built in 1946 by J. W. Davis and Tom Davis; later Jack Davis and Toliver Davis joined J. W. and Tom Davis there. (Courtesy of Louise Smith Blanton.)

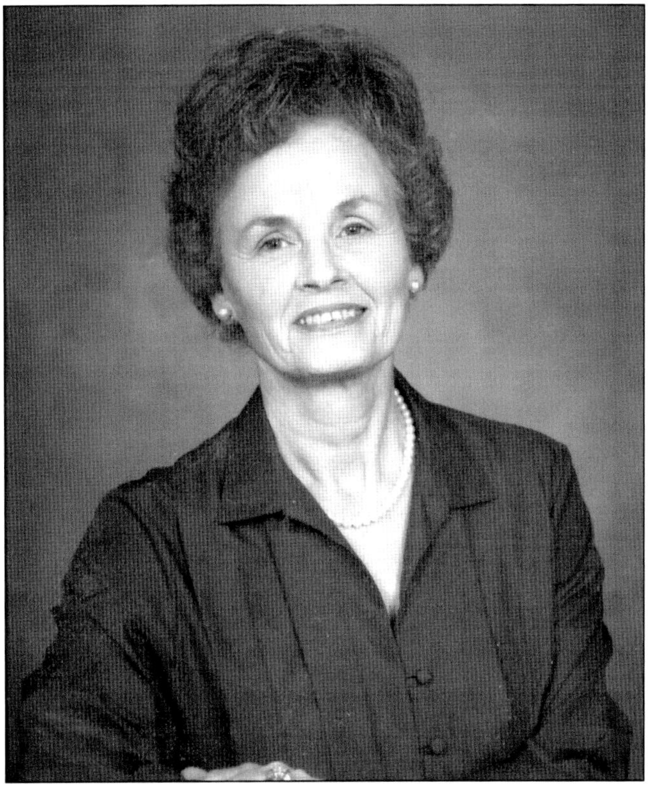

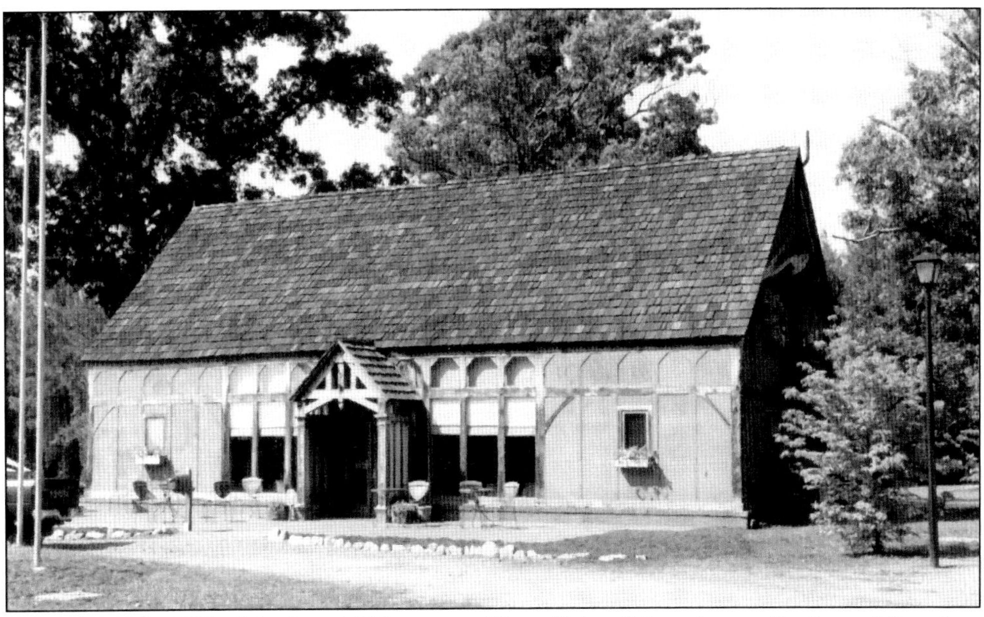

Since the early 1970s, Matthew McEnnerney, Diane (his wife), and sons, Devin and Brendan, have been active in presenting quality comedies, programs, plays, and musicals with the help of the Rutherford County Arts Council. In 2005, the council produced *Cats*. The Globe Theater on Shakespeare Drive is across from the Alexander Baptist Church on U.S. Highway 221. (Courtesy of James M. Walker.)

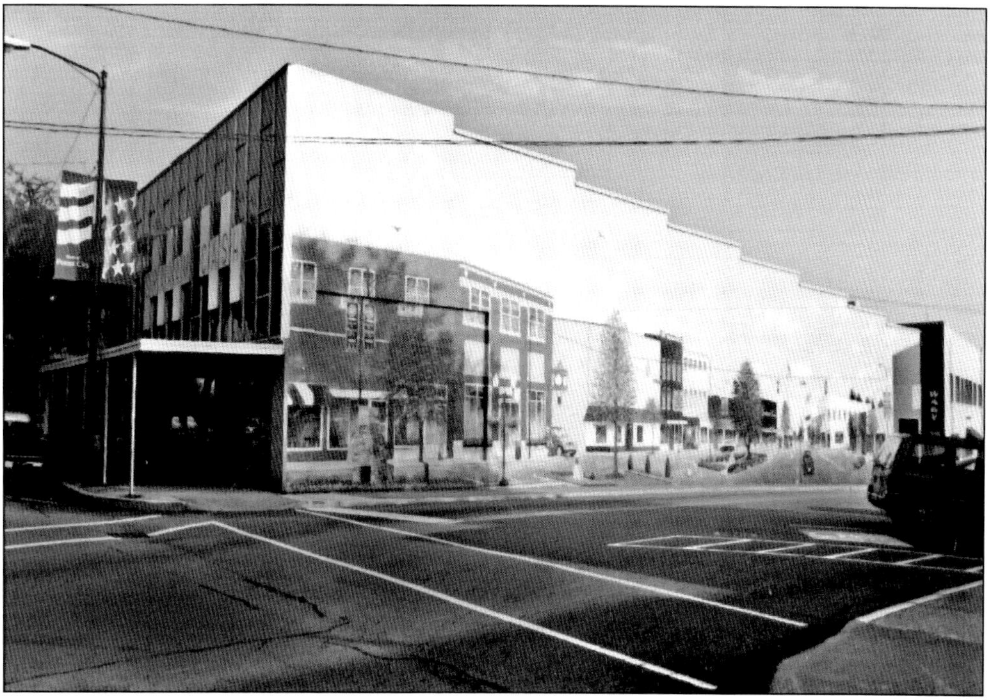

A prominent mural is evident to the traveler going west on Main Street. This mural on the side of Graham-Cash Company was the work of Clive Haynes. It shows a view of Main Street as it appears when one is traveling east. (Courtesy of James M. Walker.)

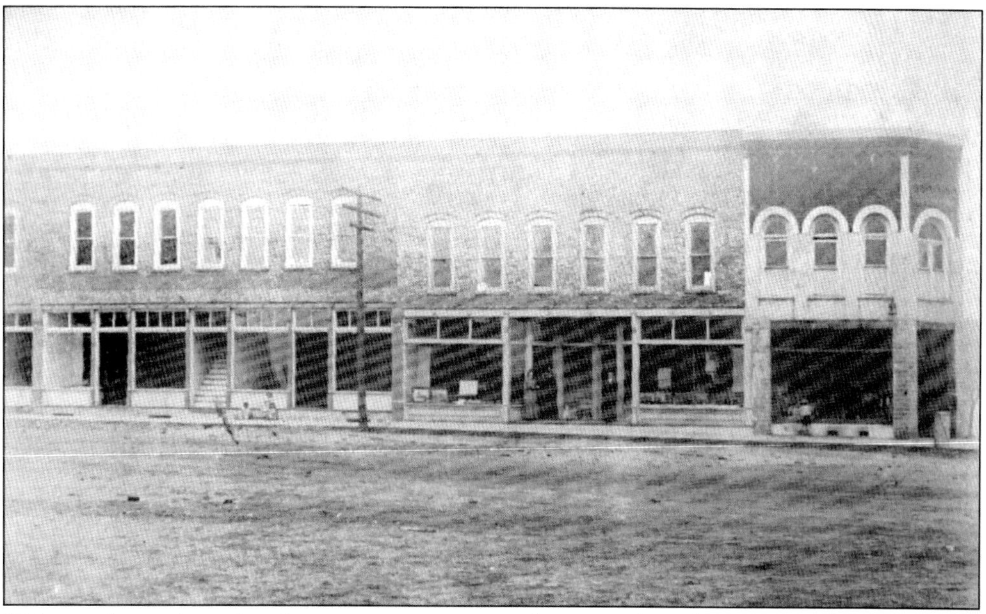

This storefront view, after the construction pictured on page four, shows an unpaved street and several unoccupied stores. Forest City continues to remember its past; one of the imminent markers, selected by the 225th Anniversary Committee of Rutherford County, will be for Clarence Griffin. Historic storefronts in downtown Forest City are themselves monuments to the past—and present. (Courtesy of Paul Tim Jones Jr., Daniel King, and Beth King.)

Three

Schools
Educating Our People

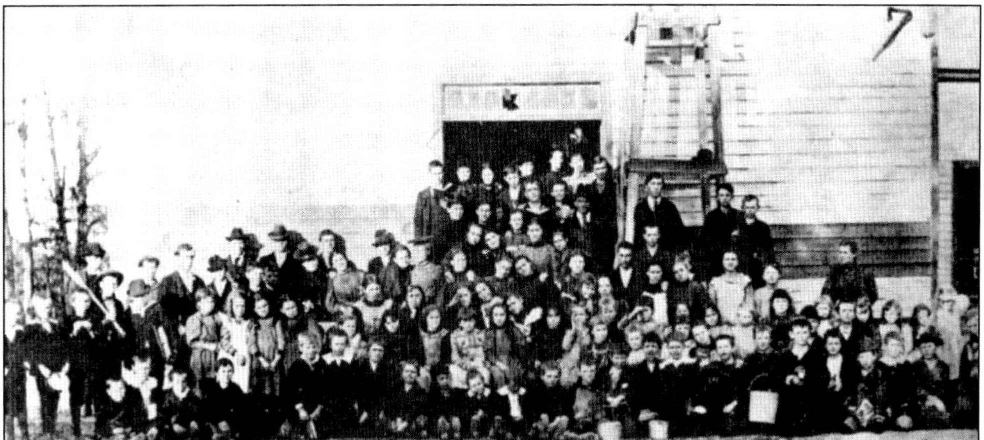

Although the North Carolina Constitution of 1776 made it compulsory for the North Carolina General Assembly to provide schools for the state's people, it was 1842 before formal public education in Rutherford County began. Field schools often met in buildings of scraped logs, but an 1873 county vote defeated a special school tax to finance a county school system. In 1874, the one-story Burnt Chimney Academy (30 by 45 feet) opened; trustees were Rev. C. B. Justice, Housen Harrill, Thomas Wilkins, J. W. Davis, and George Bostic; directors were Rev. J. H. Yarboro and Prof. Burwell ("Bert") H. Bridges. The school was near the old Cool Springs High School. (Courtesy of First Baptist Church and Betty Jo Carpenter.)

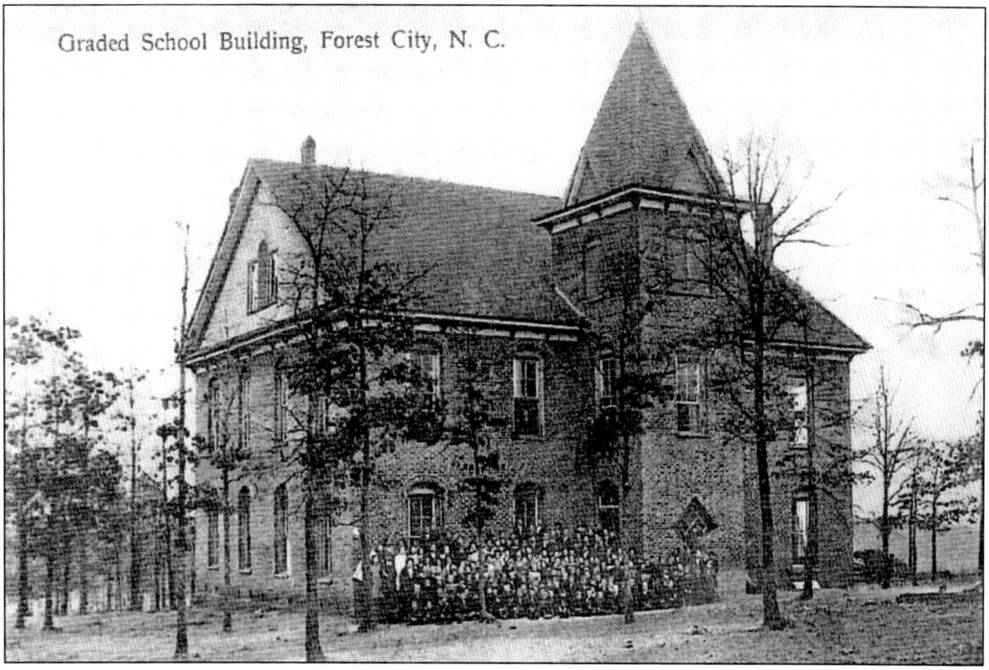

With the 1901 election of C. B. Aycock as governor, education received a giant boost. Forest City particularly benefited. By 1904, the construction of the Forest City Graded School was complete. Located at North Broadway and Trade, the two-story brick structure with its many windows provided a much-improved facility. Forest City children attended the school for 20 years. (Courtesy of Daniel King and Beth King.)

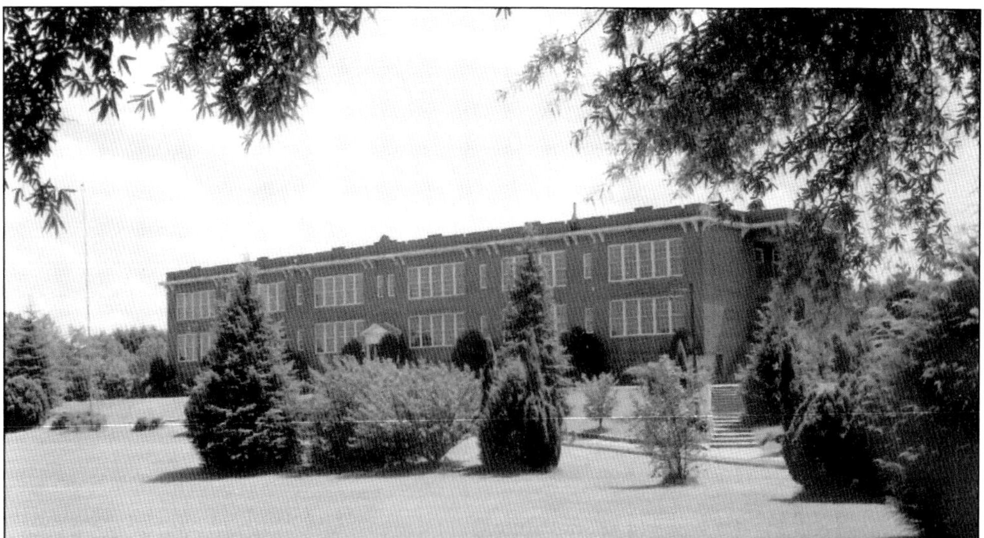

During the 1920s, a golden age for school construction, Forest City gained a massive red brick elementary school (1922). Just off the Old Caroleen Road, the facility remained in use until fire destroyed it in the 1960s. Robert M. Watkins helped with landscaping; the principal had him pull the yellow bitter weeds. Robert still works for others: Relay for Life, the First Methodist Church, and wherever else he is needed. (Courtesy of Robert M. Watkins.)

Robert Watkins attended Forest City Elementary School; he was seven years old and in first grade at the time of this photograph. Robert quipped, "Here I am in my hand-me-down clothes and an unhappy expression on my face." The lad was actually well-dressed for the era—the beginning of the Great Depression. (Courtesy of Robert M. Watkins.)

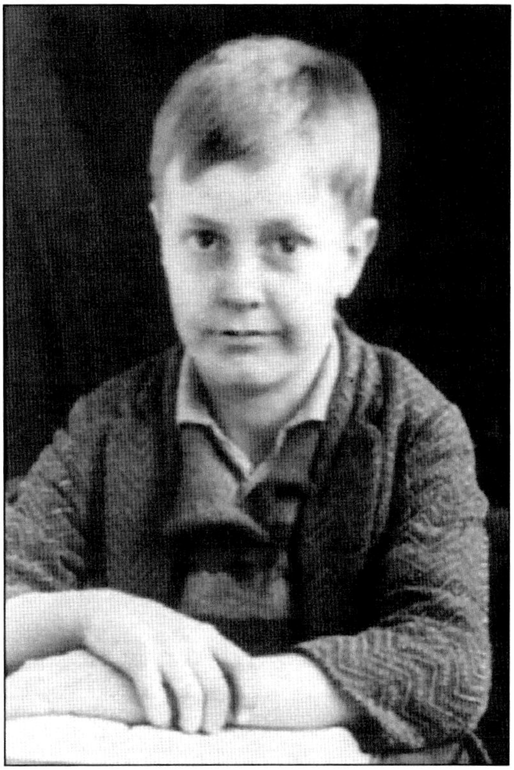

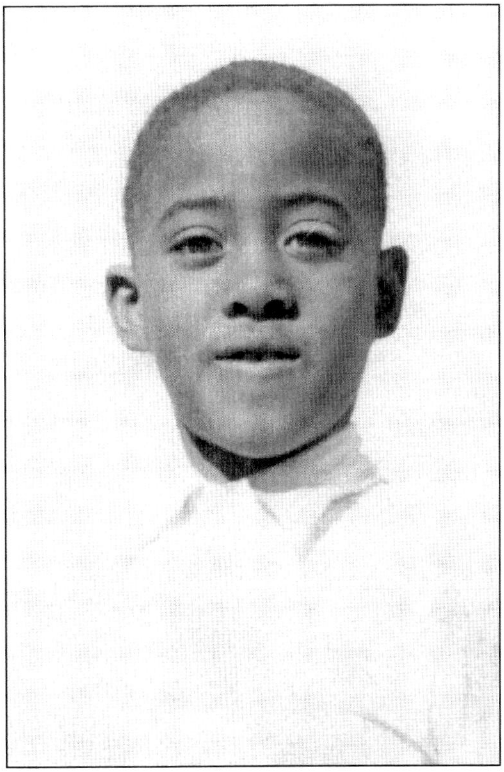

Milton Robinson Jr. attended Doggett Grove Elementary School. Here is Milton Robinson Jr. as a second-grader on April 1, 1947. The school had three rooms: one for grades one, two, and three; one room for grades four and five; and the third room for grades six, seven, and eight. (Courtesy of Milton Robinson Jr.)

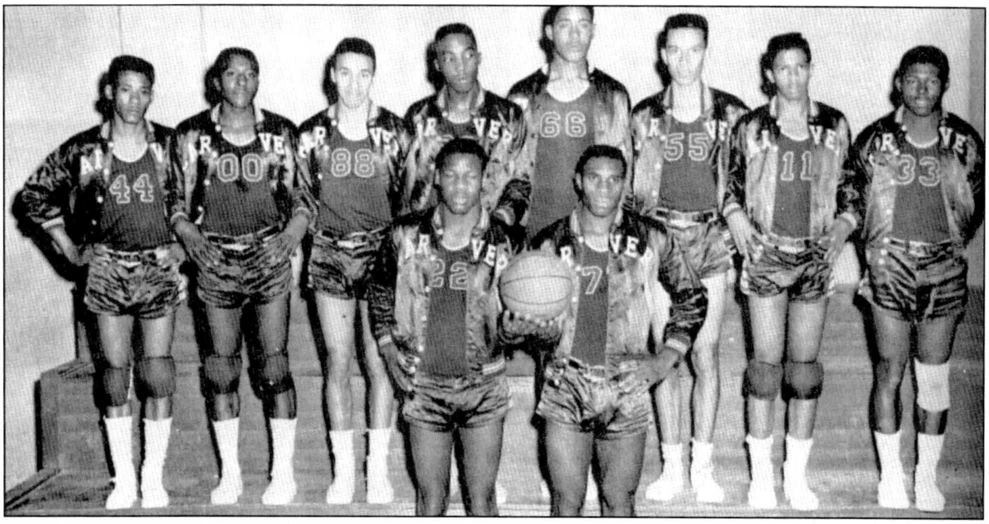

Milton Robinson Jr. attended Grahamtown High School in Forest City. With consolidation, New Hope School, Carver High School, and Dunbar Schools opened in the early 1950s. Milton played for the Carver High School Eagles Basketball Team coached by Mr. W. H. Knight in 1958. From left to right are (first row) Archie Simons and Paul White; (second row) Lewis Black, T. J. Logan, Jimmy Duffy, Curtis Logan, Milton Robinson Jr. (#66), James Logan, Robert Miller, Lynal Ray. (Courtesy of Milton Robinson Jr.)

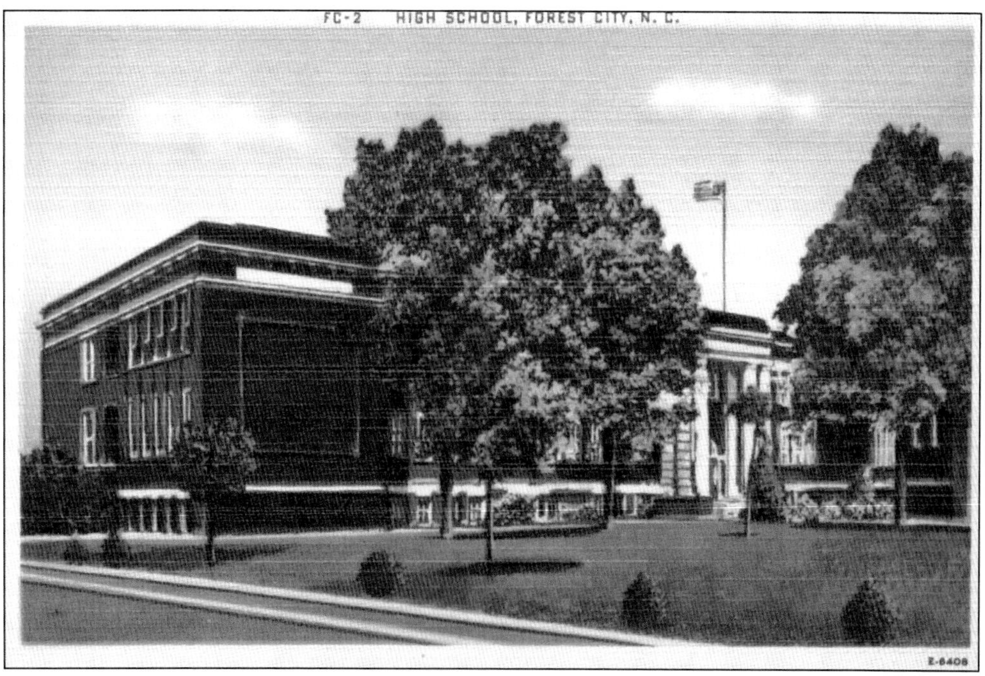

The West Main Cool Springs building has served as a high school (1925–1962), a junior high, and now the Administration Building for the Rutherford County Schools. The National Register of Historic Places added the building to its list in 1999 because of its Classical Revival style, its place in social history, and its service to education. Louis Humbert Asbury and H. A. Kistler were the architects, builders, and engineers. (Courtesy of the authors.)

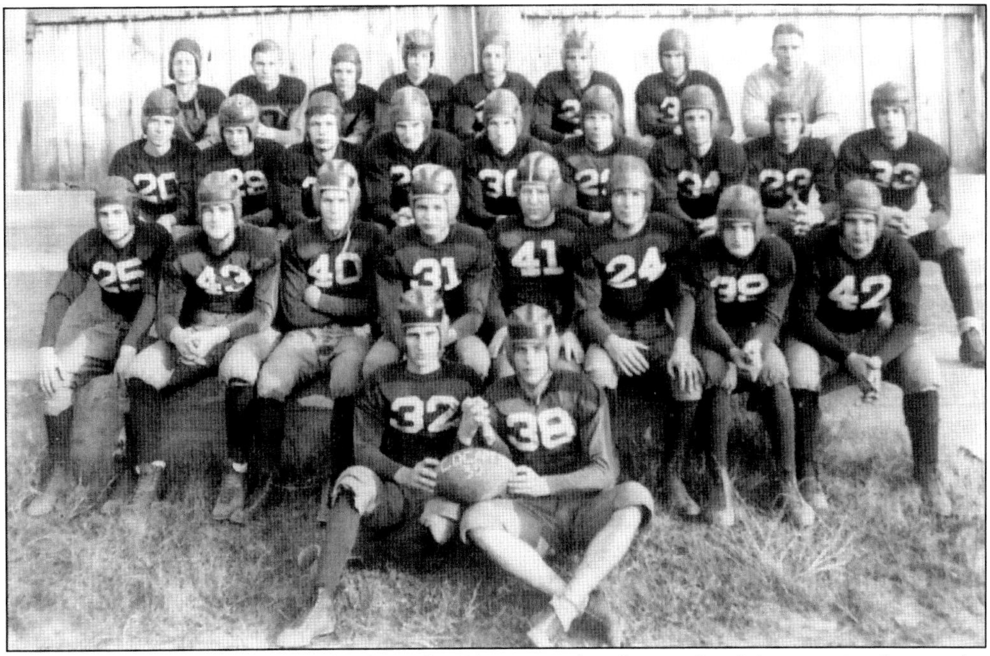

Public schools, private schools (Anath Christian Academy, the Masters Academy, the Tabernacle of Praise Christian Academy, and Trinity School), and a charter school (Thomas Jefferson Classical Academy) are available. Forest City has always supported education and high school athletics: from the Golden Tornados at Cool Springs High School to the present-day Cavaliers of East Rutherford High School. This 1939 Golden Tornados photograph includes cocaptain Ross Hudson, #38. Ross is sitting on the ground on the right. (Courtesy of Mrs. Ross (Elaine) Hudson.)

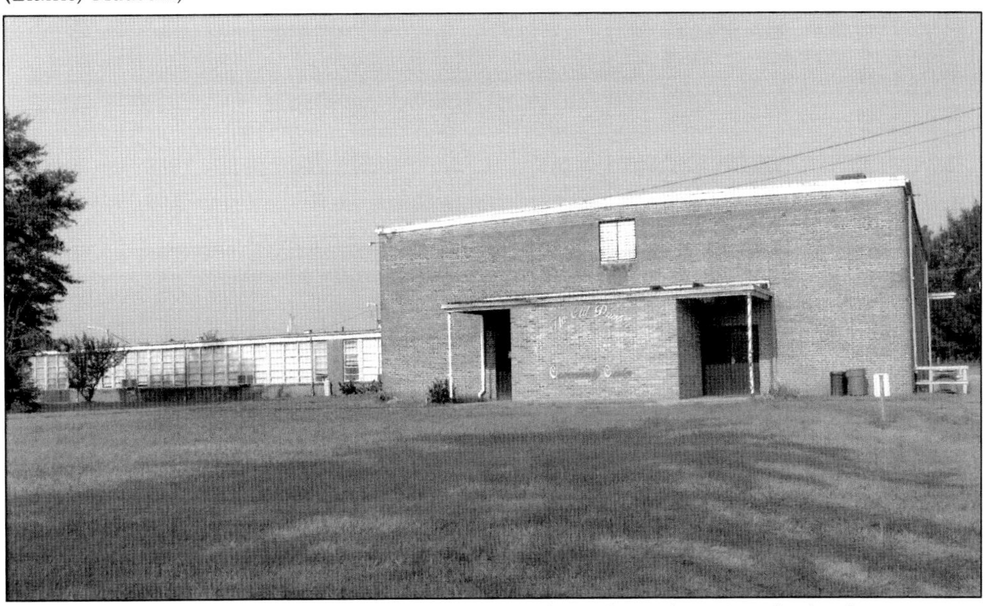

Located on 421 Hardin Road is Dunbar School. Built in the early 1950s, the brick structure is still in use as the Old Dunbar Community Center. Directly across the street is the Maimy Etta Black Fine Arts Museum and Historical Society. (Courtesy of James M. Walker.)

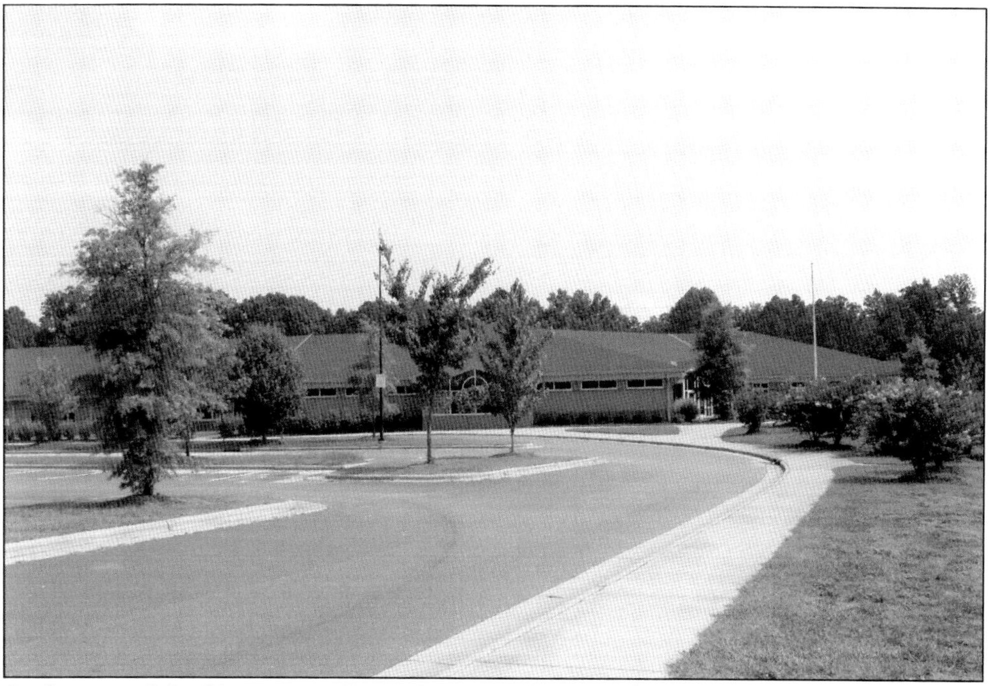

At the turn of the 21st century, Forest City opened a new school for grades four and five. The new school is Dunbar Elementary School, named in honor of the great African American poet Paul Dunbar. The school is at 286 Learning Parkway. (Courtesy of James M. Walker.)

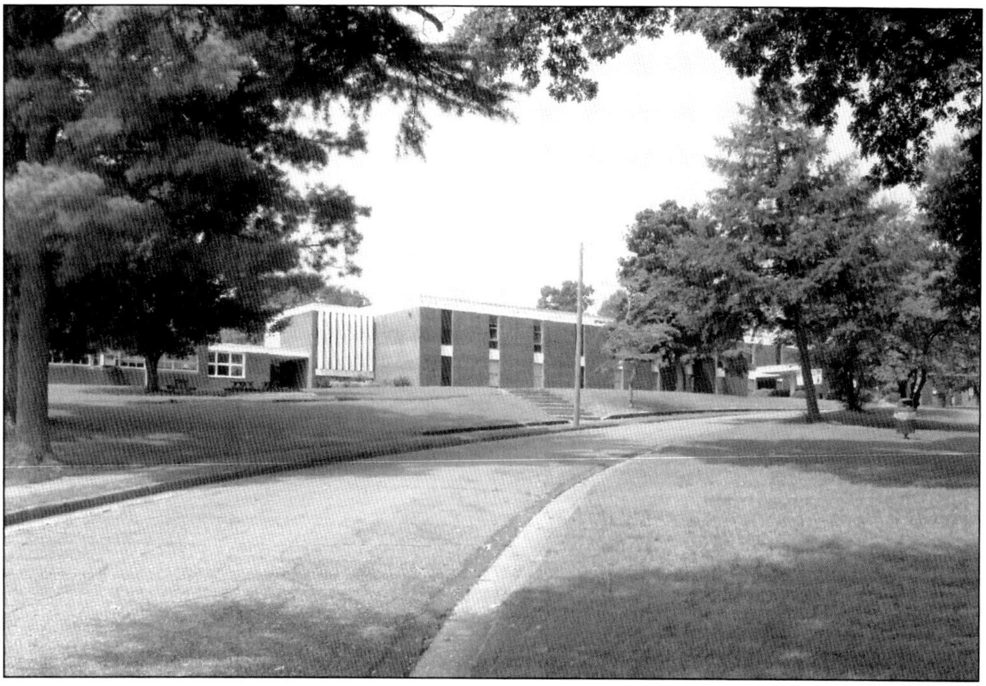

Located at 140 Old Caroleen Road is the Forest City Elementary School for kindergarten through third grade. This mid-1960s structure replaced the building that burned in the 1960s. (Courtesy of James M. Walker.)

Four

PEOPLE
Making the Town

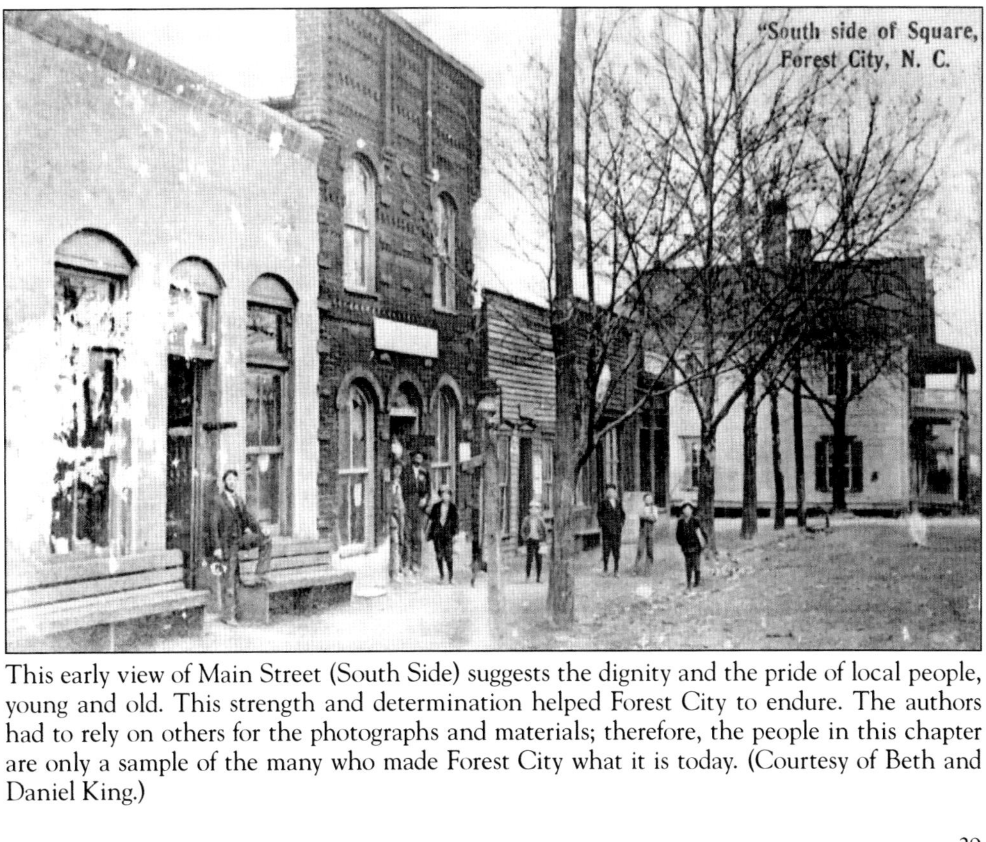

This early view of Main Street (South Side) suggests the dignity and the pride of local people, young and old. This strength and determination helped Forest City to endure. The authors had to rely on others for the photographs and materials; therefore, the people in this chapter are only a sample of the many who made Forest City what it is today. (Courtesy of Beth and Daniel King.)

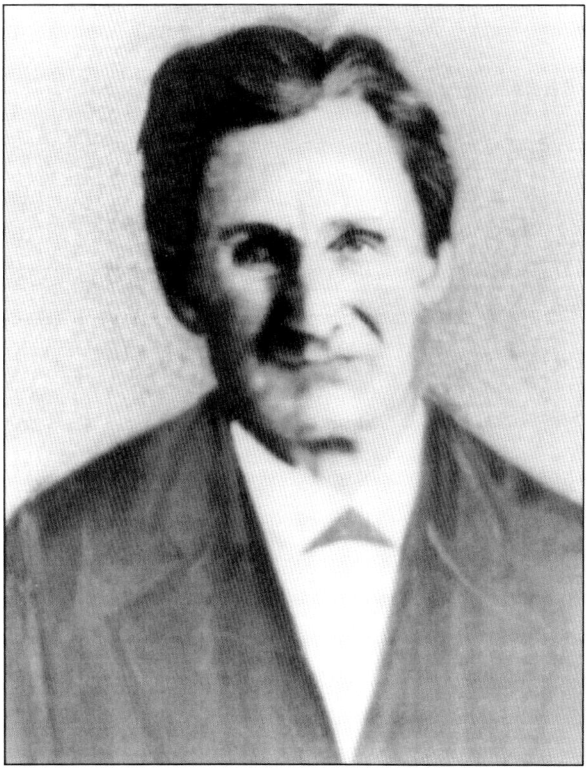

William Harrill preferred the title "elder"—instead of "reverend," "preacher," or "pastor." This first pastor of the Cool Springs Baptist Church (serving 1858–1867) ranked as a foremost revivalist; he baptized more than 1,500 people. A blacksmith and a cabinetmaker, Elder Harrill missed only one service—and that was because of illness. (*First Baptist Church: 1848–1939*; *Our Heritage, 1848–1991*). (Courtesy of First Baptist Church.)

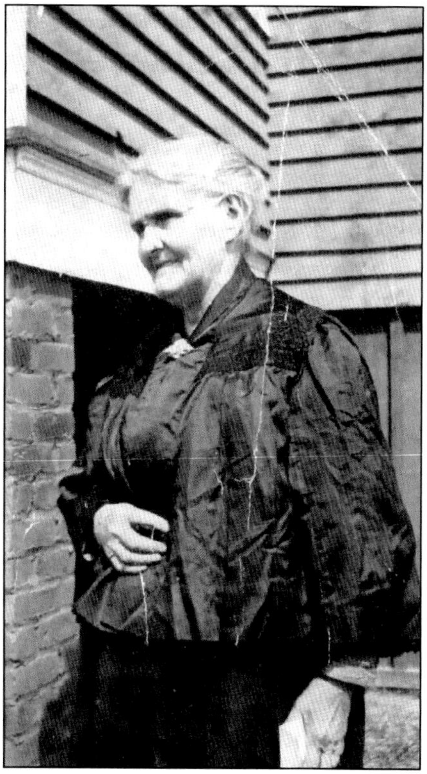

Catherine Mahala Suttle Harrill (June 1, 1845–January 5, 1920) married Robert McBrayer Harrill on June 30, 1860. Their home was on West Main Street beside what is now the Rutherford County Schools Administration Building. She and her husband donated land for the use of educating the citizenry. (Courtesy of Colleen Jenkins Biggerstaff.)

Robert McBrayer Harrill (1837–1914) made the stipulation that if the use of the donated land was ever for other than educational purposes, it would revert to the heirs. Robert and Catherine Harrill are buried in the Old Cool Springs Cemetery located on Vance Street. (Courtesy of Colleen Jenkins Biggerstaff.)

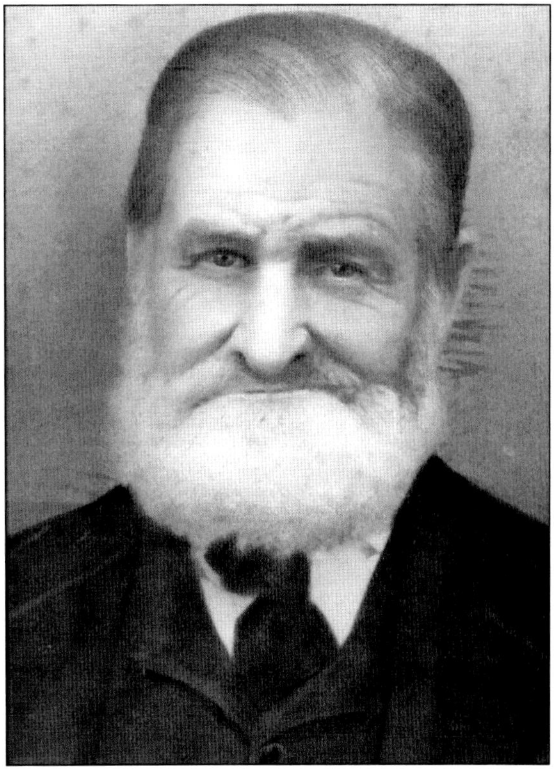

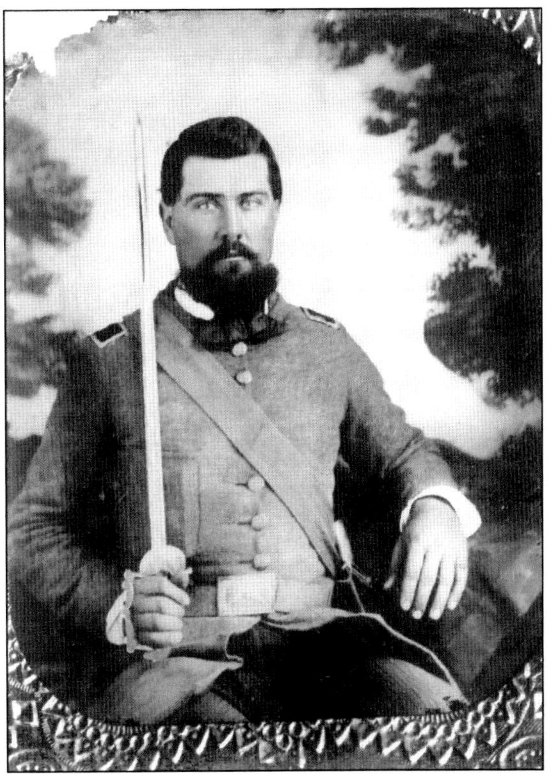

Representing the 1,734 Confederate soldiers from Rutherford County is David Beam Harrill, Company B, 34th Regiment, NC Troops ("Sand Run Yellow Jackets"). First Lieutenant Harrill was present at the surrender at Appomattox in April 1865. A Florence Mills stockholder, "Uncle Dave" was a county merchant and Sara Blanton Johnston's great-grandfather; he paid for Sara's mother, Mildred Henrietta Coffield Blanton, to attend Asheville Home School and Asheville Normal School. (Courtesy of Sara B. Johnston.)

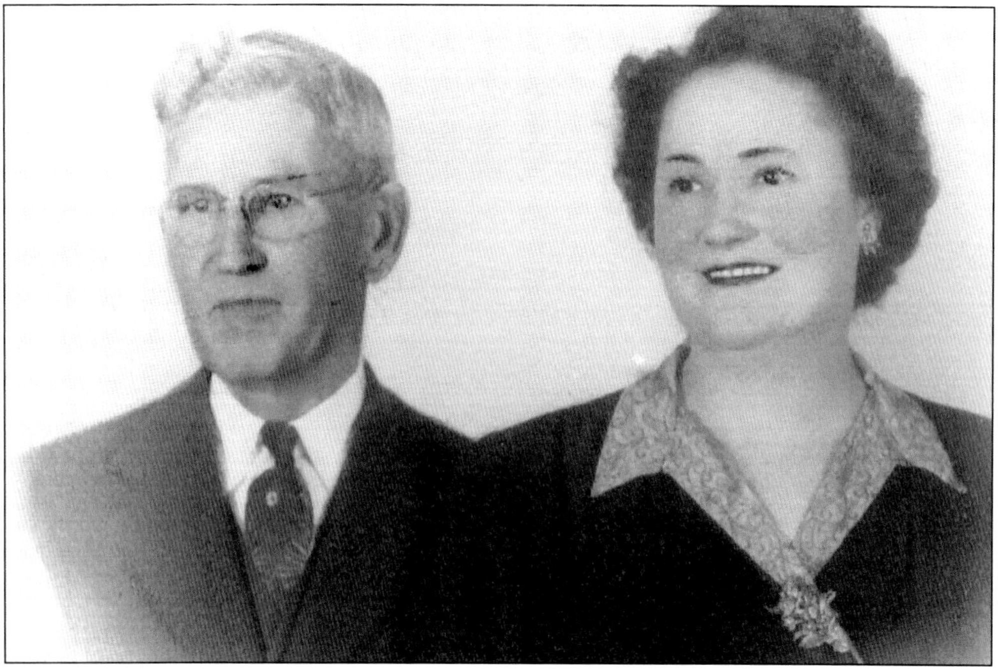

Local business executive James Willis Griffin Sr. purchased the Horn Theatre and renamed it the Pastime. He purchased the Romina Theatre from Walter H. Haynes. Pictured here are James Willis Griffin Sr. and his wife, Alice Grace Griffin, for whom he named the Grace Theatre. Clarence Griffin commended J. W. Griffin Sr.'s pressing the sale of war bonds during World War II (Griffin, 84). (Courtesy of Melinda Griffin Peterson.)

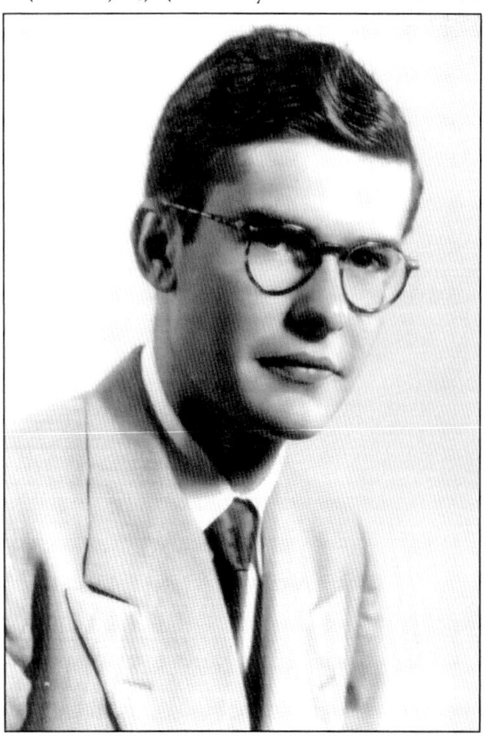

James Willis Griffin Sr.'s son, James Willis Griffin Jr. (December 16, 1920–June 27, 2001), followed in his father's successful footsteps and started the Griffin Theatre (June 8, 1949–June 1972). Pictured here is James Willis Griffin Jr., the father of Melinda Griffin Peterson, Jimmy Griffin, Mark Griffin, and Gary Griffin. (Courtesy of Melinda Griffin Peterson.)

Cleo King Padgett was president of the Forest City Betterment Club in 1914 when it began its Main Street beautification project. The landscaped medians and fountain still exist. Tildon Rucker Padgett helped establish Padgett and King Funeral Home, the first purpose-built funeral home in Rutherford County. Padgett and King also opened a furniture store on the south side of Main Street. (Courtesy of Melinda Griffin Peterson.)

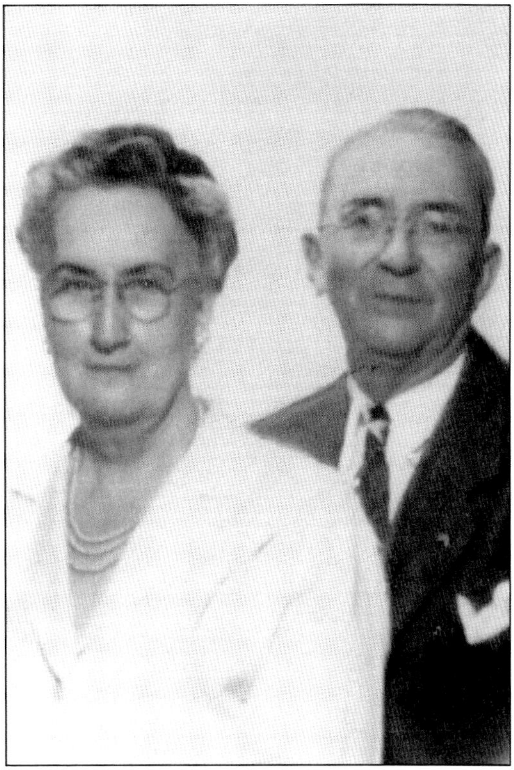

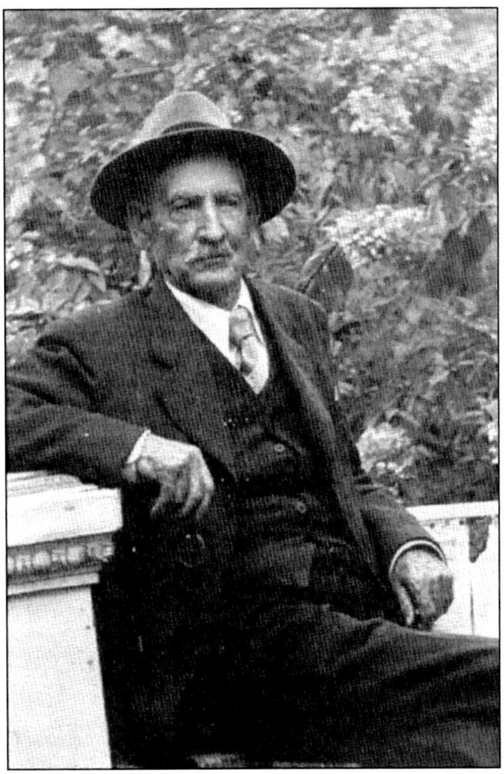

Will McArthur (left), uncle of W. H. ("Bill") McArthur, was one of the earliest photographers in the county. Postcard companies relied on his sharp, clear, glass-plate negatives to depict accurately the Forest City area. Some of his work is evident in the postcards of the Mabry Hotel, the streets of the town, and the local churches. (Courtesy of W. H. McArthur.)

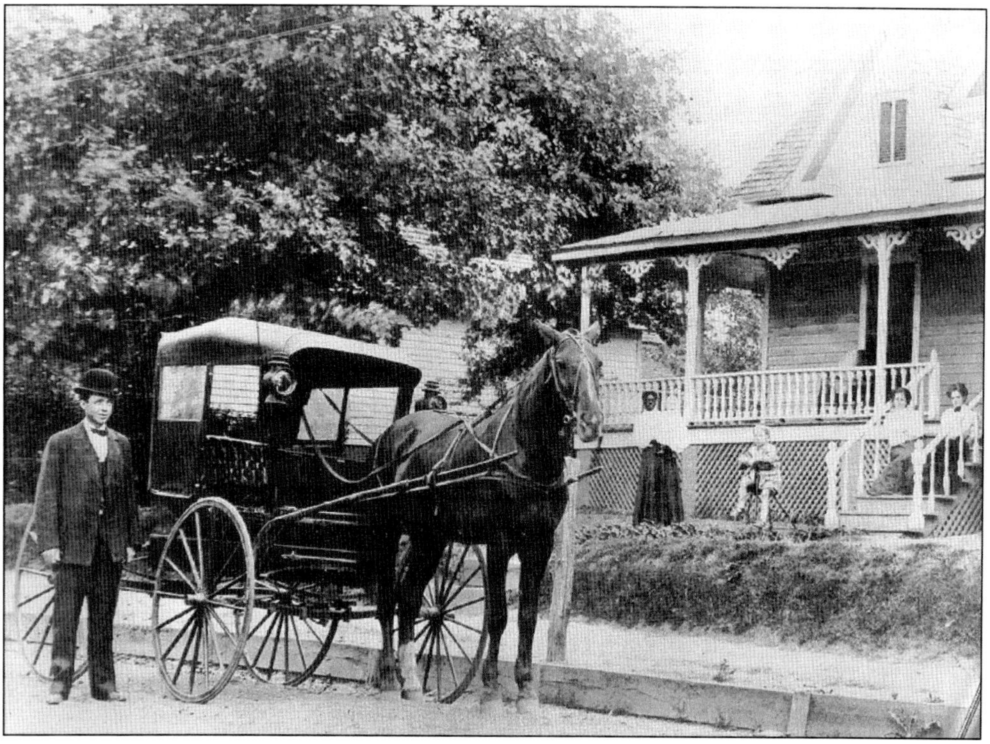

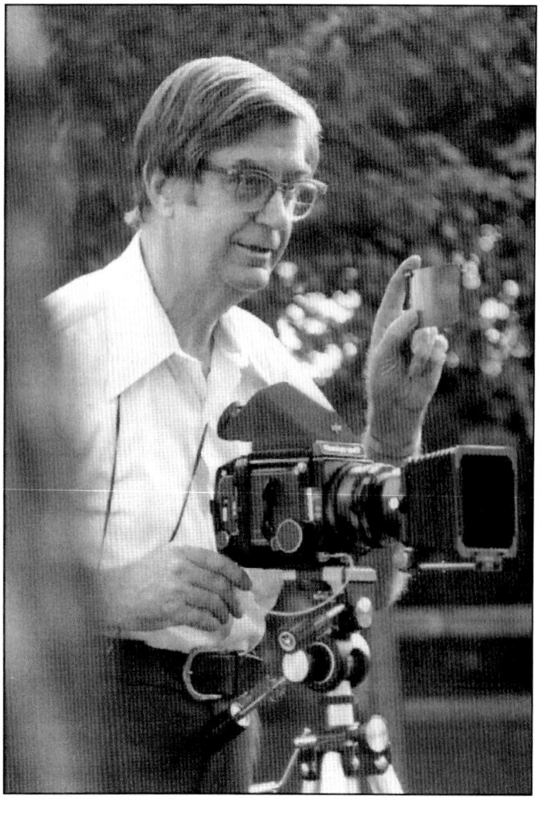

This Will McArthur photograph shows Dr. W. C. Bostic Sr. on Cherry Mountain Street before paved sidewalks and paved streets. The latticework conceals the porch underpinnings; gingerbread at the top of the porch shows well in the photograph and indicates the pride that the homeowner took in the residence. (Courtesy of Robert M. Watkins.)

After serving in World War II as an 8th Air Force fighter pilot, Robert M. Watkins began an apprenticeship with photographer J. T. Gilbert, whose studio was over Ivey Drum's Restaurant, called Ivey's Restaurant. In 1959, Robert Watkins purchased Gilbert's Studio, which was still on the south side of the square. Later Watkins moved his studio to his home at 114 Webb Street in Forest City. (Courtesy of Robert M. Watkins.)

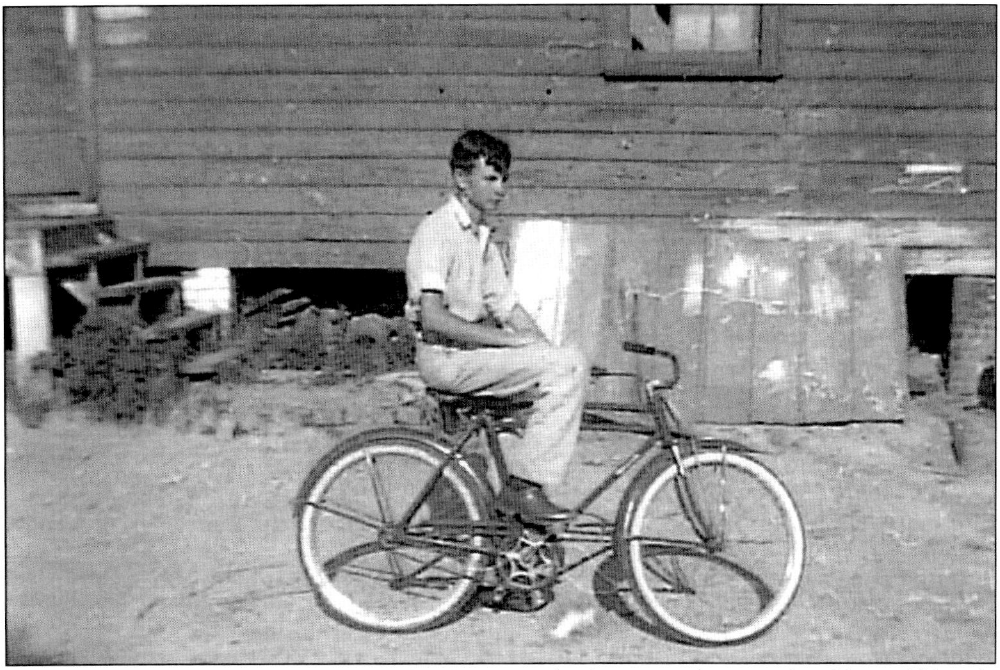

W. H. ("Bill") McArthur furnished this late-1930s/early-1940s photograph of himself beside McArthur's Tin Shop, now McArthur's Industrial Sheet Metal, Inc. Forest City has benefited from Bill and Mary McArthur's generosity with their photographs and with Will McArthur's work. Bill was a combat engineer in India and Burma during World War II.

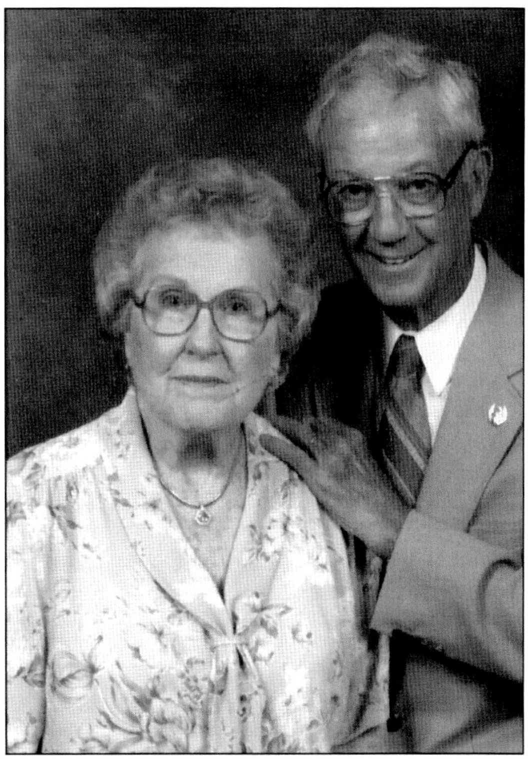

Educator Nancy Blanton Stallcup helped plan the Cool Springs Memorial Gardens when Memorial Avenue began suffering damage. Second Lt. Harold Stallcup piloted 30 missions of a B-17G with the 601st Squadron, 208th Bomb Group, 5th Air Force. After the war, he worked in bridge construction, as superintendent of County Bridge Maintenance and Construction, as superintendent for 26 counties, and as a town commissioner (1991–2005). (Courtesy of the Stallcups.)

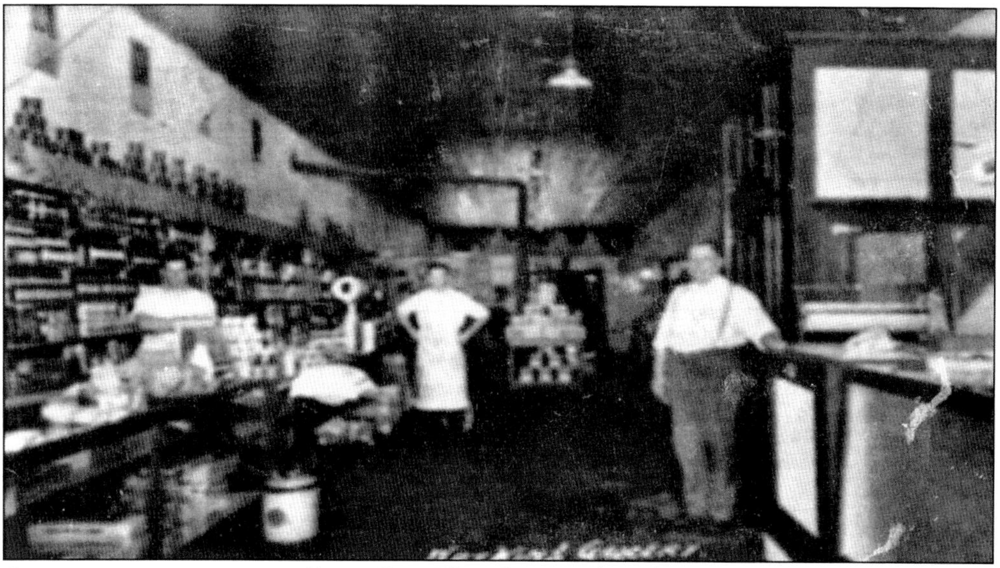

Groceries were important to Forest City. This photograph of the 1930 Watkins Grocery shows owner Edgar Watkins (with suspenders), Cecil Watkins (left, behind counter), and Ernest "Red" Watkins (center). Ernest Watkins later became manager of the Winn-Dixie in Rutherfordton. Cecil became a Winn-Dixie sales representative for the entire Southeast. Edgar Watkins ("Papa") was Martha Grace Estes's grandfather. (Courtesy of Martha Grace Estes.)

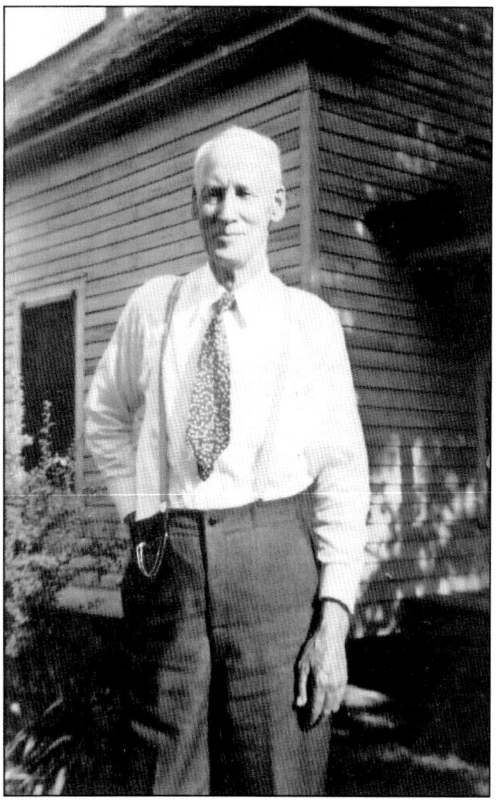

"Daddy Joe" Morris (Martha Grace Estes's other grandfather) was a grocer in a metal building near Florence Mills. Daddy Joe lived on South Broadway (where the Little Red Schoolhouse is today). Charles Vess, a local high school student, helped in the store of this Spanish-American War veteran. (Courtesy of Martha Grace Estes.)

At right are World War II veterans Charles Vess (101st Airborne Division) and his brother Guy (7th Armored Division) in the U. S. Military Cemetery in Normandy. Guy's postwar employment was with the U. S. Postal Service. After the war, Charles (left) worked in Africa for two years, earned his B.S., completed a law degree from the University of South Carolina in 1957, and worked with Western Auto (Houston and Kansas) until retirement in 1986. (Courtesy of Charles Vess.)

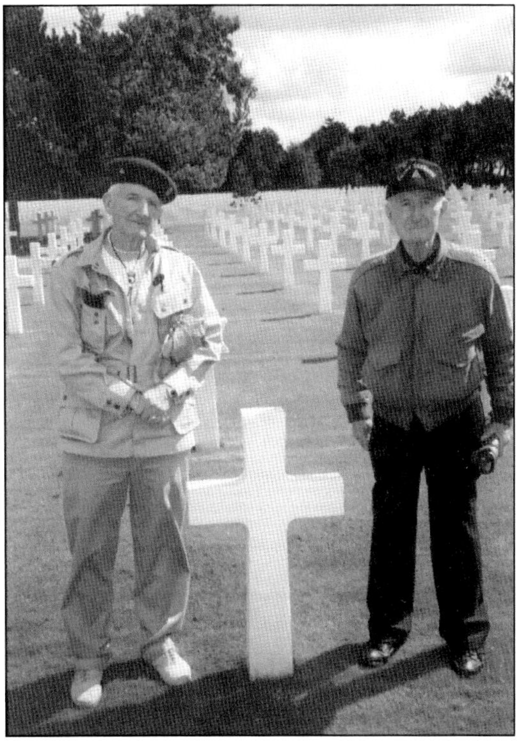

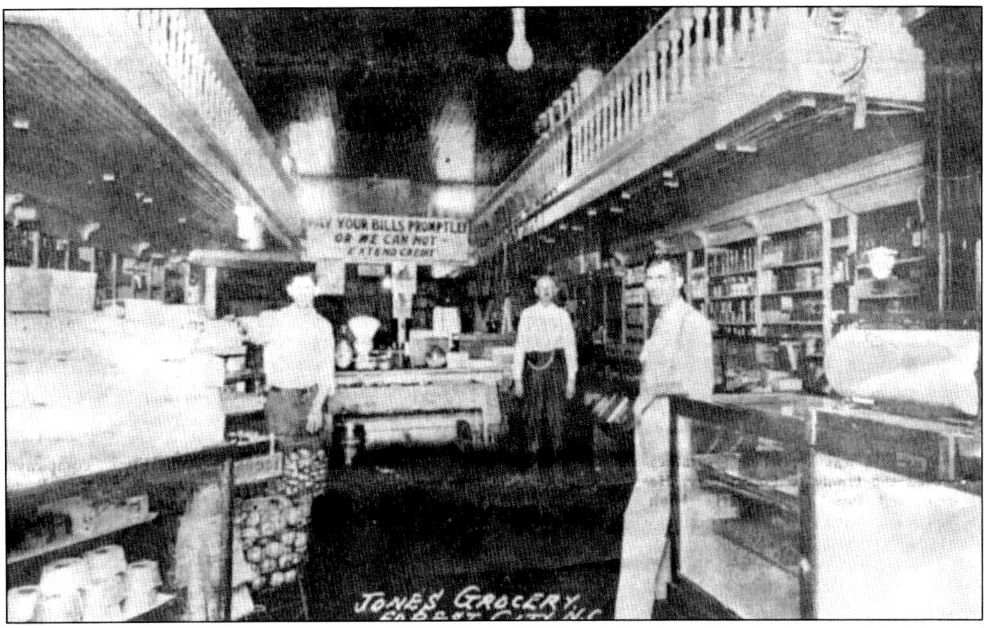

Jones's Grocery was formerly the Florence Mills Store at Cherry Mountain and Main. Pictured from left to right are Robert Blanton (delivery), "Newt" Jones (with watch and chain), and Tom Jones (co-owner). Tom's son Robert remembers unloading flour from a boxcar until his arms ached. Robert later worked at the A&P Store on West Main until it closed on February 28, 1976, at Harris Teeter for 10 years, and at Community Cash for three years. (Courtesy of Caroline and Robert Jones.)

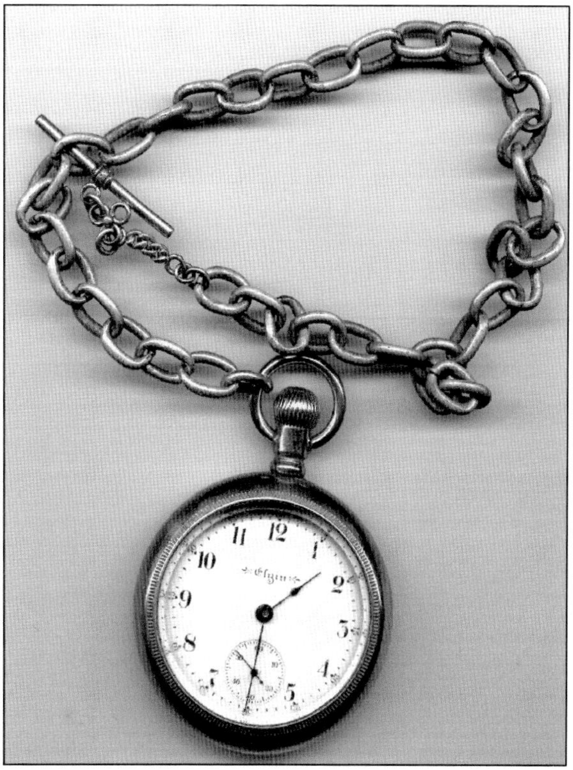

A treasured possession of Robert Jones is his grandfather Newton Jones's pocket watch and sturdy chain; the timepiece is visible also in the previous photograph. The Elgin watch still keeps perfect time and lacks the scratches one might expect from such an heirloom. The watch helped Jones close the store on time; his store stayed open until 10:00 p.m. as a service to workers of Florence Mills. (Courtesy of Caroline and Robert Jones.)

To entice customers and to reward faithful patrons, Newt Jones sometimes offered premiums. Dishes, photographs, mugs, and other gifts are still treasures of some Forest City residents. Pictured on the collectible plate above is Gen. Robert E. Lee on his horse, Traveller. (Courtesy of Caroline and Robert Jones.)

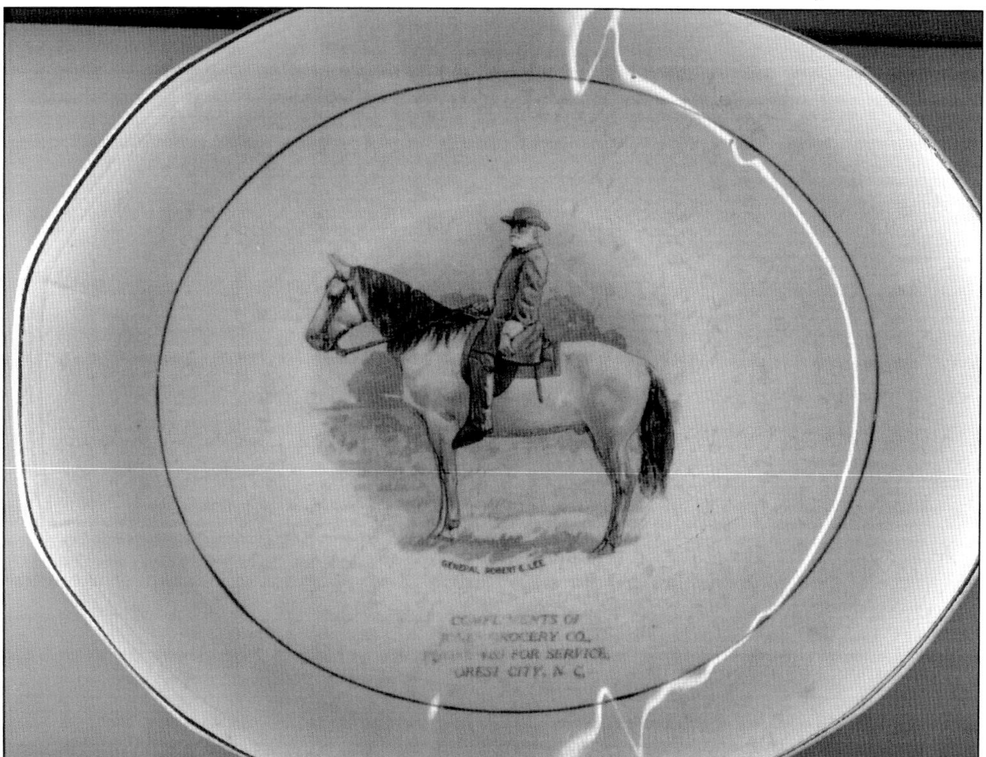

Other bonuses from Jones's Grocery that some collectors still save are the six-by-nine-inch photographs that Newton Jones offered in appreciation to his patrons. This photograph bears the inscription: "Memories of Mother. Mother, when I grow up, I'm going to buy everything from Jones Grocery Company, Forest City, North Carolina." (Courtesy of the authors.)

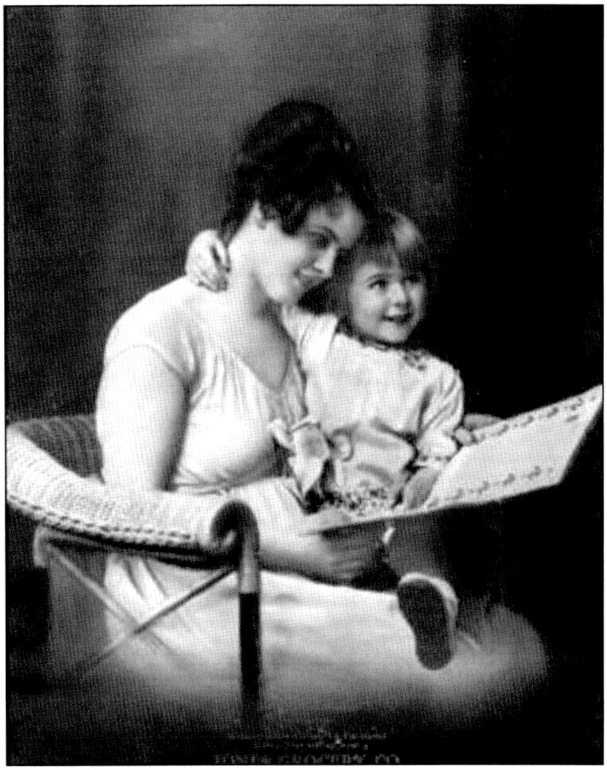

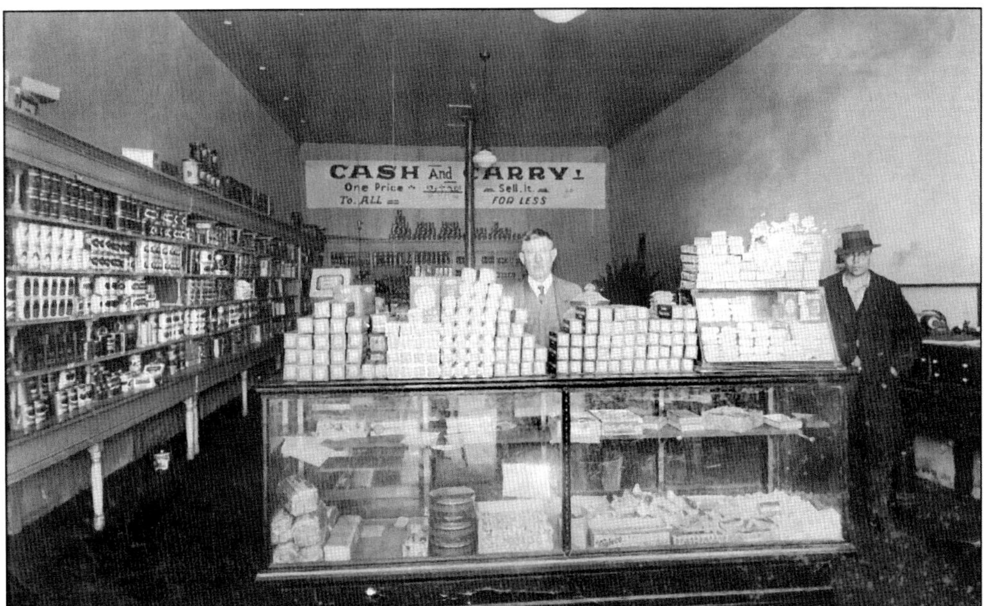

Other Forest City grocers included the Hemphills (Hemphill's Cash and Carry Grocery) and the Kings (King Brothers Grocery). In the center of the photograph of Hemphill's Cash and Carry Grocery on Main Street is Charlie Stein Hemphill; the policy of his store was to discourage the credit accumulations that were causing problems for patrons and businesses alike. (Courtesy of Jim Hemphill.)

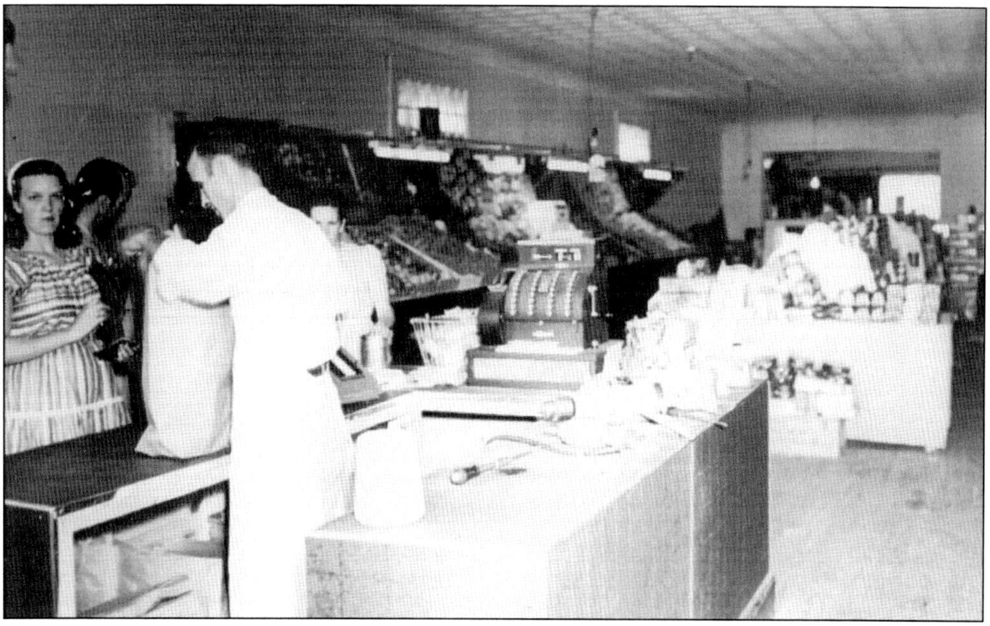

King Brothers Grocery, beside "Griff" Padgett's Barber Shop on Main Street, was popular in Forest City. At the cash register in this photograph is Willie B. King. This photograph shows fluorescent lighting, display shelves, and a cash register, which are more modern than furnishings in some grocery stores shown in this chapter. (Courtesy of Beth and Daniel King.)

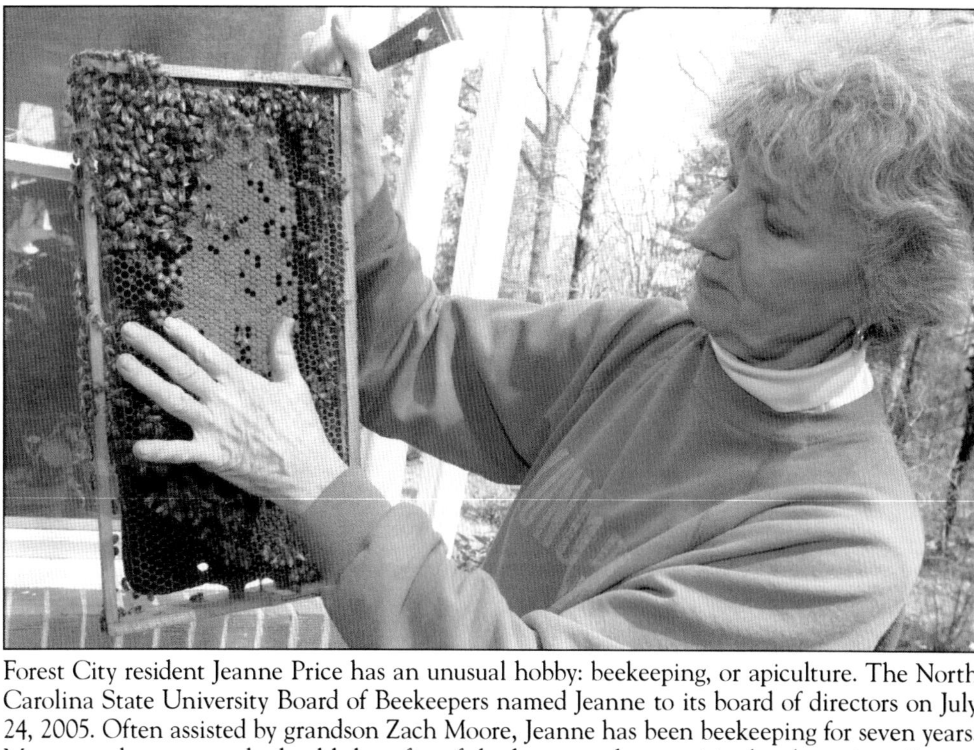

Forest City resident Jeanne Price has an unusual hobby: beekeeping, or apiculture. The North Carolina State University Board of Beekeepers named Jeanne to its board of directors on July 24, 2005. Often assisted by grandson Zach Moore, Jeanne has been beekeeping for seven years. Many people attest to the health benefits of the honey and—surprisingly—bee stings. Jeanne welcomes calls when bees swarm. (Courtesy of Angela Wyatt, *Daily Courier*.)

Local residents also consult physicians for health needs. For 40 years, Dr. Bobby England maintained a reputable family practice. His office at 124 Groce Street was a beacon to the sick. Now a North Carolina state representative, Dr. England is still active. He has held his position as athletic trainer for the football team at East Rutherford High School for the past 40 years. (Courtesy of Bob F. England, M.D.)

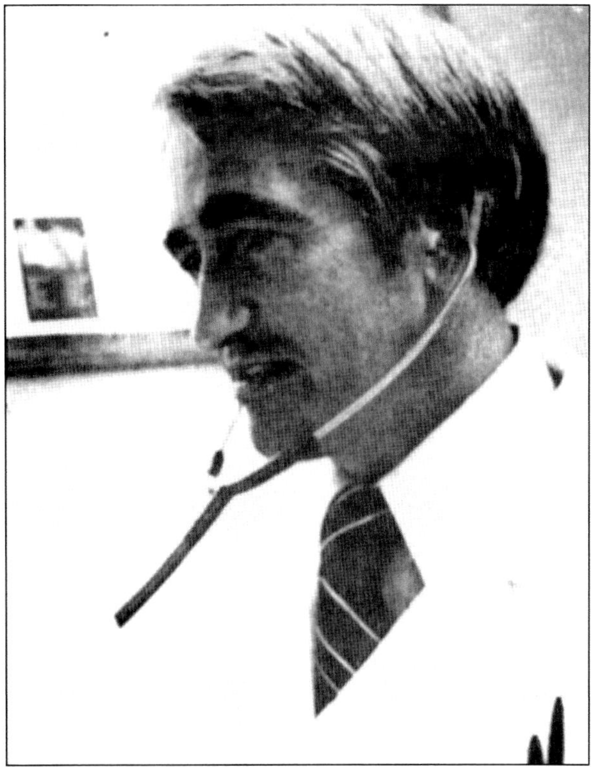

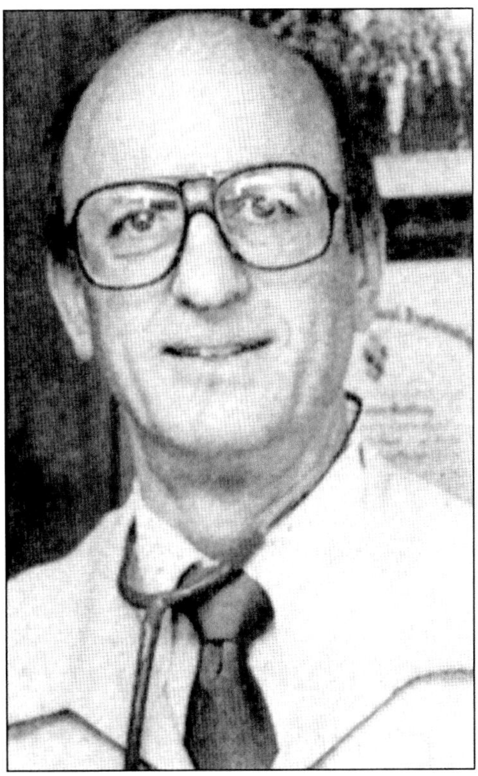

Practicing with Dr. Bobby England since their graduation from medical school was Dr. Joe Godfrey, originally from Woodruff, South Carolina. In 20 years (about 1966 to 1986) the two doctors delivered approximately 3,600 babies. Dr. Godfrey, like his medical partner, considers politics and helping his community an important part of serving others. (Courtesy of Bob F. England, M.D.)

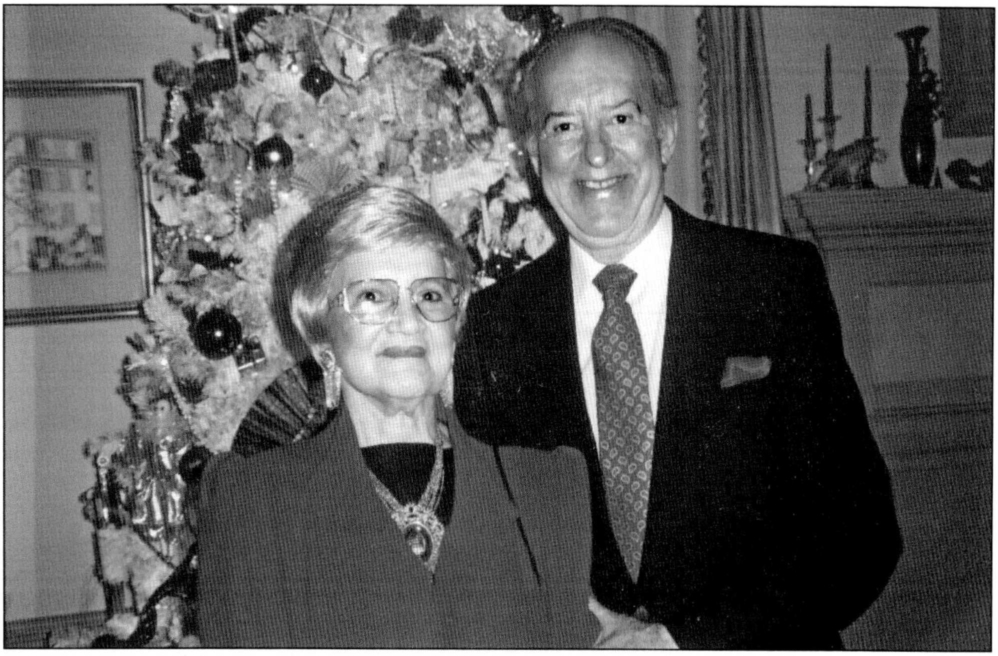

Cool Springs graduate (1941) Dr. Jack A. Wofford served in the U.S. Army Air Forces. Stationed in England, he received retraining on B-29 Bombers. A 1949 graduate of the Illinois College of Optometry in Chicago and married to Dorothy Turner in 1951, he opened his first office in the 1950s over Rose's 5-10-25¢ Store (page 111). Later offices were beside Stallings Jewelry Store and on South Broadway. (Courtesy of Dr. Jack A. Wofford.)

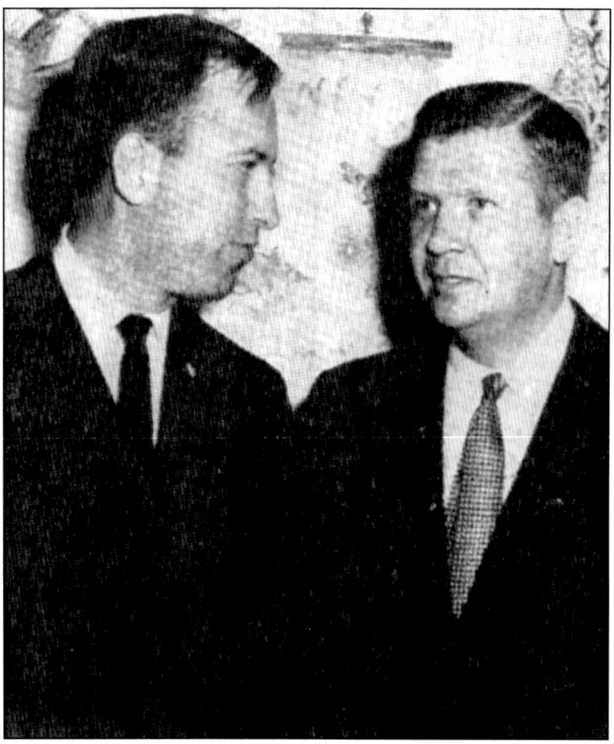

Dr. Jack A. Wofford (left), Terry Sanford's county campaign manager, shared lunch at Ron and Eddy's with Gov. Terry Sanford on April 25, 1960. Wofford, among other things, chaired the Rutherford County Democratic Party and the County Welfare Board; Sanford appointed him to the Welfare Study Commission. After Wofford's retirement after 40 years in optometry, his granddaughter, Tammy, and her spouse, Gary Edelman assumed his practice. (Courtesy of Dr. Jack A. Wofford and the *Courier*.)

Dr. W. L. Stallings was a doctor of veterinary medicine and the owner of Stallings Jewelry Store on Main Street; the jewelry store still bears the Stallings name. Robert Daniel Beason and Joy Beason Hunt now own the store. Seeing Dr. Stallings with camera in hand was not unusual. One of his most unusual shots was a self-portrait. (Courtesy of Betty Jo Carpenter and Dr. W. L. Stallings.)

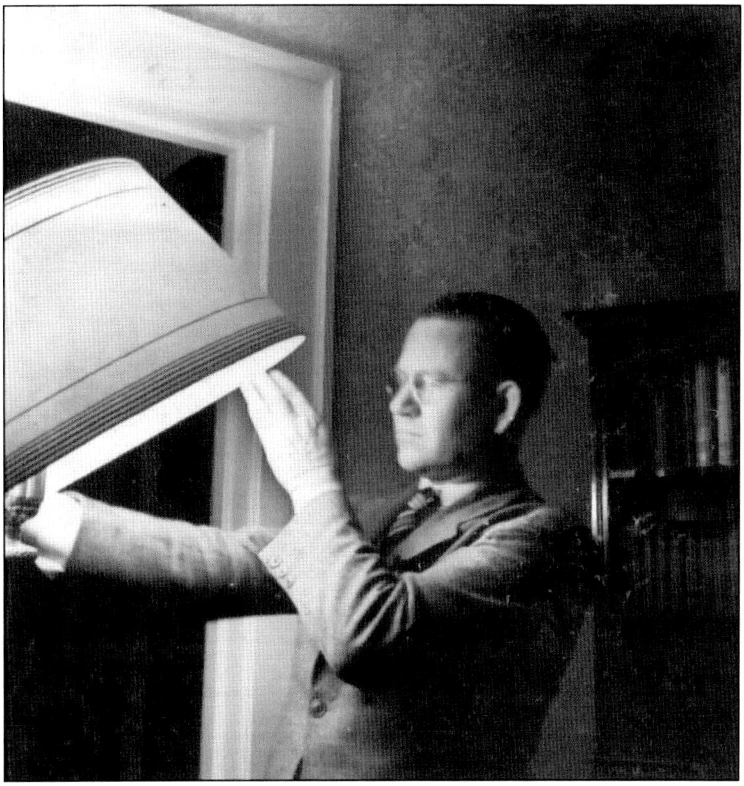

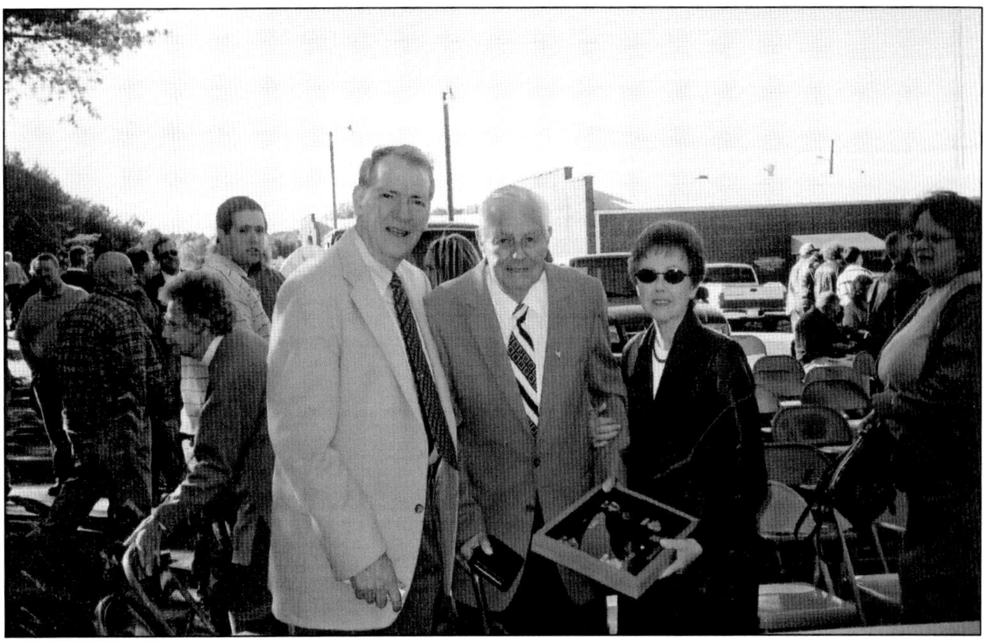

A. C. Burgess served in Okinawa in World War II. He did not receive all the decorations that he earned so Congressman Charles Taylor (left) came to Rutherford County to recognize A. C. (center) and other county veterans. Laverne Fritze is pictured on the right. A. C. remembers 10¢ lunches at Ron and Eddy's and pumping gasoline for 10–15¢. (Courtesy of A. C. Burgess.)

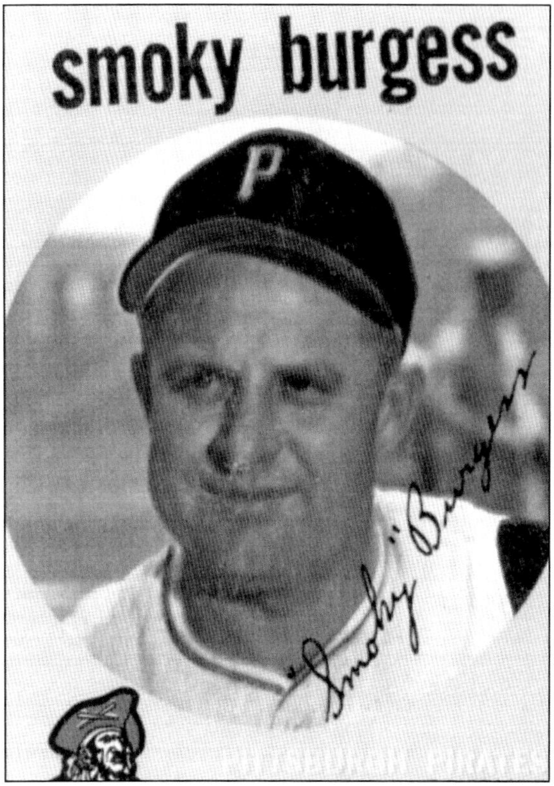

Forrest "Smokey" ("Smoky") Burgess (1927–1991), younger brother of A. C., played major-league baseball from 1949 to 1967 with various teams: Chicago Cubs, Philadelphia Phillies, Cincinnati Reds, Pittsburgh Pirates, and Chicago White Sox. Four-time All-Star and member of the 1960 World Champion Pittsburgh Pirates, he excelled as a defensive catcher and pinch hitter. He worked as a furniture mover for Grindstaff's Furniture to keep in shape. (Courtesy of A. C. Burgess.)

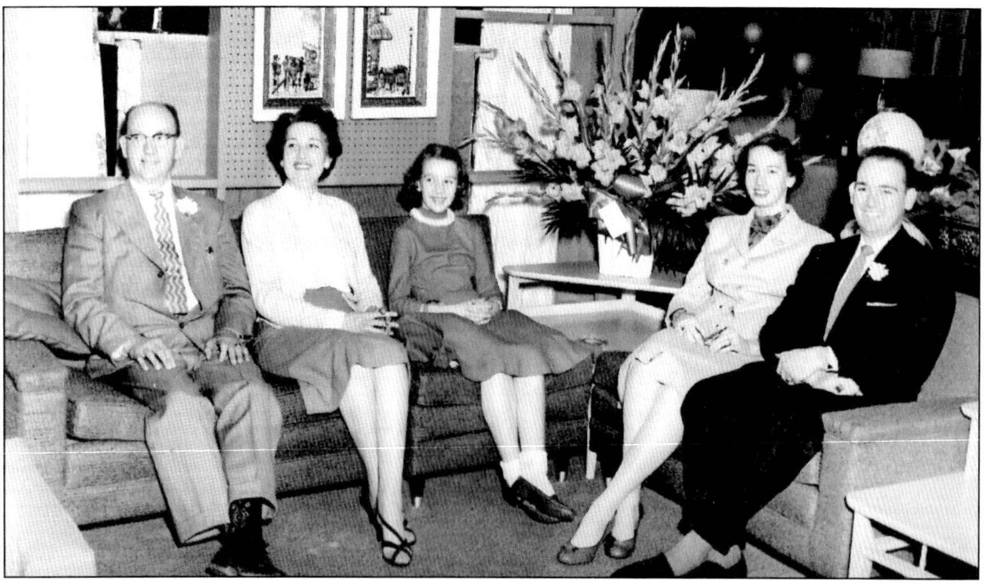

The Grindstaffs respected baseball player/scout Smokey Burgess when he worked at Grindstaff's Furniture (West Main) in the off seasons. Although the store's name and CEOs have changed since the 1950s, it is still prominent. An opening of a new addition is the occasion for this photograph. From left to right are E. M. Grindstaff (founder), Ruth Price Grindstaff, Barbara Grindstaff (Whitehurst), Carolyn Grindstaff (Barbee), and Boyce Grindstaff (husband of Dorothy Smith Grindstaff). (Courtesy of Carolyn Grindstaff Barbee.)

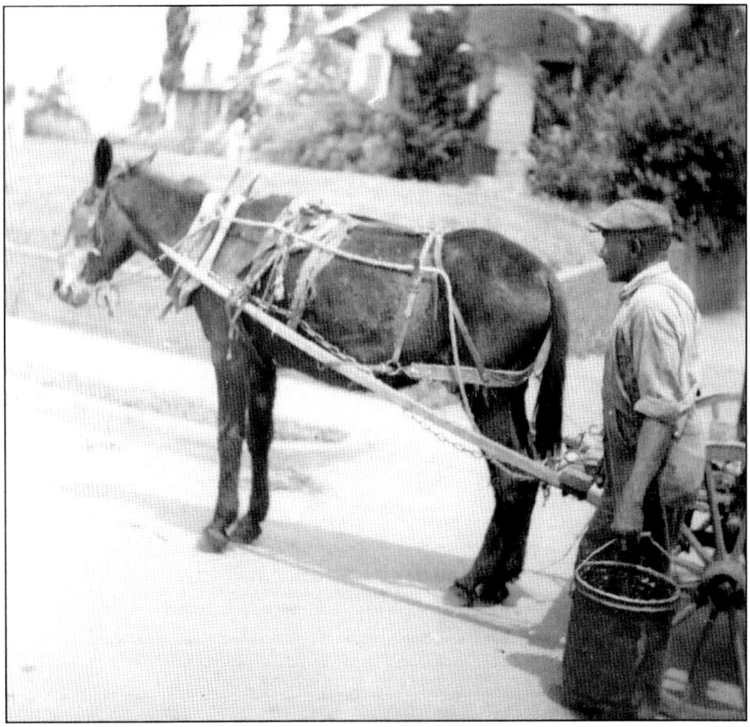

Dr. W. L. Stallings stepped out of his home on Arlington Street and photographed this service worker. A mule pulled the collection wagon from house to house. Sanitation work is still essential to Forest City today, but the vehicles have changed. (Courtesy of Dr. W. L. Stallings and Betty Jo Carpenter.)

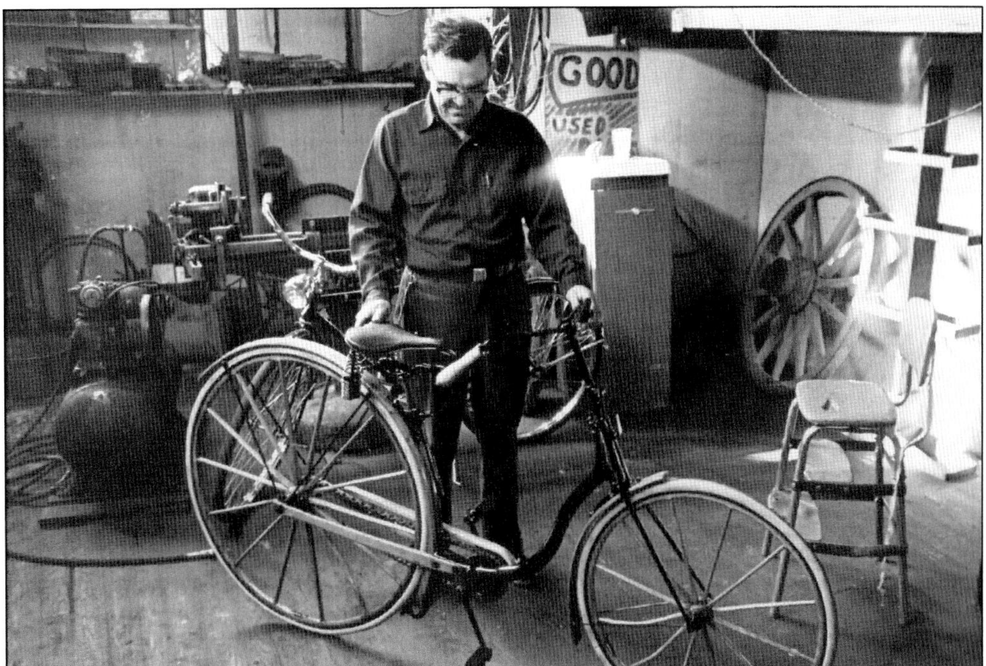

Another essential worker in Forest City was Spike Ellis. Here he examines an early bicycle for repair. The spokes on the wheels indicate the age of the bike. Residents of the town knew where to come for any repair job, large or small: Ellis's Cycle Shop on Thomas Street. (Courtesy of William Brown.)

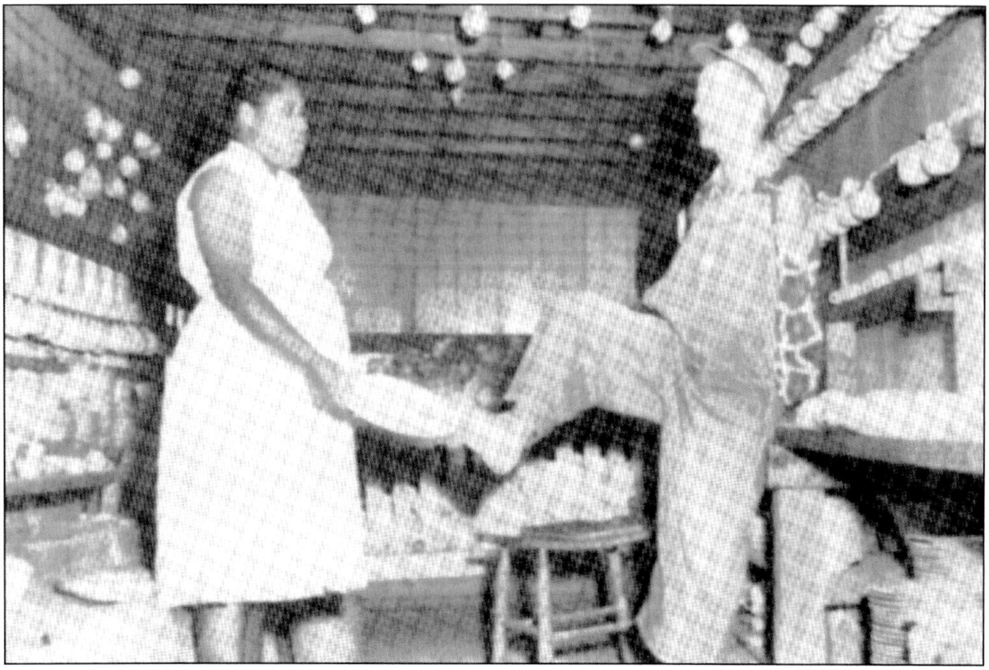

Forest City residents seeking dishes knew where to go. Just outside the city limits was the dish shop of Samuel Nunnie Tipton (1893–1963). Born without arms, Nunnie used his feet for everything—tipping his hat to changing an automobile tire—as *Ripley's Believe It Or Not* attests. Here Nunnie helps a customer with a plate. Many county residents remember well his pleasant demeanor. (Courtesy of David Daniel.)

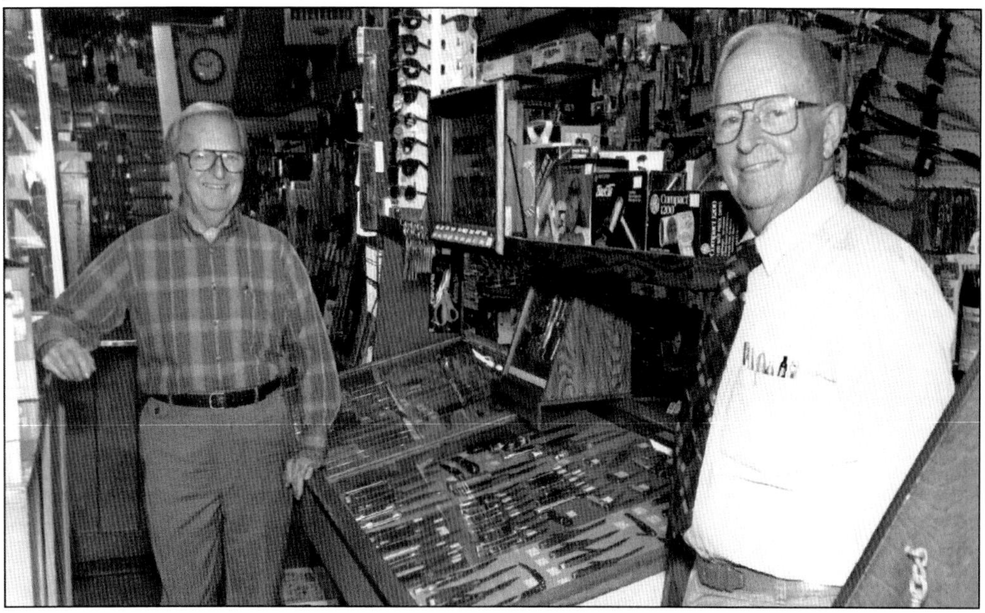

Displaying their cutlery in Logan's Hardware Store are Logan brothers James (left) and Blaine (right). The two brothers and their father, Blaine Logan Sr., operated the family business on East Main Street for many years. Honesty and dependability were their trademarks for half a century. (Courtesy of Blaine Logan Jr.)

Mary Ellen Turner Goforth and Charlie Johnson Goforth Sr. operated Goforth's Cafe in downtown Forest City for many years. Built before 1935, the tin building moved two times. Its general location is still near Davis Donuts on Powell Street. The cafe met the fire codes that required no wood in the kitchen area. These beloved grandparents of Frances Goforth Pilgrim reared her from an early age. (Courtesy of Dr. W. L. Stallings and Betty Jo Carpenter.)

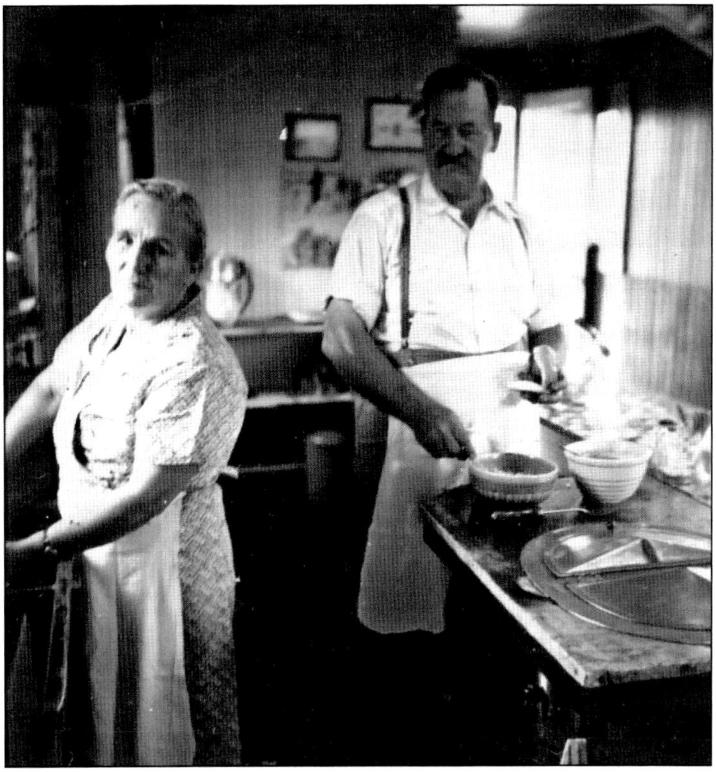

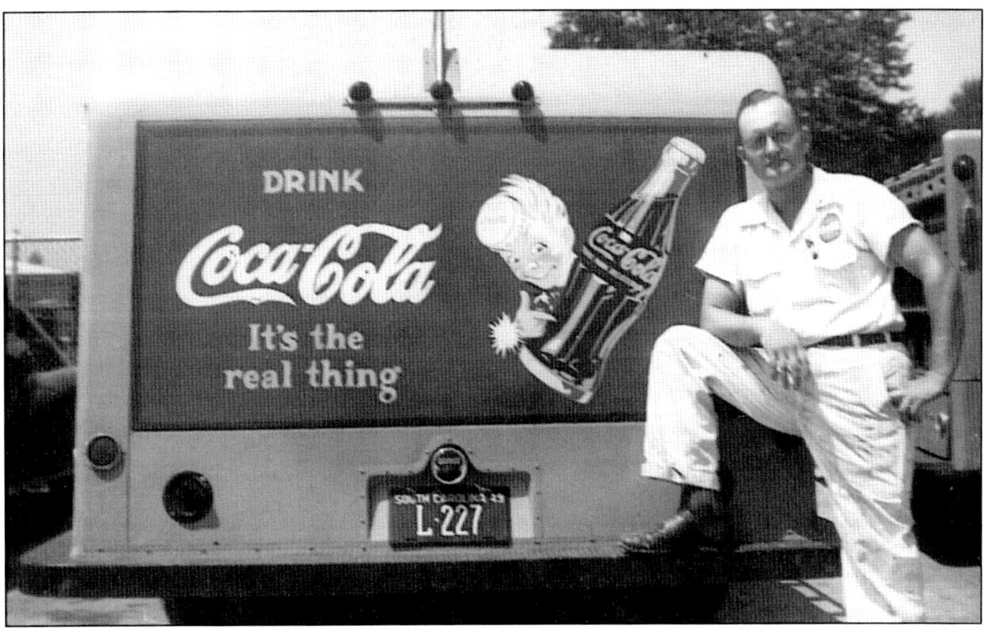

Baptist minister Rev. Albert Reeves Hastings (October 14, 1919–August 5, 1999) served 14 churches, including the Forest Lake Baptist Church. An employee of the Southern Railway, Pepsi-Cola, and Coca-Cola, here he poses in 1949 at the rear of a delivery truck announcing that Coca-Cola is "the real thing." He was the father of five children, including Frances Hastings Owens. (Courtesy of Frances Hastings Owens.)

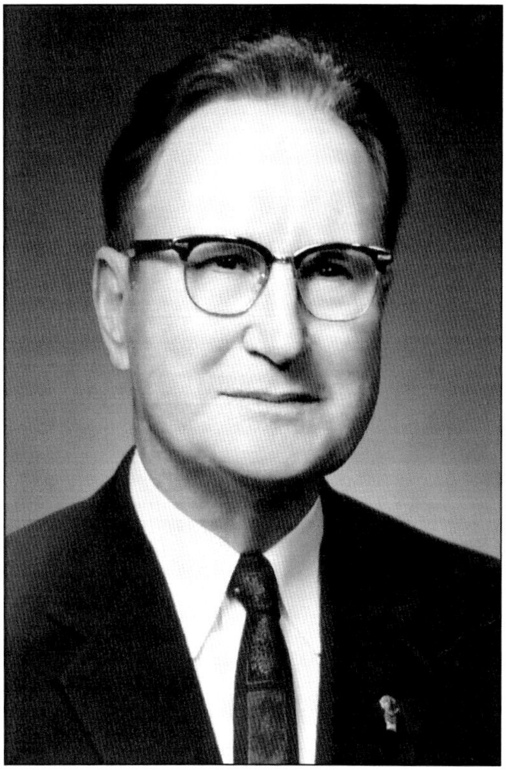

O. J. Mooneyham supervised the Works Progress Administration in North Carolina's Eighth District, established Mooneyham and Forest City Drugs, headed the county's Council of Defense during the 1940s, and (with Clarence Griffin) leased the *Forest City Courier* in 1940. "He did much of his work with a handshake," said Ruth Toney Calvert; E. A. Toney always called Security Bank and Trust "Mr. Mooneyham's Bank," because he was the founder. The East Main public library bears his name. (Courtesy of Colleen Jenkins Biggerstaff.)

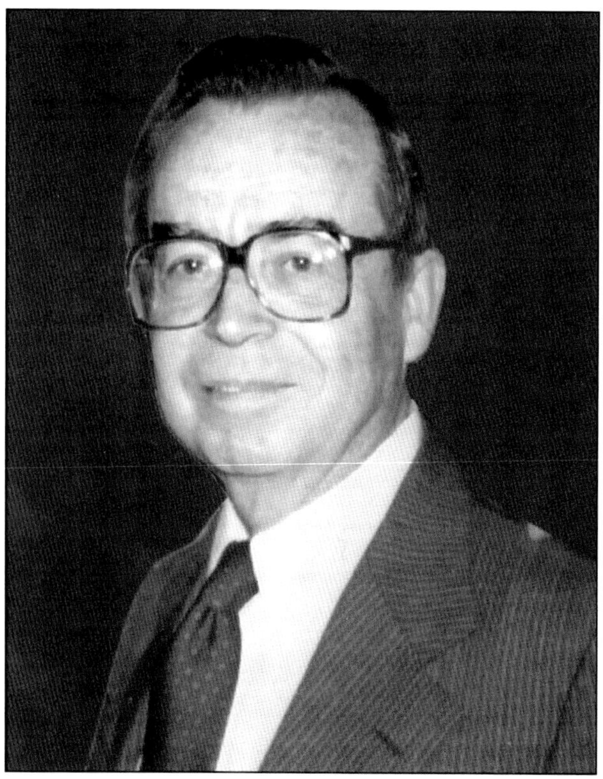

Dr. George F. Becknell (U.S. Army Air Forces) was a Duke graduate with an M.D. from the University of South Carolina. From 1951 until 1998, he practiced in Dr. Moss's Cliffside office, the Turner Building (Forest City), and the Becknell Family Practice Center (South Broadway). He met chemistry major Lathelma Towery during her senior year in college; they married in 1958. His brother was "Uncle Bud" Becknell of WAGY. (Courtesy of Lathelma Towery Becknell.)

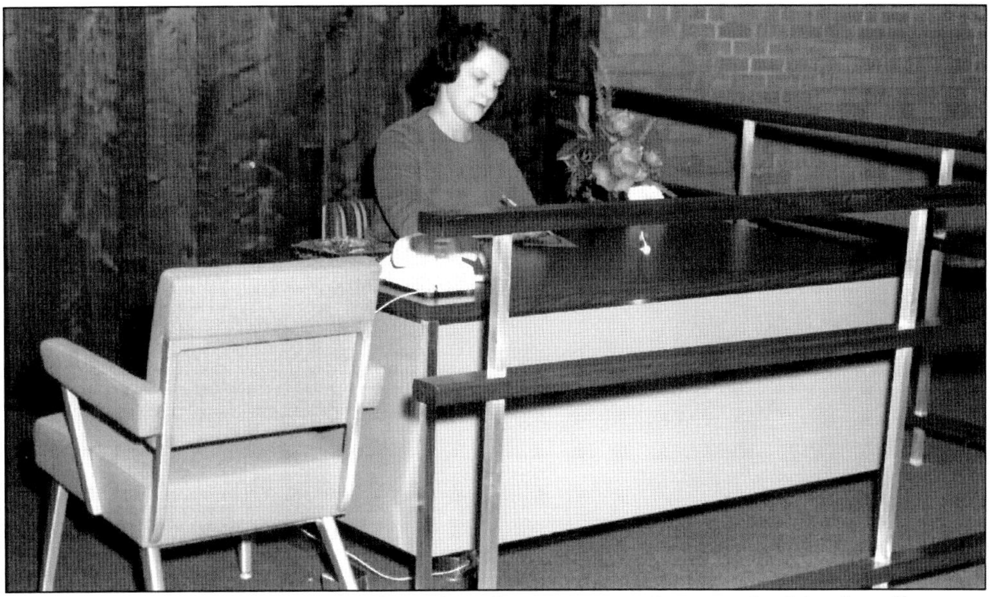

Although she is still active in church work and in preserving her own food for the off season, Colleen Jenkins Biggerstaff retired in 1989 after a successful banking career of 36 years. During her career with Security Bank and Trust, Northwestern Bank, and First Union National, she held various positions: branch manager (1953), assistant cashier (1955), assistant vice president (1964), operations officer, assistant branch manager (1985), and branch manager (1987). (Courtesy of Colleen Jenkins Biggerstaff.)

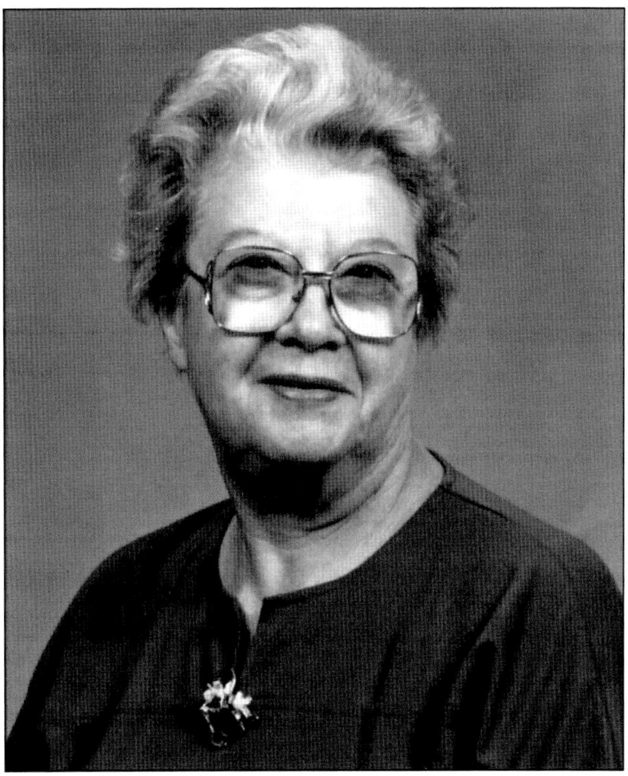

Lucille Hamrick Carpenter is another woman associated with financial institutions. Lucille went to work in 1956 after graduating from high school and completing a business education program in Asheville. She retired after 32 years with Home Finance ("Finance at Home with Home Finance"), Barclay Finance, and American Credit. Wife of World War II veteran Harmon Carpenter (deceased), she has two children, Kenny and Debbie, and is an active gardener, seamstress, and cook. (Courtesy of Lucille Carpenter.)

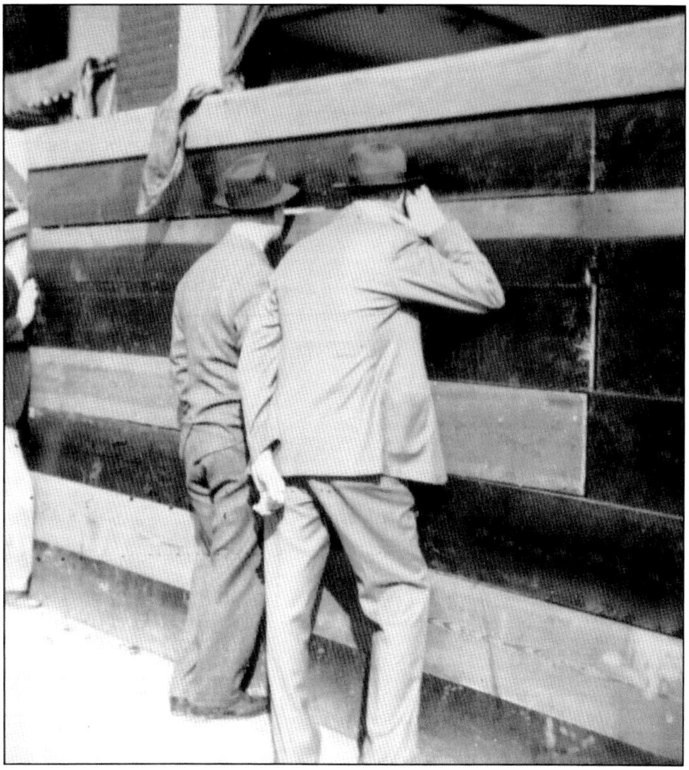

During the construction of Smith's Drugs on East Main Street, local residents watched with interest. Here Clarence Griffin (left) and J. Worth Morgan peer through the construction barricade designed to protect bystanders. Smith's Drugs opened in 1939–1940. One employee who greeted patrons was Eloise Toms, chief cook and cashier for more than 57 years. (Courtesy of Dr. W. L. Stallings and Betty Jo Carpenter.)

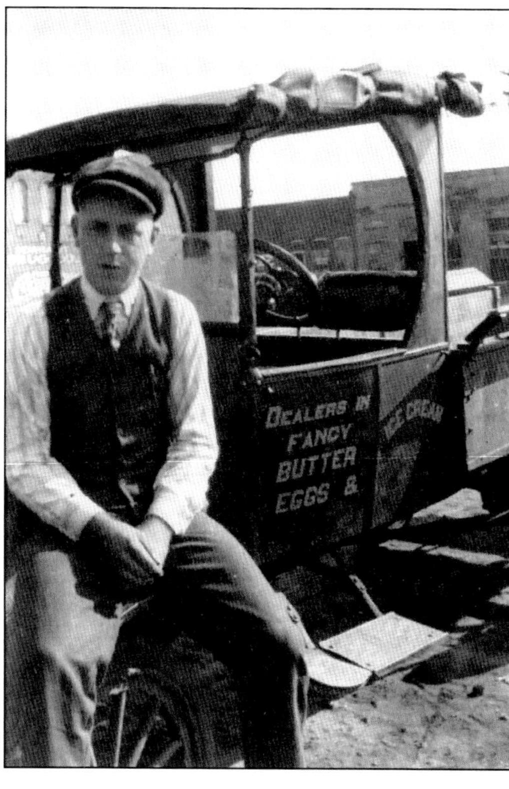

Serving as a drayman was Martin H. Mauney. His delivery vehicle promised "Fancy Butter, Eggs, and Ice Cream." Mauney poses in front of Jones's Grocery in 1916. Reinhardt Drugs is visible over Mauney's shoulder in the left corner of the photograph. The street was unpaved at that time. (Courtesy of Bill Brown.)

In front of their Arlington Street residence are Clarence Lloyd Morris Jr. (far left, born in 1930), Clarence Lloyd Morris Sr. (with cap, born in 1901), and Martha Grace Morris (future wife of Maxie Chambless Estes) on tricycle. Martha Grace remembers listening to the Victrola and early radio shows and loving music even as a child. She and her husband served as college professors in LaGrange, Georgia. (Courtesy of Martha Grace Morris Estes.)

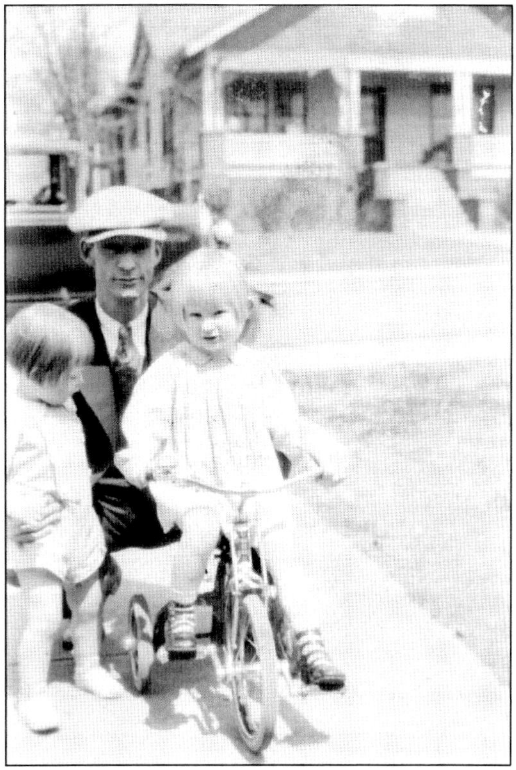

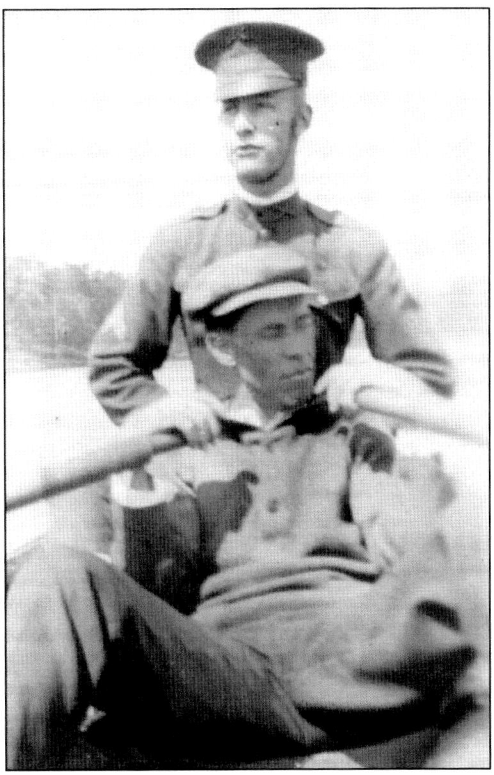

Joseph Morris ("Daddy Joe," grandfather of Martha Grace Estes) was born in 1873 and served in the U.S. Army during the Spanish-American War. Morris (pictured here in uniform and sitting upright) attained the rank of corporal in the infantry before his discharge. After the war, he operated a small grocery near Florence Mills before his death in 1941. (Courtesy of Martha Grace Estes.)

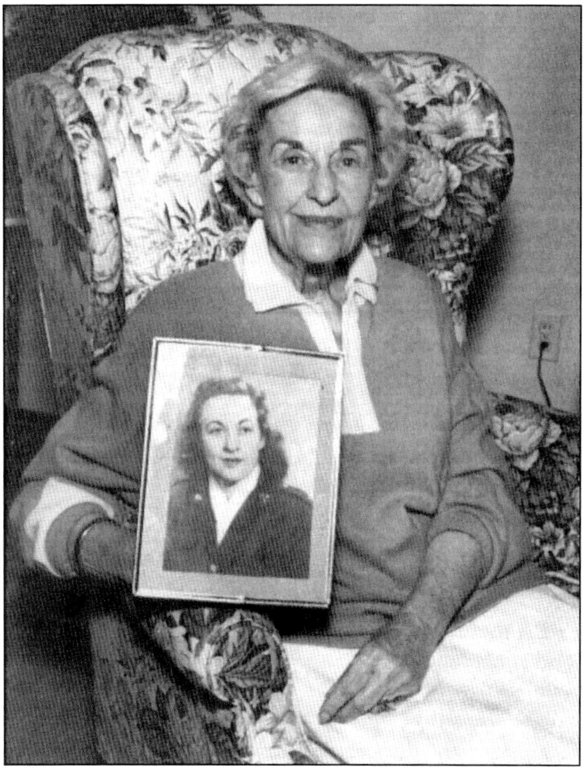

Lt. Evelyn Morris (Mrs. Jim Ferree) served in the U.S. Army Nursing Corps. From 1943 until 1945, she served in North Africa, Italy (Naples), Guam (Pacific), and Okinawa. She worked at the health department for 32 years. Her brother John Morris (infantry) died in action. Their siblings are O. W. Morris (former principal of Cool Springs High), G. Arnold Morris, Robert Morris, and Walda Morris (Mrs. Dewey Carpenter Sr.). (Courtesy of Evelyn Morris Ferree.)

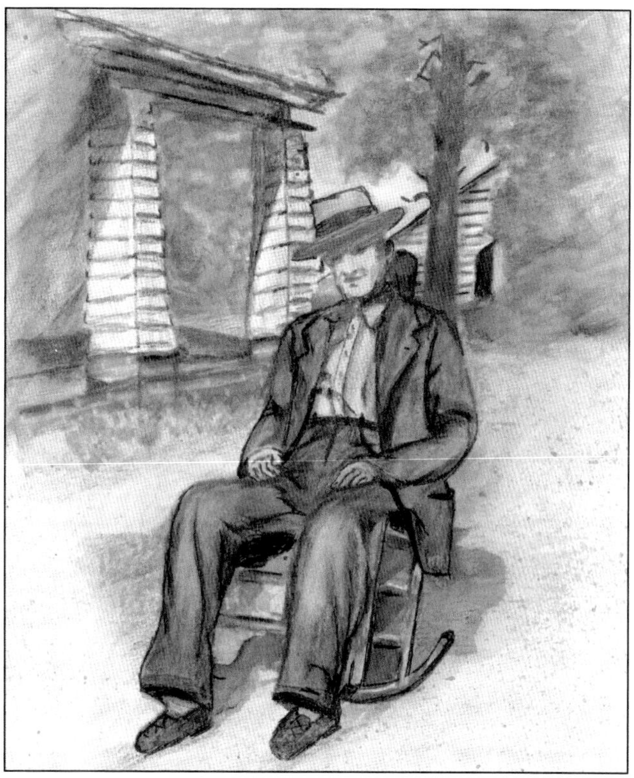

This painting of Adam Price (1870–1960), with his barn in the background, is by his great-granddaughter Jane Thompson Gurley. Price was a cotton farmer in the Forest City area. His family was usually in the top three in cotton production in the entire county. Jane's grandmother, Selma Jane Price Harrill, provided the photograph from which Jane was able to make her painting. (Courtesy of Jane Thompson Gurley.)

Bob Morgan (page 2) served in the U.S. Navy during World War II. Morgan has served on the Economic Development Commission, the Tourist Development Authority, the County Planning Commission and the Local Transportation Board (with Harold Stallcup). He helped coach the East Rutherford High School tennis team, which broke the winning streak of Hickory High School. He and his camera are familiar sights in Forest City. (Courtesy of Bob Morgan.)

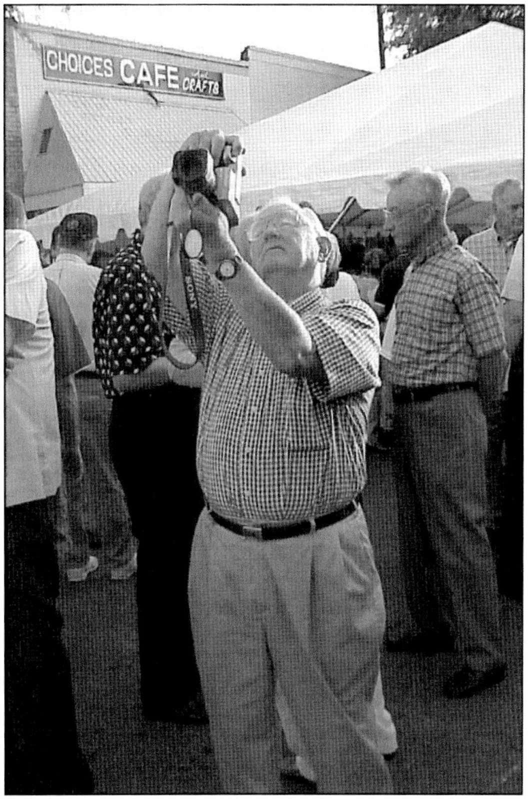

Danielle Withrow has served as town planner since 2000. She is planning a museum in the Florence Mills Building. Danielle received her baccalaureate from UNC-Chapel Hill and her master's in public administration from North Carolina State. Grover Bradley, mayor at the time of the photograph, is a World War II veteran, businessman, and civic leader; he served as mayor from 1995 to 2003 and council member from 1990 to 1995. (Courtesy of Bob Morgan.)

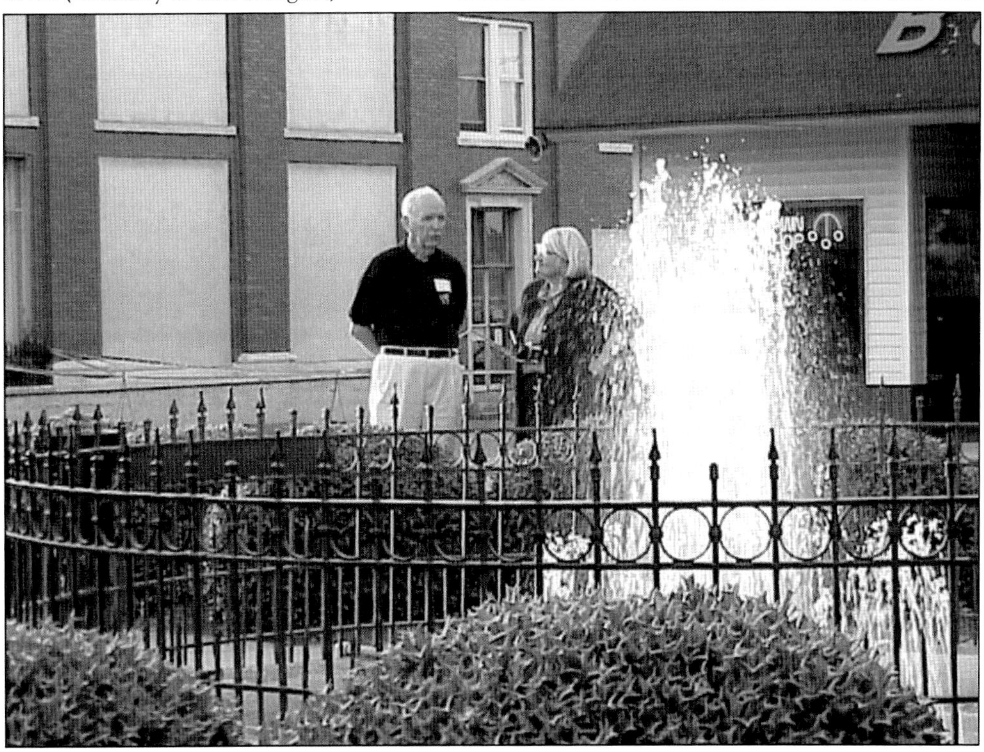

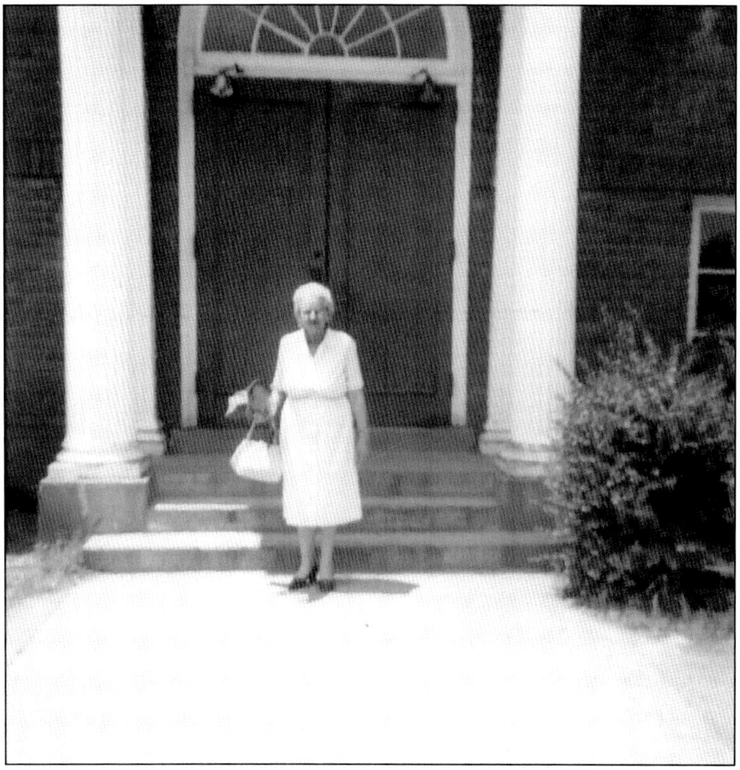

Ottilie Long taught first grade at Forest City Elementary School for over 30 years. Here she leaves the front door of the school for the last time in 1962. Ottilie was a sister of Katie Long and Mary Thompson Long (Hair), an aunt of David Brown, and a daughter of Johnny Long, who owned Long's Drugs (Mill Street and East Main). (Courtesy of David Brown and Mary Thompson Long Hair.)

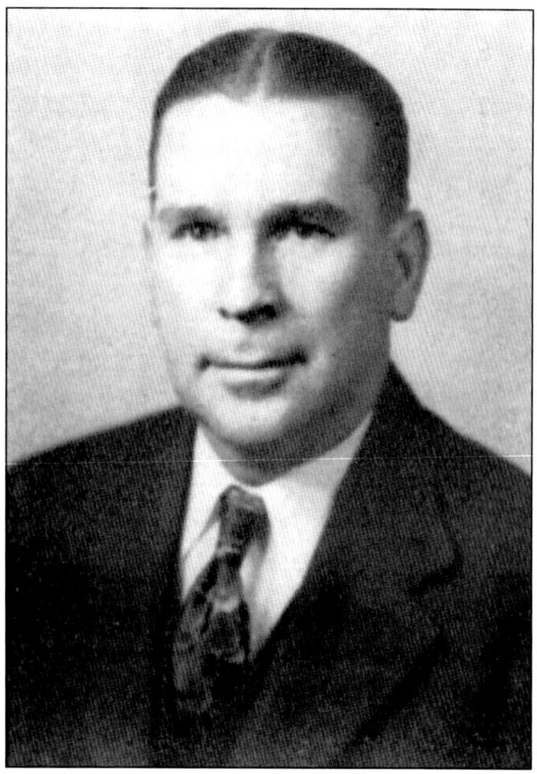

E. V. Seitz was an educator in Rutherford County and veteran of World War II. He served as both teacher and principal during his tenure at Cool Springs High School. In his memory, the most outstanding male athlete at East Rutherford High School receives the E. V. Seitz Award. (Courtesy of Martha Grace Estes and Helen Cole Krause.)

Dee Christopher Cole—"Music Man"—started the county band movement. He served in the 117th Infantry during World War II and attended the Cincinnati Conservatory of Music. Here Cole waves farewell at the end of the last concert he conducted. The East Rutherford High School Band was honor guard at Cole's funeral in 1974. He received a posthumous induction into the North Carolina Bandmasters Association Hall of Fame. (Courtesy of Bob Morgan and Helen Cole Krause.)

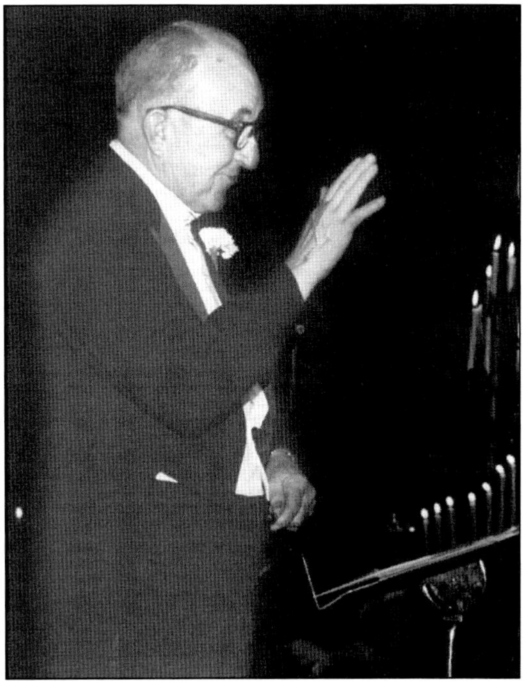

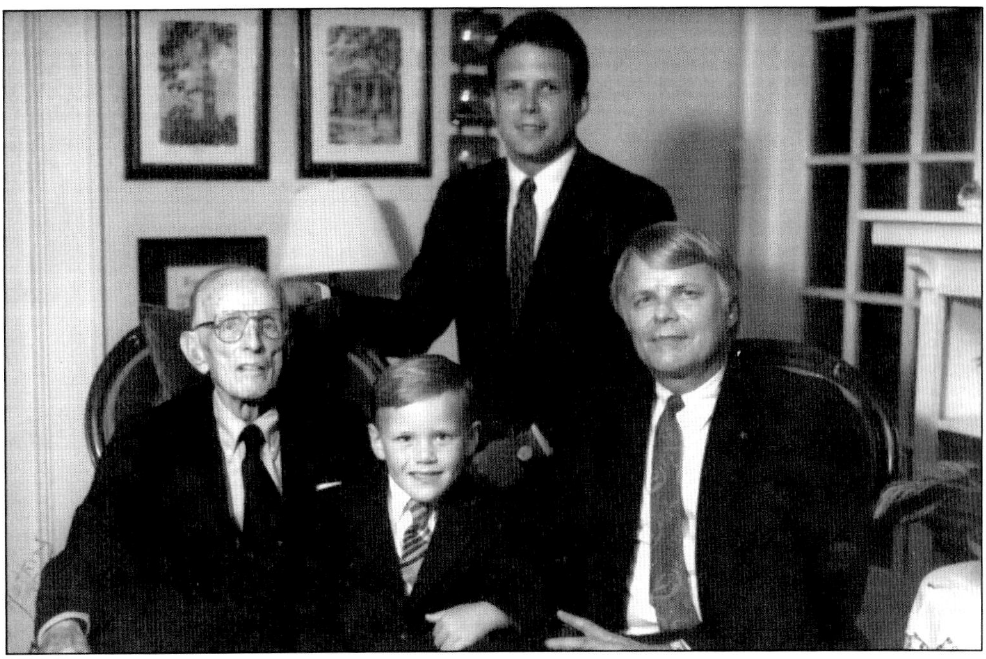

University of North Carolina graduate and World War I veteran Charles Z. Flack Sr. (1893–1991) helped his father, A. B. Flack, with Flack's Hardware on Main Street, graduated after 10 grades, took the 11th grade, and graduated again. He was mayor (1929–1931) during town hall construction for $35,000 on Powell Street. Pictured here from left to right are C. Z. Flack Sr., C. Z. Flack IV ("Chad," an outstanding baseball player at UNC-Chapel Hill in 2005), C. Z. Flack III ("Tripp," with Blanton-Flack), and C. Z. Flack Jr. ("Chuck," businessman/politician). (Courtesy of C. Z. Flack Jr.)

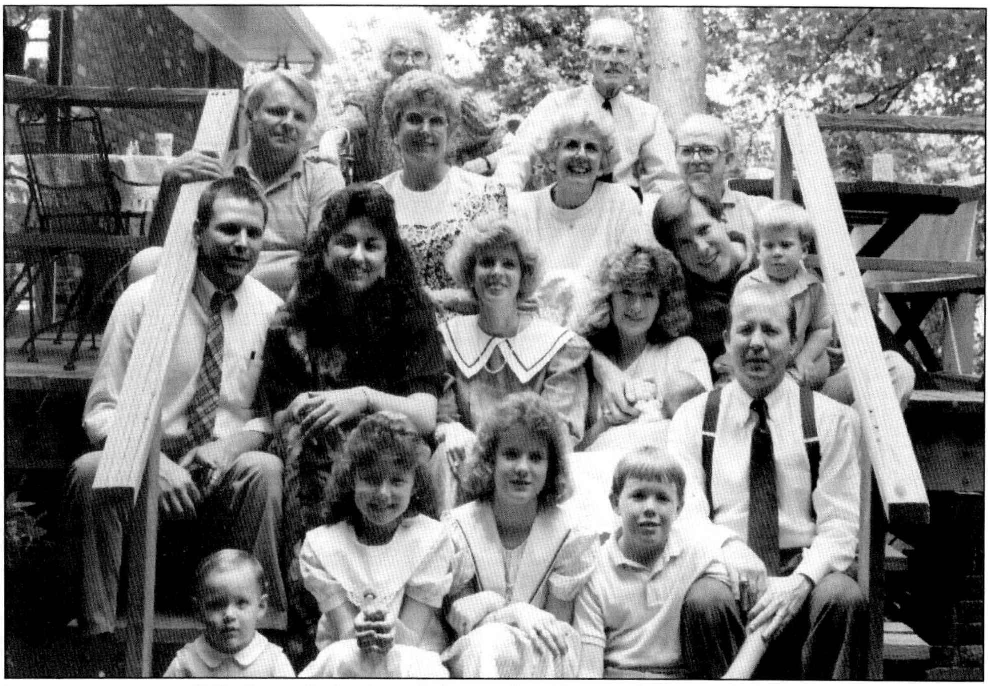

Four generations of Flacks include, from left to right, (first row) C. Z. Flack IV, Ashlea Elizabeth Flack (a pharmacist), Meghan Caroline Lamb, Brett Thomas Lamb, and James Thomas Lamb; (second row) Charles Z. Flack III, Angela Guy Flack (a pharmacist), Caroline Ann Lamb, Deborah B. Baynard holding Devon Elisabeth Baynard, and Paul Thomas Baynard Jr. with Paul Cameron Baynard; (third row) Charles Z. Flack Jr., Jane Sawyer Flack, Caroline Flack Baynard, Paul Thomas Baynard, Blanche T. Flack, and Charles Z. Flack. (Courtesy of Caroline Flack Baynard.)

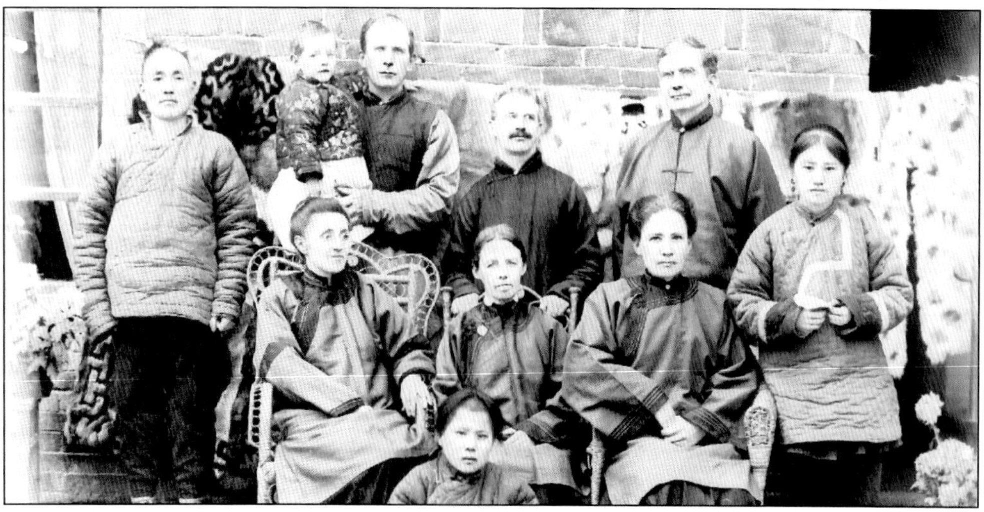

This 1910–1911 photograph made in Pochow, China, shows the grandchildren of John Bostick. Three served as missionaries to China from the 1890s to 1943—a total of 111 years among them. They are Attie Texas Bostick (far right of first row, seated), Wade Bostick (third row, holding child), and George Pleasant Bostick (standing at far right, behind Attie Texas Bostick). The rugs behind the missionaries are of dog skin. (Courtesy of First Baptist Church and Betty Jo Carpenter.)

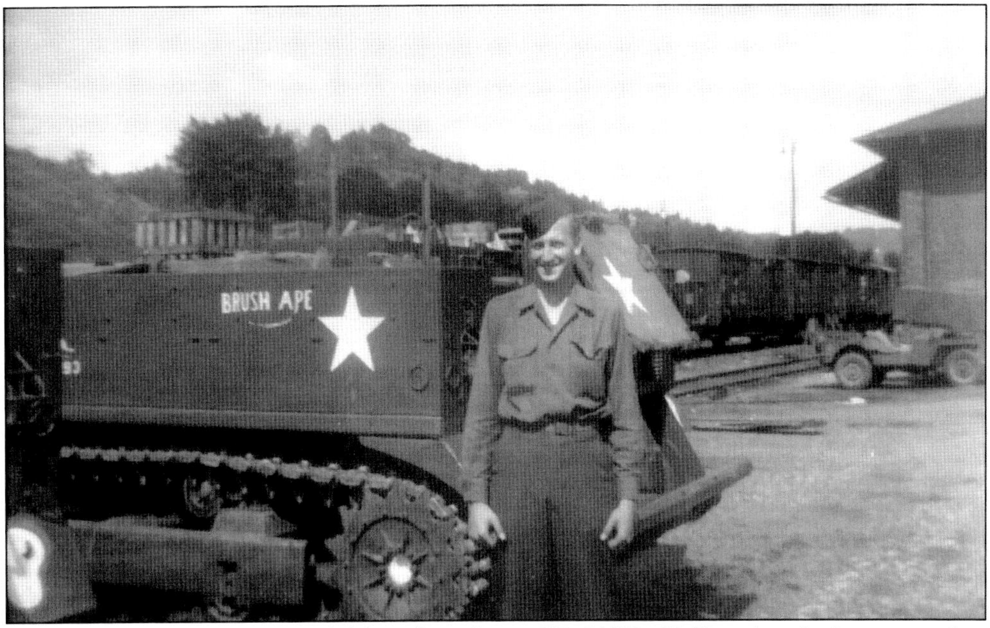

Sgt. Tom Brown served in the field artillery during World War II. He is beside the tractor that pulled his 105-mm Howitzer. In the European Theater of Operations, he earned the Good Conduct Medal, the EAME Campaign Medal with at least three Bronze Service Stars, and the Meritorious Unit Citation. After the war, he was in Battery A, 112th Field Artillery Battalion of the North Carolina National Guard. (Courtesy of Tom Brown and David Brown.)

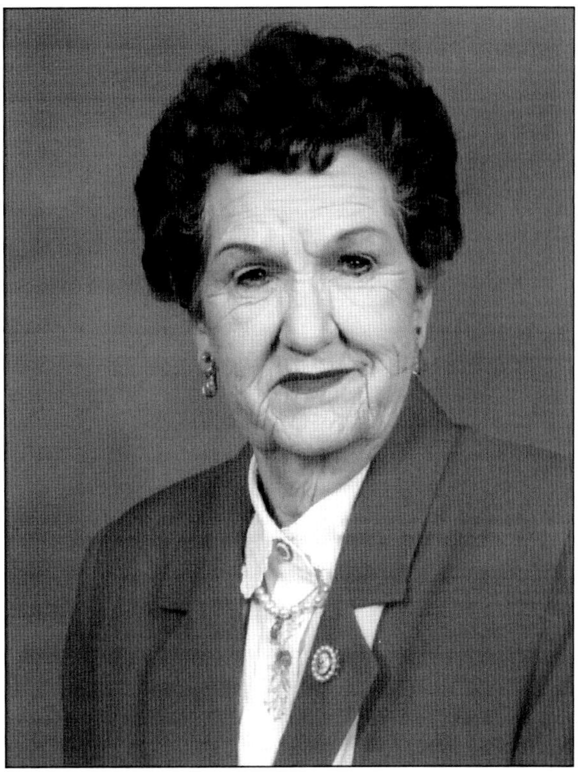

Mae Settlemyre Blanton, a 1946 Cool Springs graduate, was a 4-H Club Leader for 17 years. Mae was county president for four years during her 15-plus years with the Home Demonstration Club. Mae helped to start the Vocational Rehabilitation Workshop. Her only brother, James Settlemyre, was a World War II veteran and a POW for a year. (Courtesy of Mae Blanton.)

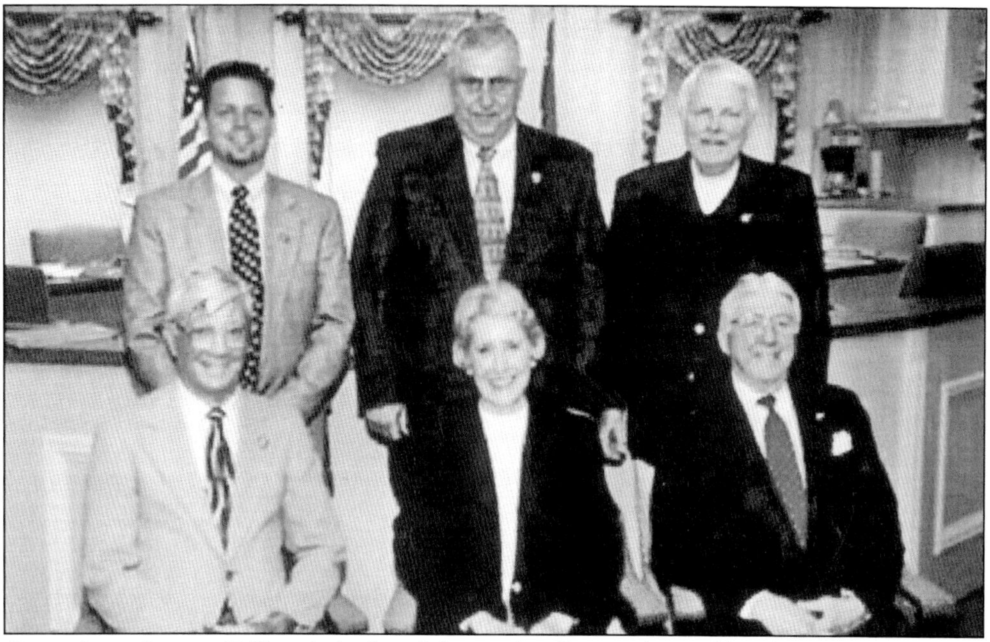

Council members in 2005 include, from left to right, (first row) Harold Stallcup, Helyn Lowery, and Mayor James Gibson, who has presided over the city council since 2003; (second row) Jack Murphy (now replaced by David Eaker), Tommy McBrayer, and C. Z. Flack Jr. Mayors serve two-year terms; council members, four. The city manager, the town's chief executive officer, is responsible for the execution of council policy and the management of city departments/services. (www.TownofForestCity.com.)

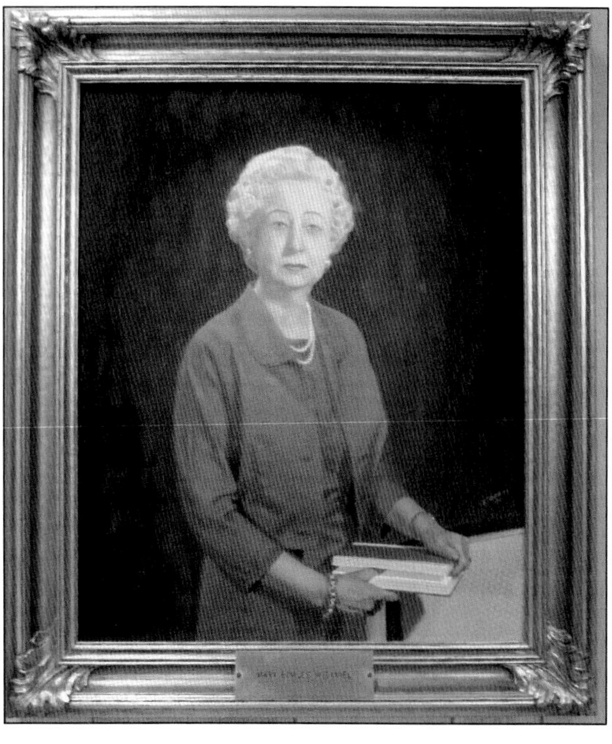

Mary Bowles (Mrs. Arthur) McDaniel served both the Forest City Public Library and the Mooneyham Public Library. Many patrons remember climbing the steps beside the fire and police departments on Powell Street to access the volumes. Current library staff members include Rita Womack, Sue Toms, and Mary Sandra Costner. The use of Robert Watkins's portrait of Mrs. McDaniel is courtesy of the Mooneyham Public Library. (Courtesy of James M. Walker.)

Five

HOUSES
Plain and Simple, Ornate and Grand

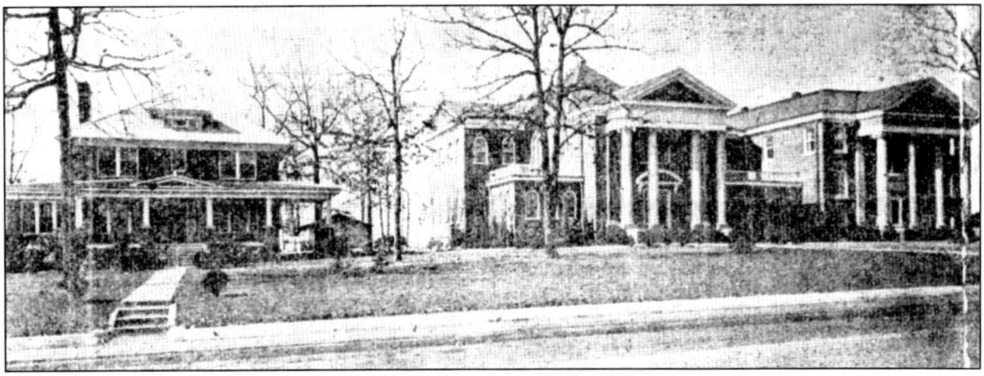

Housing and shelter are basic needs. The assorted styles of homes reflect the area's assorted residents. Some important homes still exist; others do not. The remaining chimney of the James McArthur House, for which Burnt Chimney got its name, is gone; so is the parsonage at Church and West Main for the First Baptist/Forest City Baptist Church. (Courtesy of First Baptist Church and Betty Jo Carpenter.)

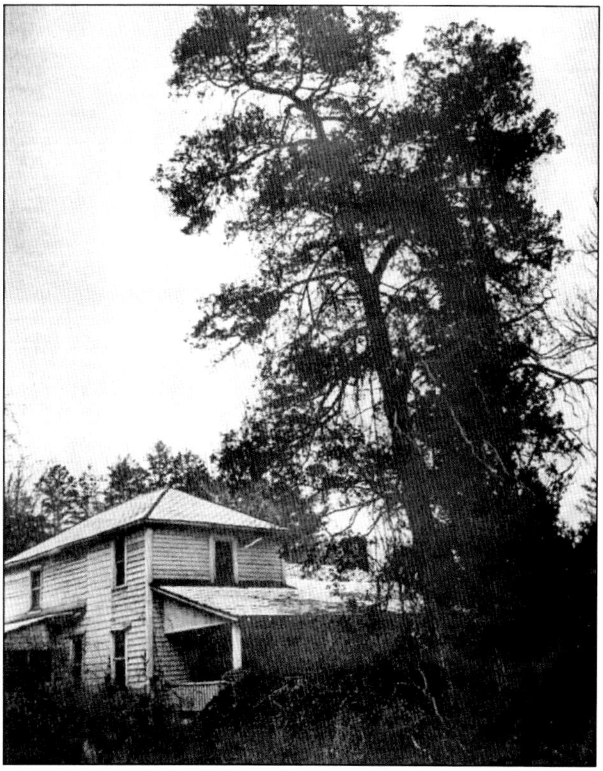

In 1977, the oldest house still standing in Forest City (according to the *Centennial Edition* of the *Forest City Courier*) was the Harrill-Lowrance House on Cherry Mountain Street. Martin J. Harrill, son of Elder William Harrill (pastor of Forest City Baptist Church), built the original home in 1849 to which later owners added rooms and floors. (Courtesy of the *Daily Courier* and Jim Brown.)

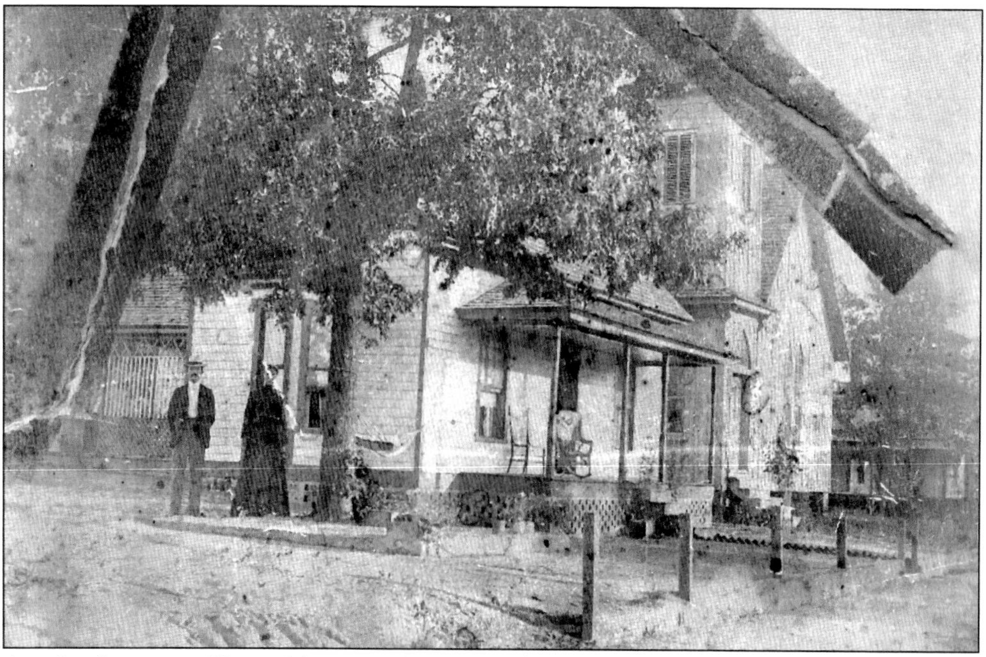

Another home on Cherry Mountain Street was the Brackett House, located beside the First Presbyterian Church. D. O. Brackett, director of music for First Baptist Church, resided in the Brackett House, a frame structure characterized by a bay window. (Courtesy of the First Baptist Church and Betty Jo Carpenter.)

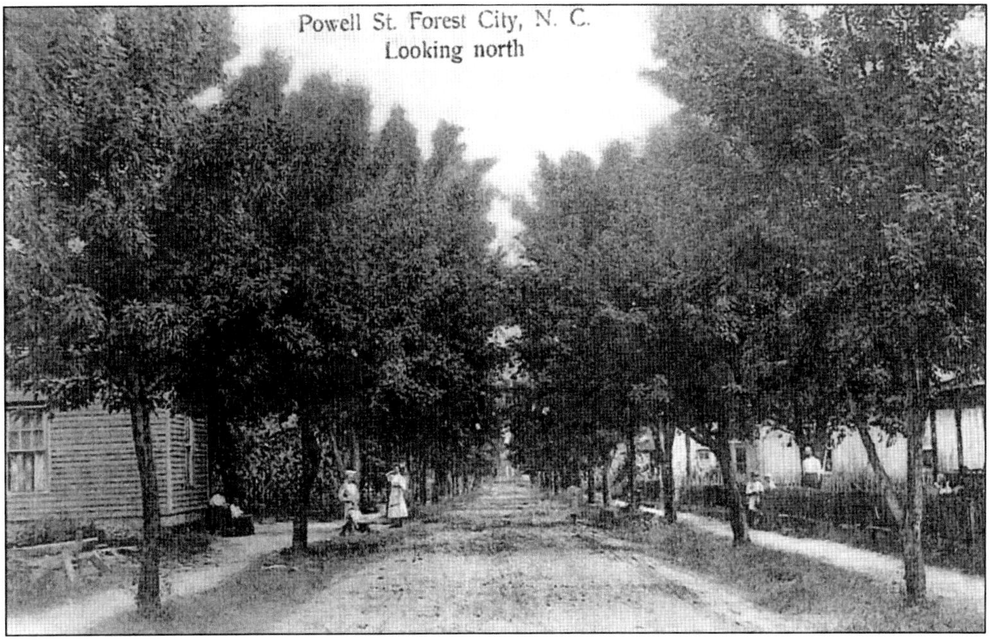

This early postcard view of the tree-lined Powell Street shows the residents in their business-as-usual activities. The scene predates roads and sidewalks. There is a definite lack of traffic on this day. (Courtesy of Beth and Daniel King.)

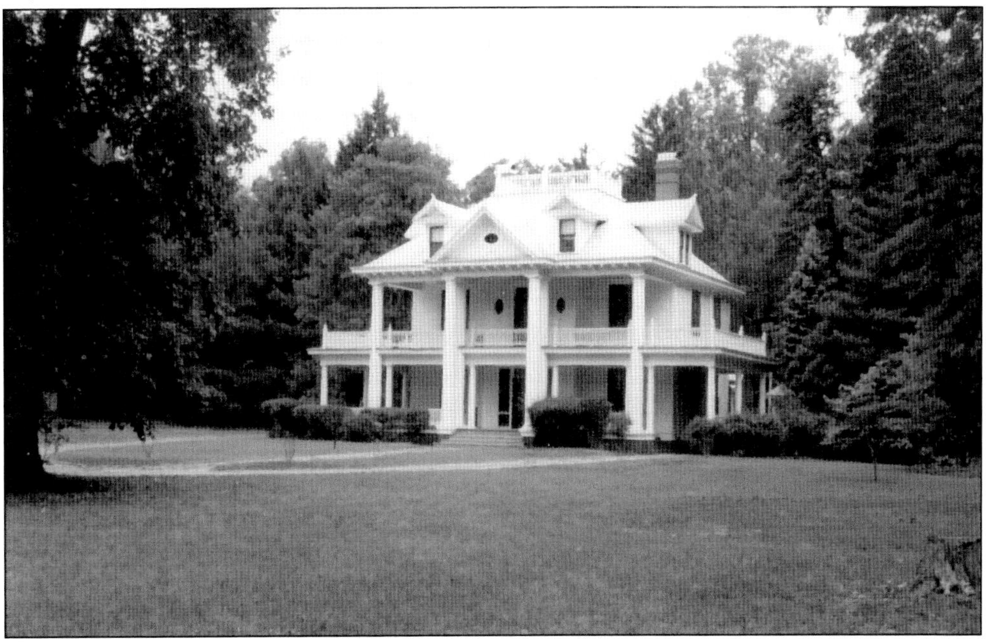

The James Dexter Ledbetter House (building #82003511) became a part of the National Register of Historic Places in 1982. Built in 1914 for a founder of the National Bank of Forest City, the Ledbetter House (on Highway 74) is a single-dwelling home representing both the Colonial Revival and the Classical Revival styles. Robert Ewart Burns, electrician and one of the first employees of the Cliffside Steam Station, upgraded the electrical wiring. (Courtesy of James M. Walker.)

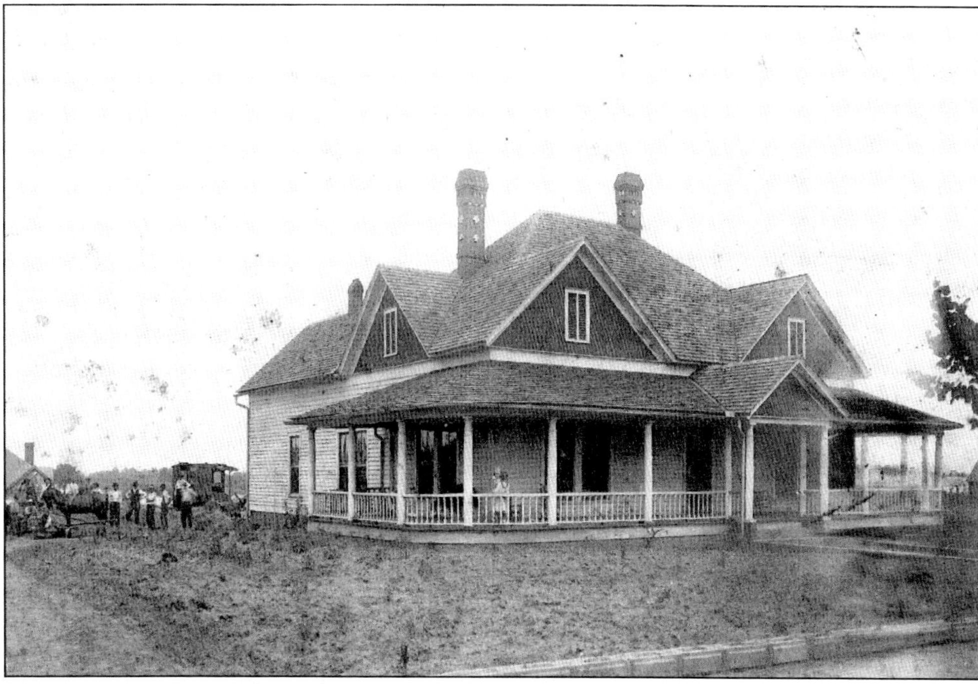

The King House, once located on present-day Broadway, is no longer standing. This postcard shows the massive front porch with modest columns and banisters. (Courtesy of Beth and Daniel King.)

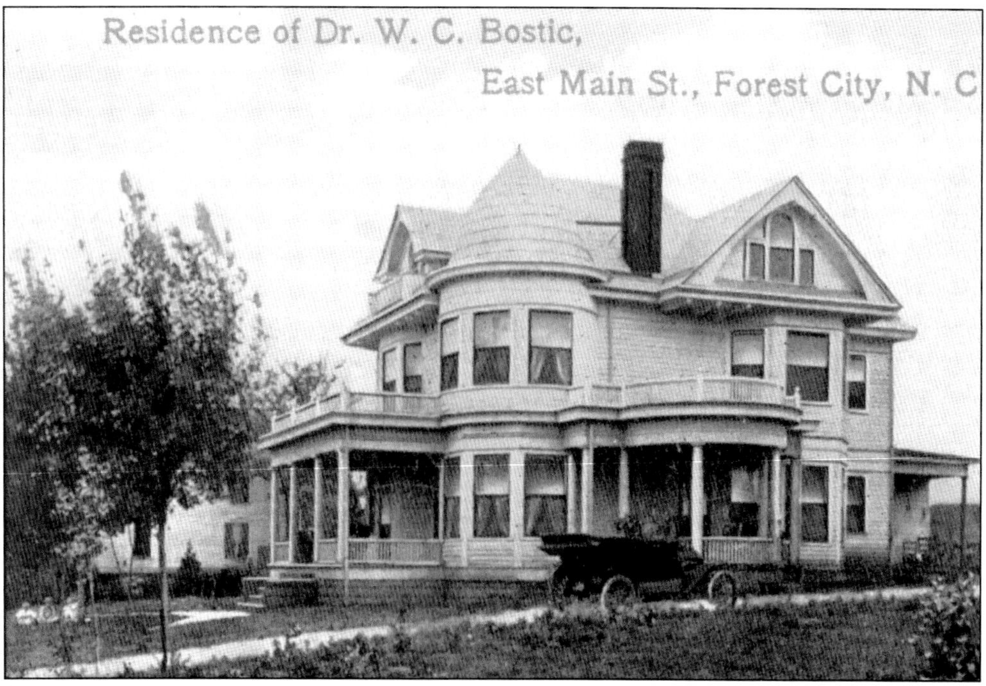

The home of Dr. W. C. Bostic, according to this early postcard, was on East Main Street. The turreted, two-story dwelling included a porch from which the family could enjoy tranquil evenings. (Courtesy of Beth and Daniel King, Robert Jones, and Paul Tim Jones Jr.)

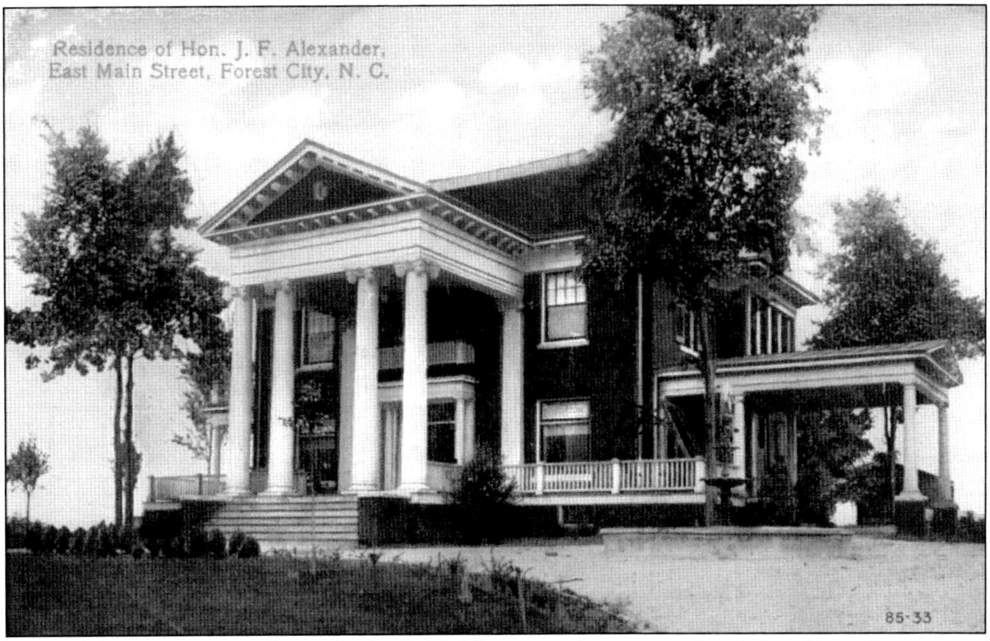

The home of Hon. J. F. Alexander (1859–1925) was at the current East Main Street location of the Bell South Central Office. Griffin calls Alexander a "Forest City lumberman, businessman, textile manufacturer . . . Assemblyman" (170). He helped financially with the construction of the Forest City Baptist Church (1914), its Education Building (1925), and the Alexander School for Homeless Children at Union Mills. (Courtesy of Beth and Daniel King, Robert Jones, and Paul Tim Jones Jr.)

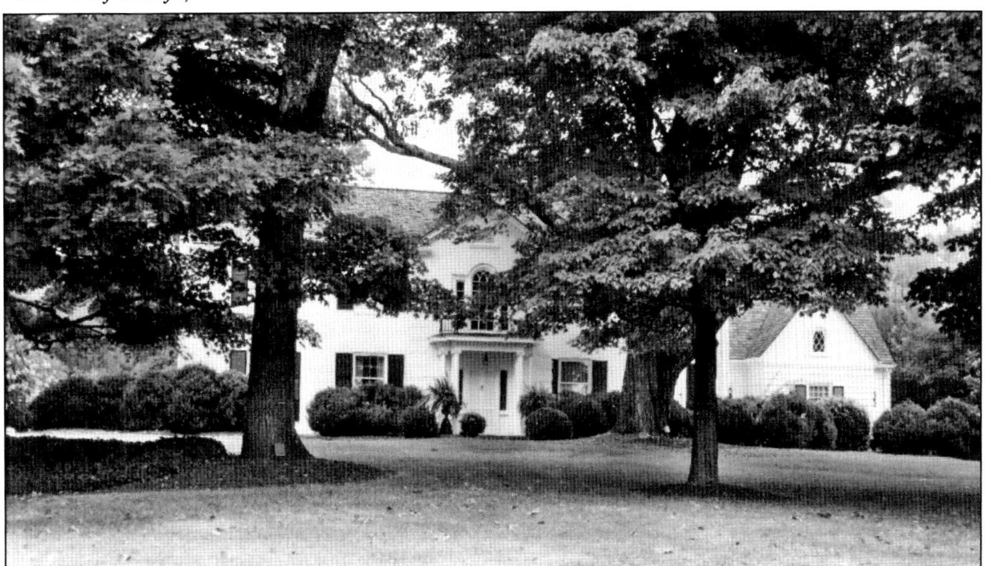

On October 15, 2001, the T. Max Watson House at 297 East Main Street became a part of the National Register of Historic Places. Watson was general manager of the Sterling Hosiery Mills in Spindale, county commissioner, appointee of Gov. Clyde R. Hoey to the State Highway Commission, and director of the First Industrial Bank of Forest City and Rutherfordton. (Courtesy of James M. Walker.)

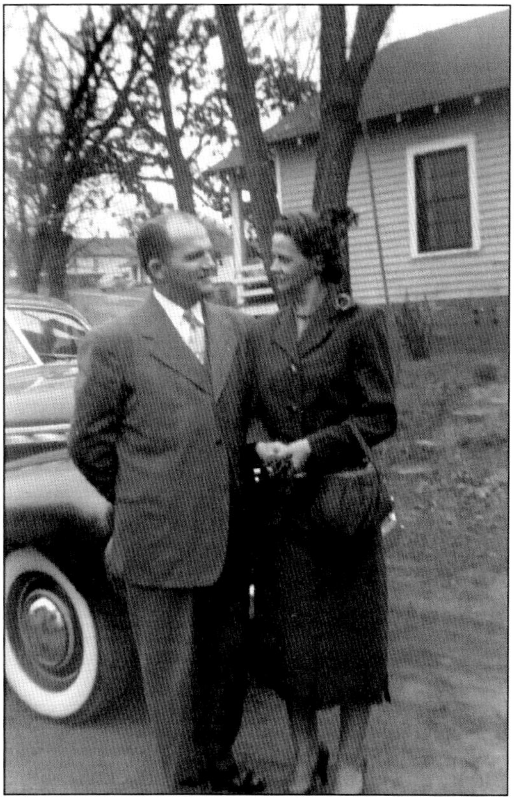

Paul Tim Jones Sr. and his wife, Annabelle, occupied this three-room house (to which they added a room) with their only son, Paul Tim Jones Jr., who now holds baccalaureate and master's degrees from Western Carolina. Residences like this to house the Florence Mill workers sprang up in the vicinity of employment. R. R. Haynes and his daughter Florence, after whom her father named the mill, were instrumental to the town's growth. (Courtesy of Paul Tim Jones Jr.)

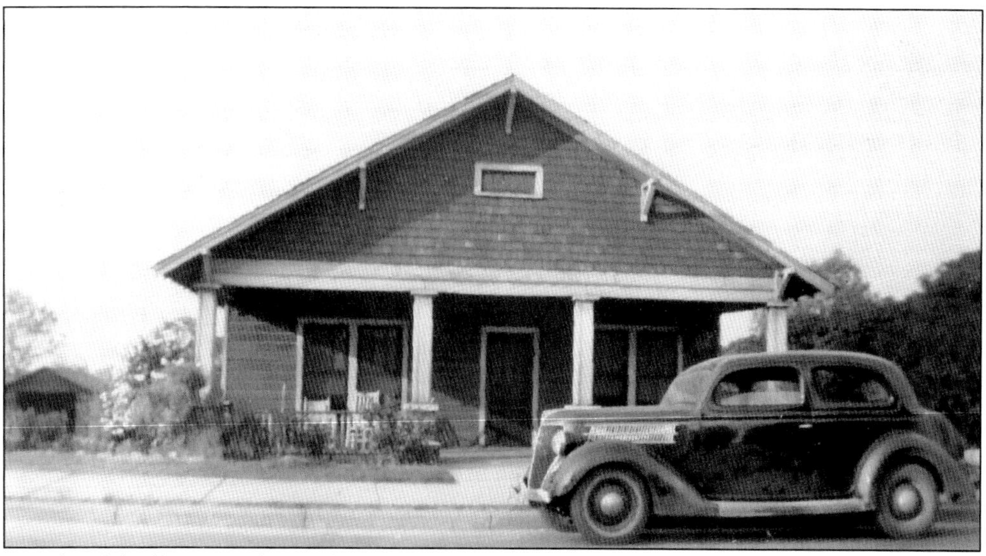

A style of dwelling popular in the 1930s and 1940s in Forest City was a single-family home on its own lot. This Arlington Street home was the 1939 residence of Dollie and Edgar Watkins, the grandparents of Martha Grace Estes. After the death of Edgar Watkins, Clarence Lloyd Morris Sr. paid the taxes and remodeled the Arlington dwelling; he, his wife, their children, Dollie Watkins, and one of Martha Grace's aunts moved into the Arlington Street home, still a residence. (Courtesy of Martha Grace Estes.)

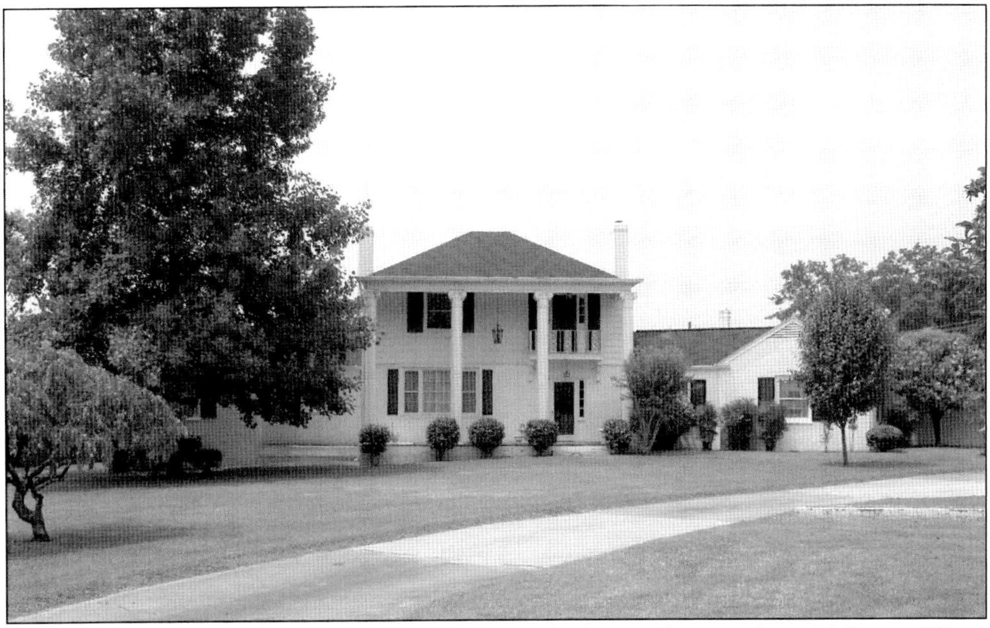

This stately home (300 Westview Drive) was the residence of Dr. William McBrayer Elliott (1904–1972), who practiced medicine for 37 years. The white brick courtyard provides privacy from the busy Municipal Golf Course and Hardin Road. Attorney George R. Morrow and his family later bought the house. (Courtesy of James M. Walker.)

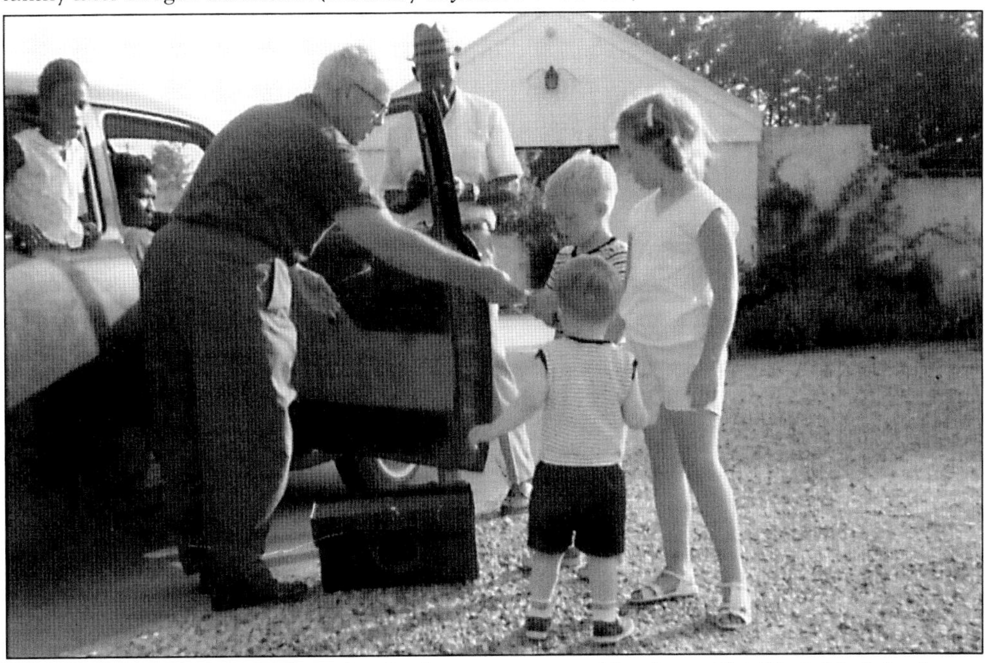

Patients often came to Dr. Elliott for after-hours treatment. Here he and his "little black bag" meet patients. With him are three of his grandchildren: William M. Elliott II (child with his back to the camera), Susan Wynn, and Jeffrey Peters (the tall blonde boy). Susan and Jeff became doctors because of the many house calls they made with their grandfather. His daughter Diane Peterson writes that her "only regret is that my dad never knew this." (Courtesy of Diane Elliott Peterson.)

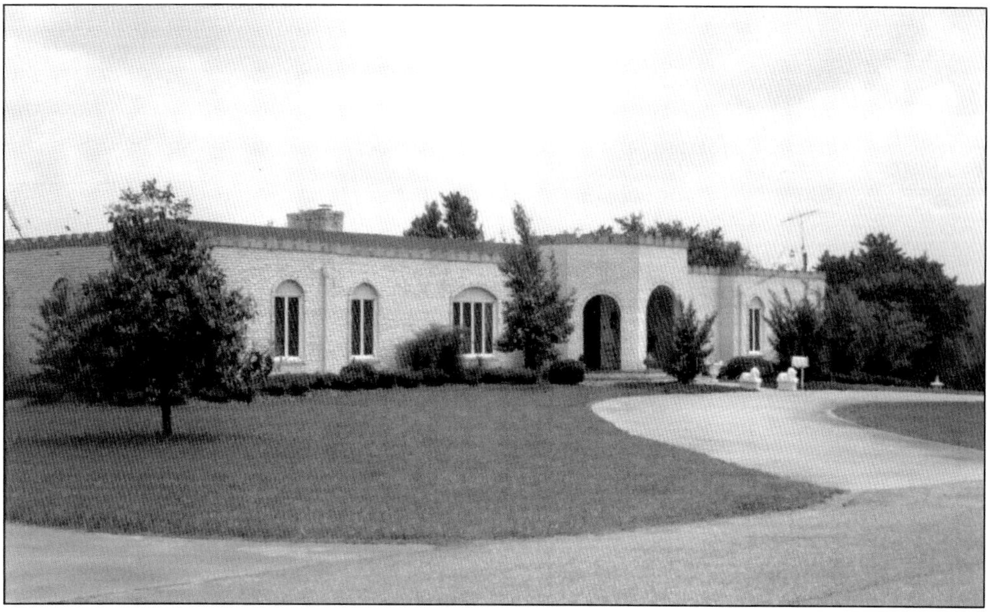

In 1977, Rutherford County Home Economics Extension Agent Jeanne Ware presented a slide program called "Two Hundred Years of Rutherford County Heritage." One of the homes she featured was one with Mediterranean styling. Located off Hudlow Road, the magnificent grounds include a grand white-brick dwelling with arched windows. Outdoor sculptures welcome visitors; indoor and outdoor fountains create tranquility. (Courtesy of Carolyn Grindstaff Barbee.)

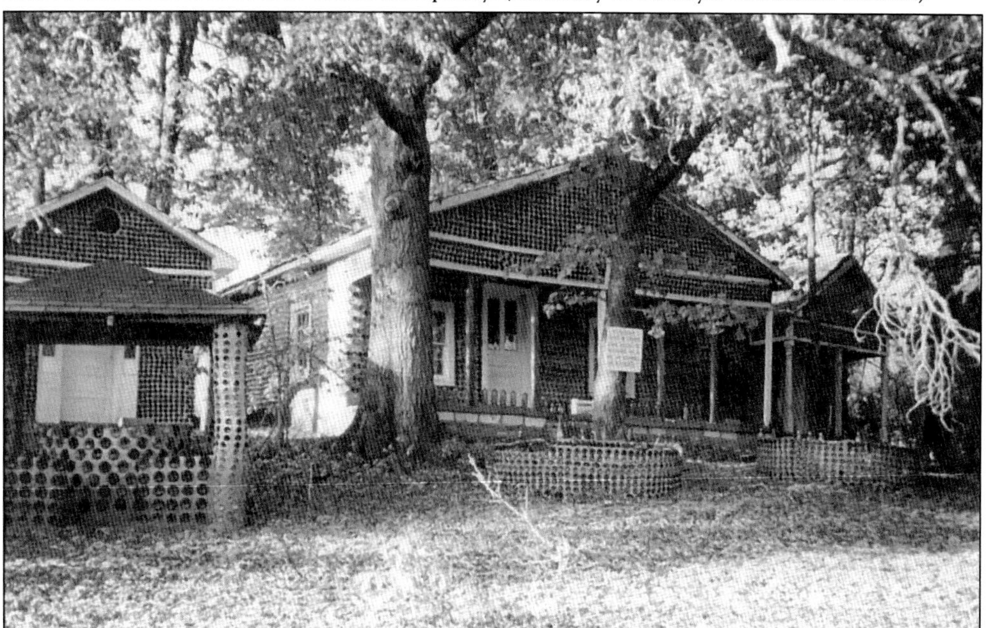

Created by Charles Yelton, the three Cherry Mountain Street bottle houses are the area's most unusual houses; the Yeltons recorded 15,000 visitors. *The Daily Courier* from March 9, 1983, called them "the ultimate answer to roadside litter." Yelton built the first bottle house using 11,987 bottles in 1971; by 1974, he had completed all three. Realtor Todd Lavender and Grant Hardin provide more photographs and information about bottling in their book *Crown Jewels.*

Six

Relaxation and Entertainment

Enjoying Life

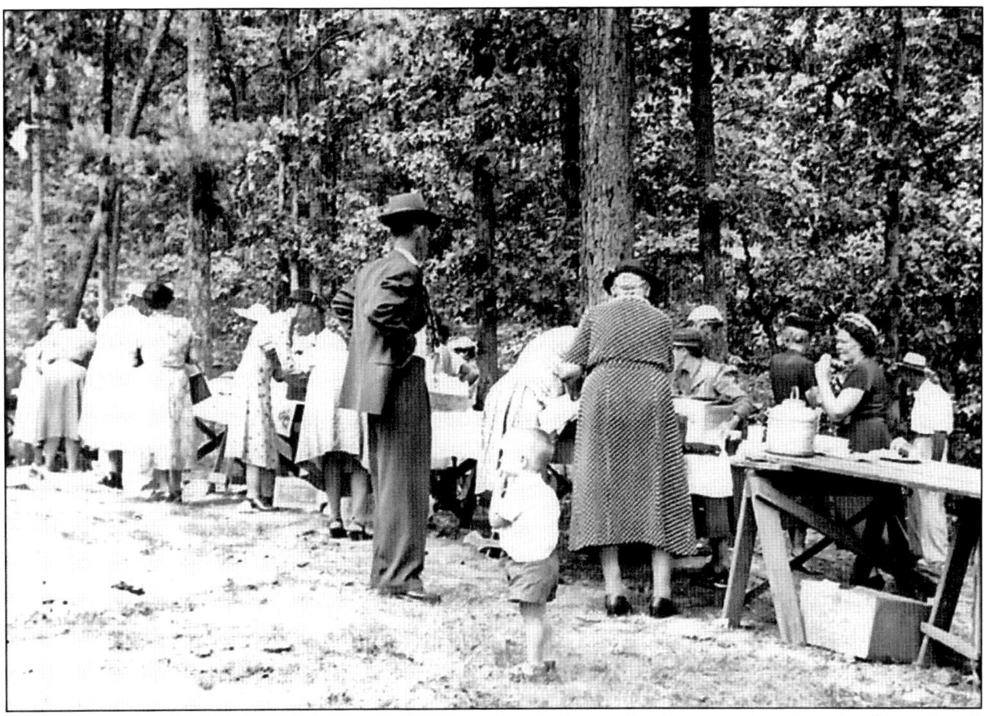

Since earliest times, much relaxation has centered about the home, the church, the school, and the community. Dinner-on-the-grounds has long been a favorite social event in many of the local churches; often members of other churches bring a covered dish and join in the food and fellowship—especially during homecomings and memorial days. (Courtesy of Rebecca Jane Harrill Thompson and Jane Thompson Gurley.)

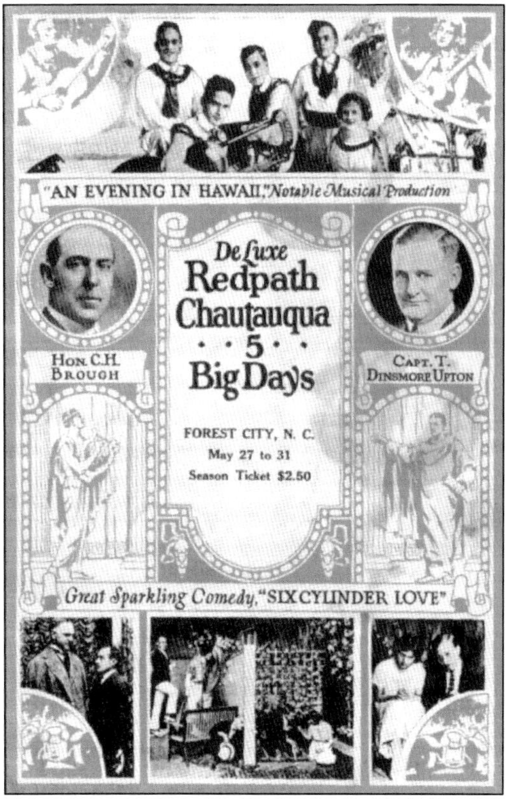

Open-air tents and later school auditoriums were convenient sites for plays, speeches, assemblies, vaudeville, and other performances. The Chautauqua programs—often lasting several days—presented music, drama, comedy, and readings for the congregated audiences. Still in existence, the Chautauqua programs maintain their historical purposes. The "Sparkling Comedy *Six Cylinder Love*" came to Forest City in the early 1920s. (Courtesy of Martha Grace Estes.)

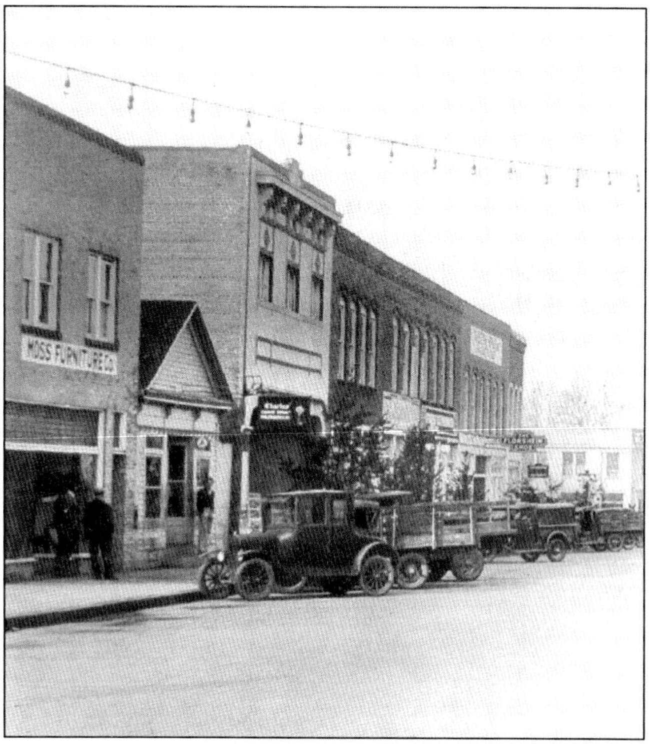

A popular form of entertainment from the 1920s was to watch a film at the Forest City theatre named the Horn. The Horn next became the Pastime. J. W. Griffin Sr. later named the theatre the "Grace" in honor of his wife. This 1931 photograph shows the theatre as the third building from the left. (Courtesy of Robert M. Watkins.)

J. W. Griffin Sr. purchased the Romina (designed by R. E. Carpenter Sr.) from Walter H. Haynes. The $125,000 Romina had a curtain, a 28-by-14-foot stage, carpeting, leather seats, a domed ceiling, dressing rooms, and vaudeville show equipment. It was the first county theatre to show a sound picture on January 1, 1930. (Courtesy of David Daniel.)

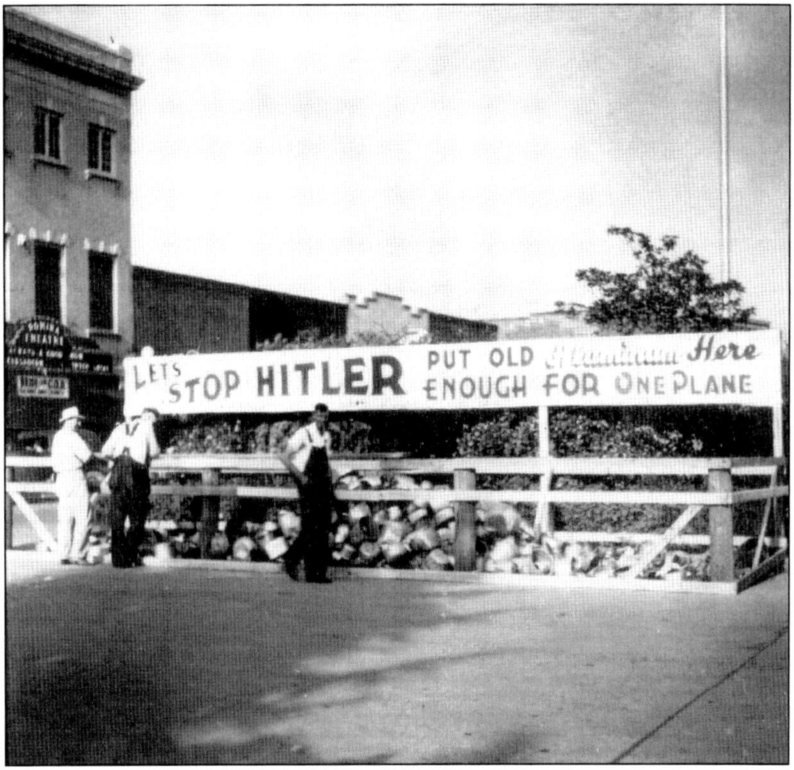

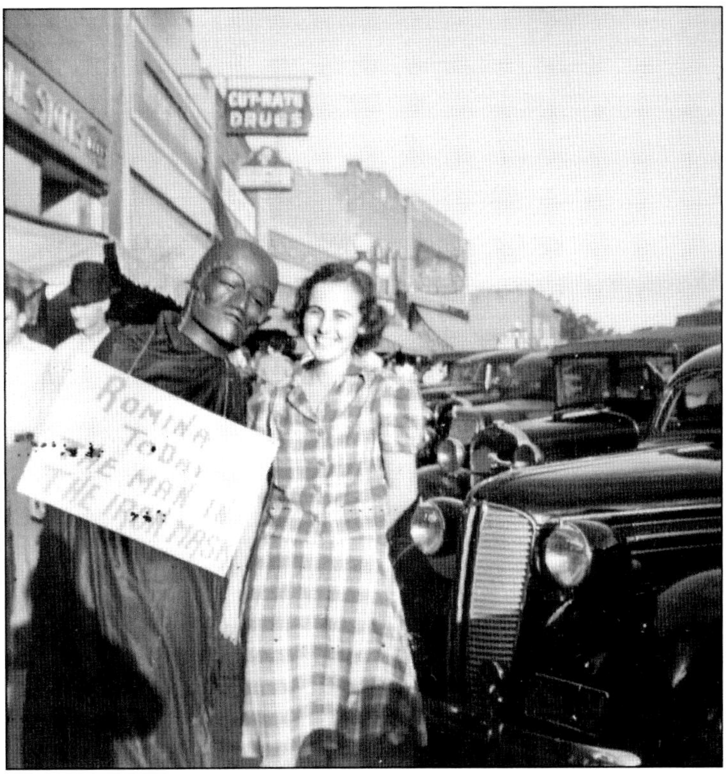

The cinema occupied an important part of the lives of area youth and adults. To advertise *The Man in the Iron Mask* in 1939, for instance, a person could pose with a character in costume on Main Street. (Courtesy of Dr. W. L. Stallings and Betty Jo Carpenter.)

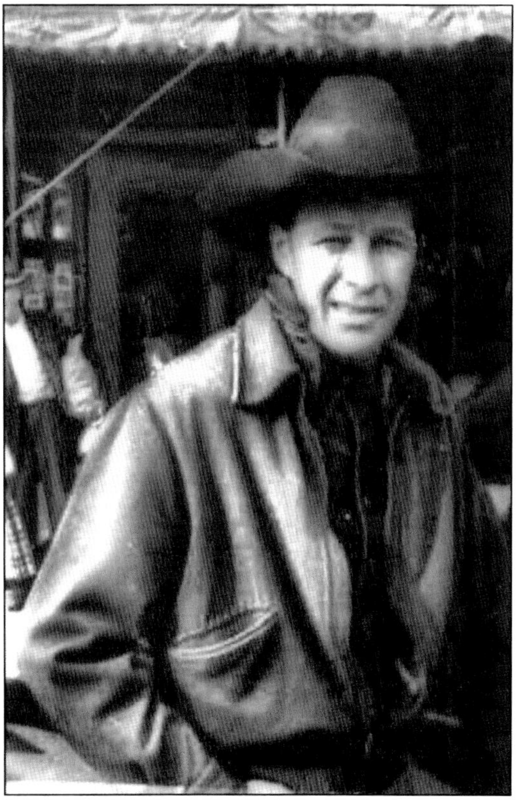

In the 1940s, Wild Bill Elliott visited Forest City. During 1940–1954, he made the top-10 motion picture poll every year. With "Side Kick" Little Beaver (played by Robert Blake), he starred as Red Ryder in 16 films. Wild Bill carried his stag-handled, two-gun six-shooters with the butts forward. His shirt was buckskin and fringe, not the standard "storm flap." (Courtesy of Bill McArthur.)

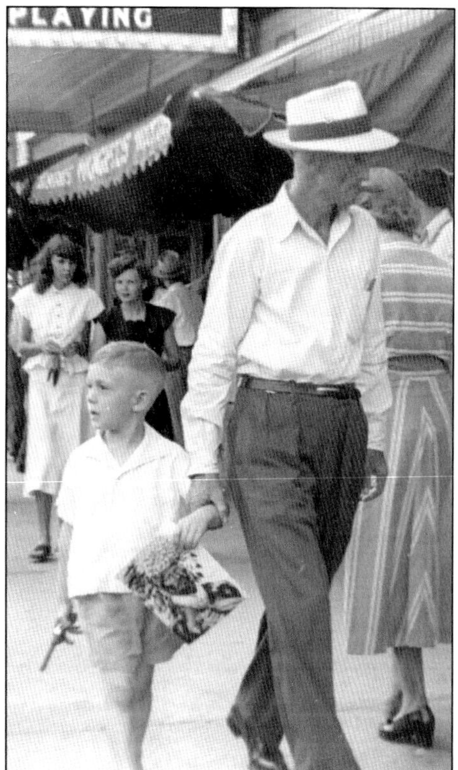

Saturday afternoons with a cowboy feature and a serial cliffhanger made idyllic moments for young and old alike. This late-1940s photo of Sherwood Withrow and his young son, Scott, shows the influence of movies on Scott's life; Scott is holding a Tarzan comic book and grips his six-shooter for protection as he walks under the Romina marquee. (Courtesy of Scott Withrow, park ranger at Cowpens National Battlefield Park.)

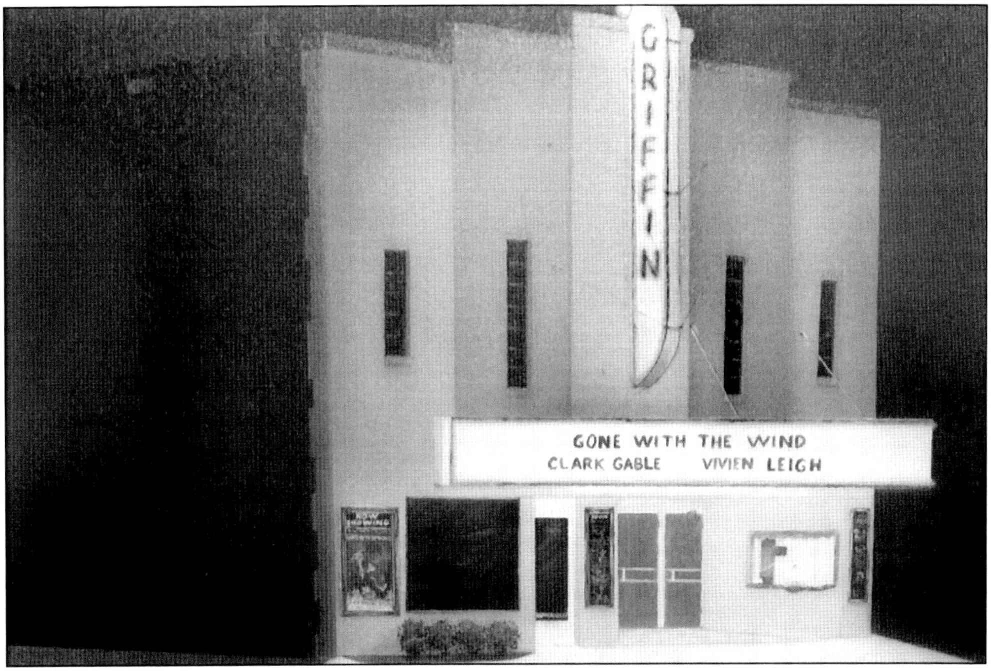

Located across from the First Baptist Church, the Griffin Theatre (open from June 8, 1949 to June 1972) showed first a new release: *Mr. Belvedere Goes to College*, starring Clifton Webb and Shirley Temple. Owned and operated by James Willis Griffin Jr. (December 16, 1920–January 27, 2001), the theatre no longer stands, but this photo records the structure and announces the re-release: *Gone With the Wind*. (Courtesy of Melinda Griffin Peterson and Jimmy Griffin.)

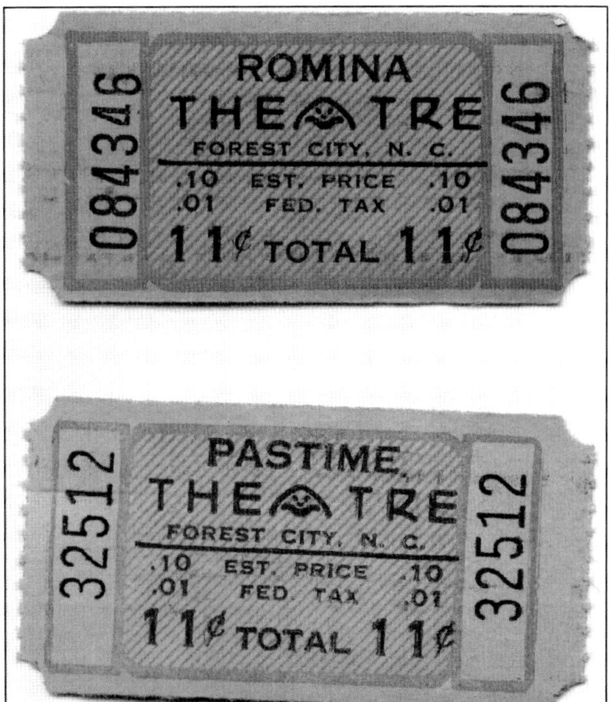

This ticket from the Romina Theatre shows an admission price of 11¢. The ticket, however, is no longer valid because the Romina Theatre no longer exists, except in memory. The Horn Theatre, across the street from the Romina, carried the name Pastime for a while. Later its name became Grace in honor of the owner's wife. (Courtesy of Melinda Griffin Peterson and Jimmy Griffin.)

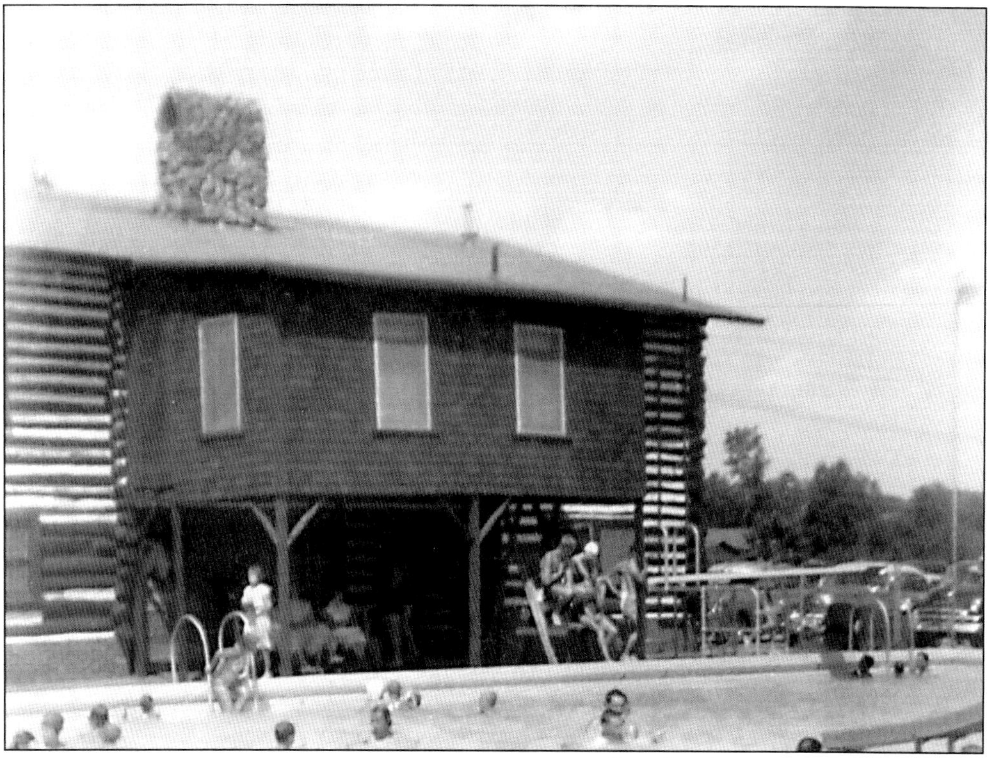

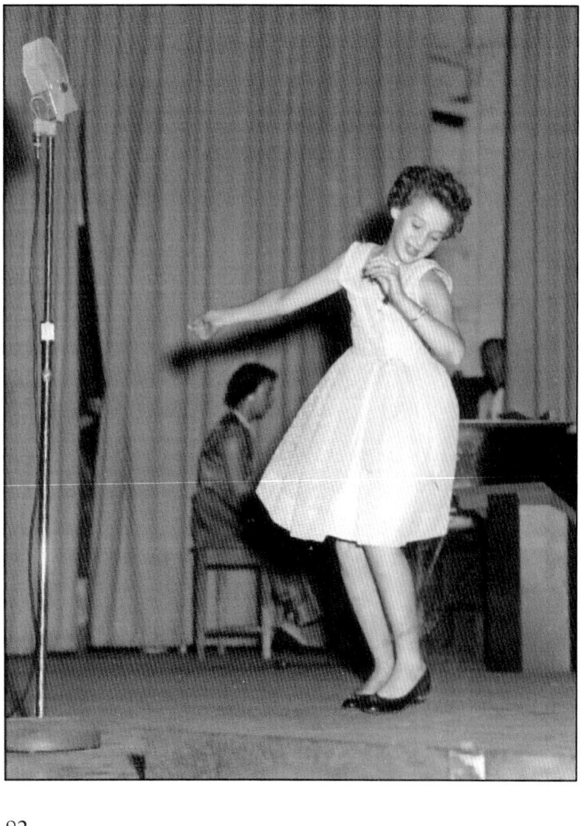

Broadus Green supervised the construction of the Clay Street Park and Pool, built with WPA labor and funds; this is a 1952 view of the pool with the clubhouse visible. The facility is still in use in 2005 as the Callison Recreation Center. The Woman's Club Building, an important accomplishment of area women, was at the front of the log structure. (Courtesy of Carolyn Grindstaff Barbee.)

At a 1950s Cool Springs High talent show, Carolyn Grindstaff plays piano for sister Barbara. Barbara Grindstaff competed on *Arthur Smith's Talent Show* and (at age 10) on the national *Ted Mack's Amateur Hour*; she was one of 27 performers to represent America in a 1957 tour of Europe. She spent her 1958 summer performing abroad. She took national honors in a United Nations Oratorical contest. (Courtesy of Carolyn Grindstaff Barbee.)

Barbara Grindstaff (Bobbi Staff), Cool Springs graduate in 1961, did summer stock in *Guys and Dolls* (1962); she performed for Dutch Queen Juliana and Pres. Lyndon Johnson in 1963. Her RCA recording contract produced *Where the Red Roses Grow*; *Have Mercy, Mr. Lonely*; *Where Did the Summer Go*; and *I'm Available*. She appeared daily on George Hamilton IV's show and often on the *Grand Ole Opry*. (Courtesy of Carolyn Grindstaff Barbee.)

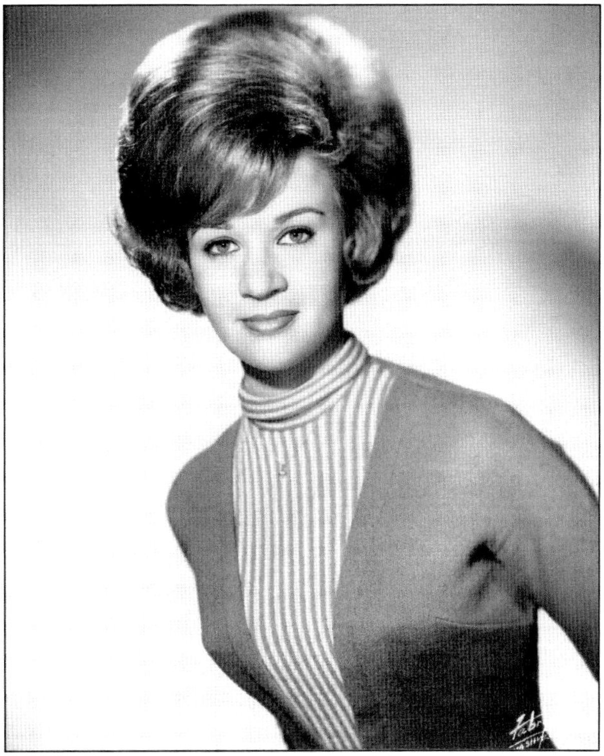

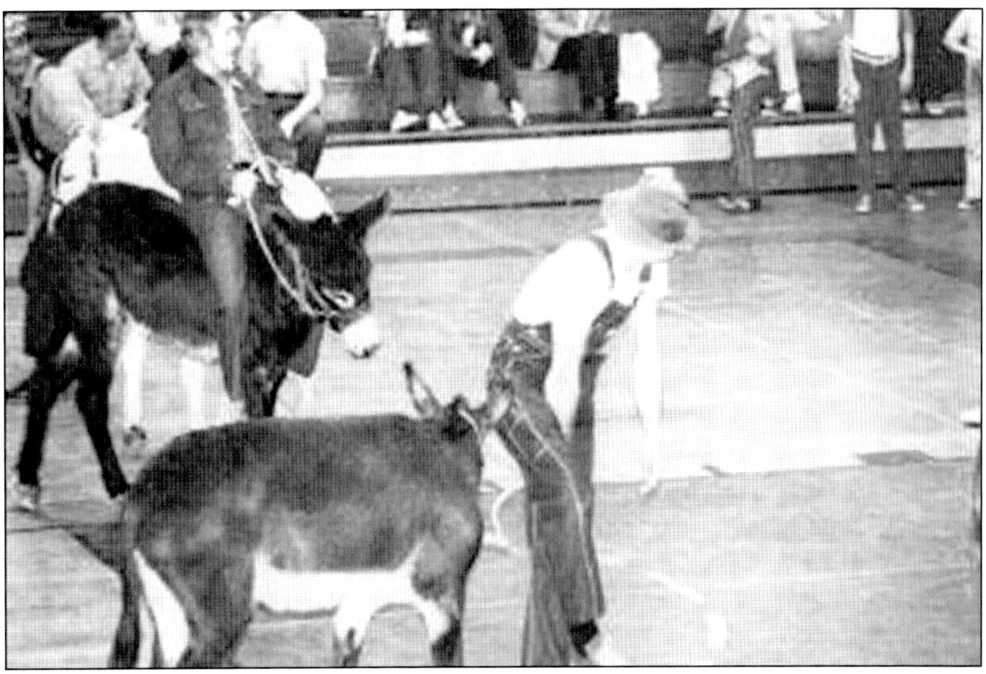

To raise money for the community, the public service workers sponsored a donkey basketball game in Cool Springs Gymnasium. Dr. Bobby England, a local physician, demonstrates his equestrian skills on a donkey. England's comment was, "That was the slowest donkey I have ever seen." (Courtesy of Bobby England, M.D.)

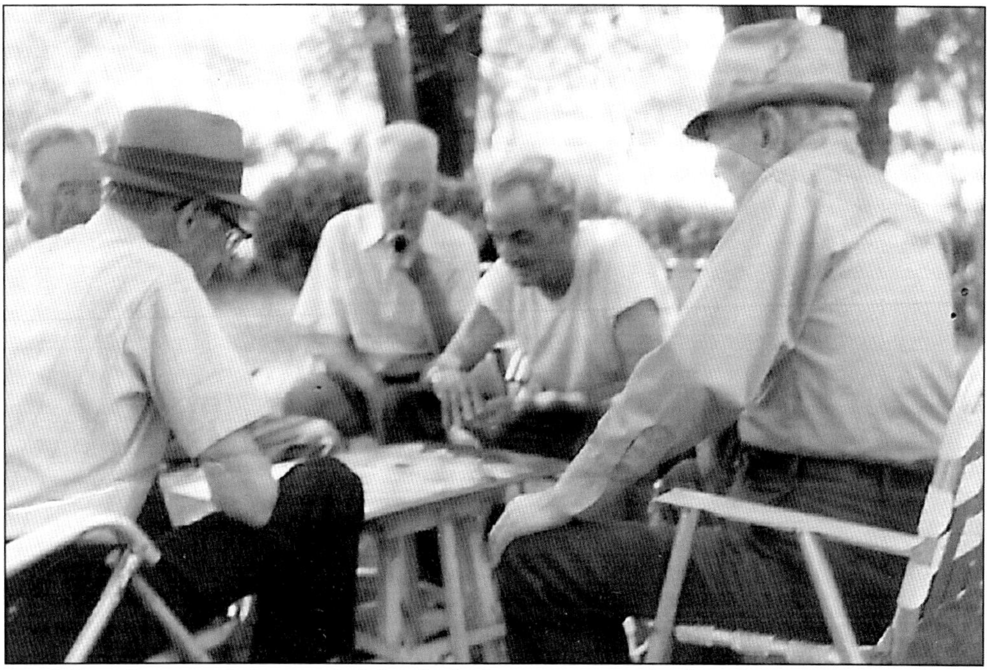

South Broadway regularly provided the shade for competitive checker players. Here Clark Miles Harrill (on left, wearing hat) and his cousin and next-door neighbor, Bryan Randall (opposite Harrill, playing checkers), participate in a 1978 neighborhood tournament. (Courtesy of Rebecca Jane Harrill Thompson and Jane Thompson Gurley.)

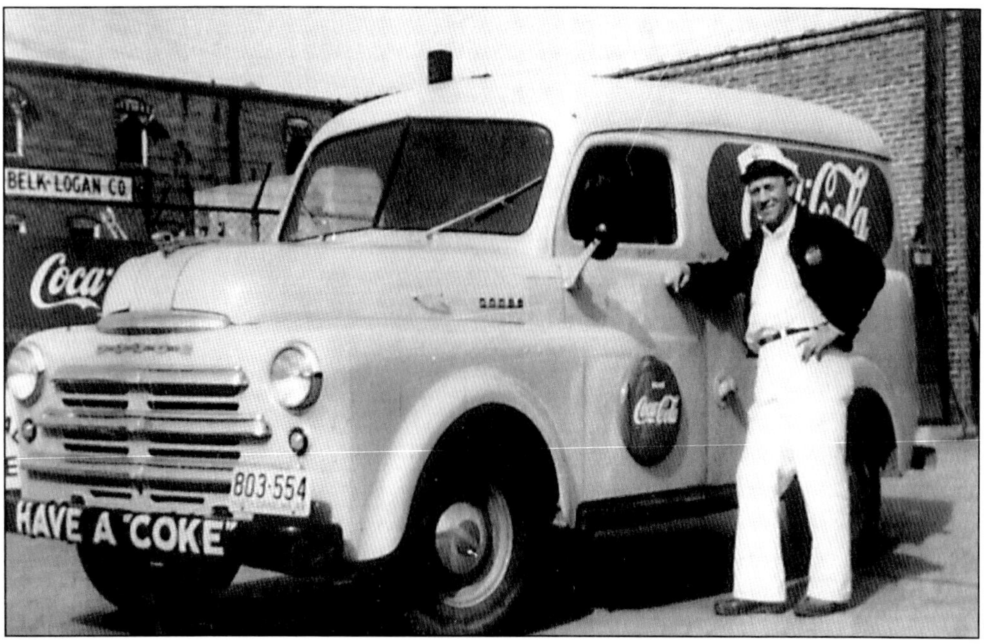

Here Ernest Pilgrim poses beside his yellow Dodge Coca-Cola truck. This 1949 vehicle is parked adjacent to the Coca-Cola Bottling Company on Depot Street. In the background is the rear entrance to the Belk-Logan Company. The Coke slogan invites the reader to "Have a Coke." (Courtesy of Frances Goforth Pilgrim.)

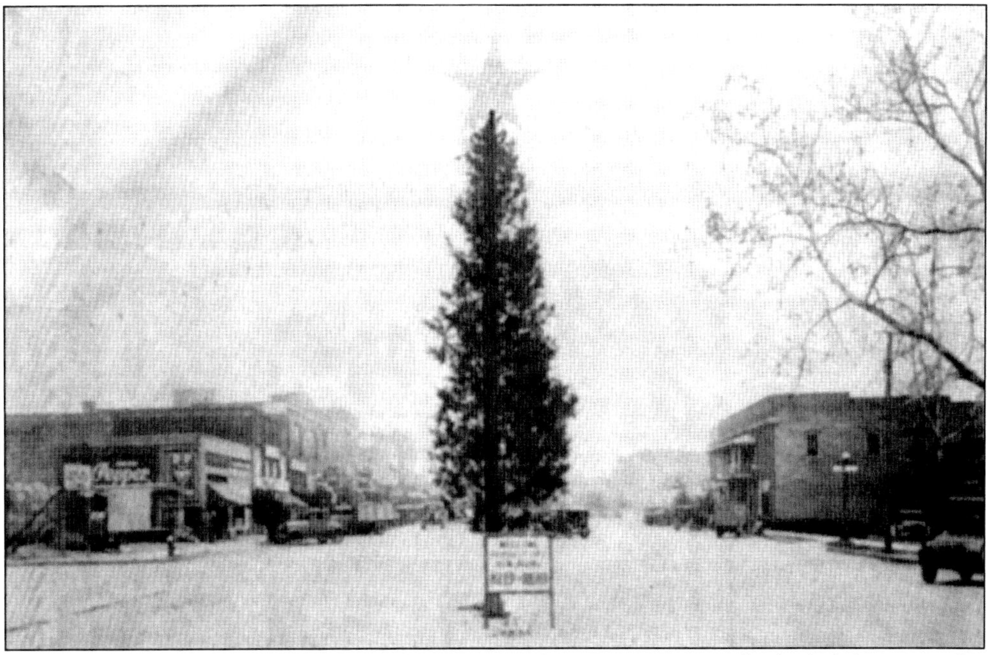

Forest City residents have long enjoyed decorating their town—especially for holidays. Broadus Green was instrumental in decorating the town from the mid-1930s. This 1937–1938 photograph shows the Christmas tree with its star at the top and strings of lights spanning Main Street. Green initially procured the trees, made the strings of light, and constructed the five-pointed star. He had only 200 allotted lights for his display. (Courtesy of Mary Lee Curtis.)

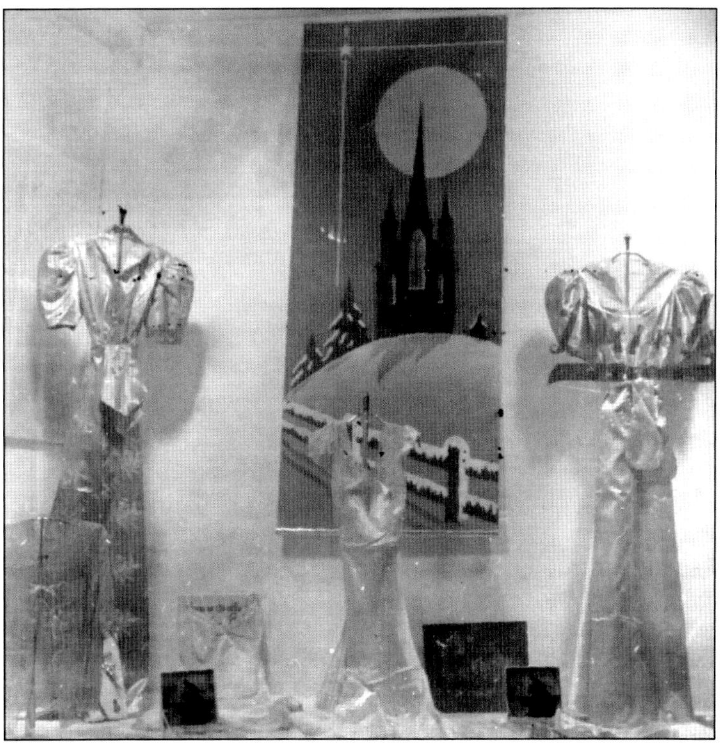

This 1939 window at the Davis Sisters on West Main provided gift-buying ideas for the season. Molly Harrill Davis originally started the Davis Shop in the 1930s. Her daughters (Ala Mae Davis Carpenter, Viola and Judy, Joanne Butler, Jenny, Winnie Davis Gill, and twins Lib Davis Dalvey and Mary Davis Wiley) helped area women dress appropriately for every occasion. (Courtesy of Dr. W. L. Stallings and Betty Jo Carpenter.)

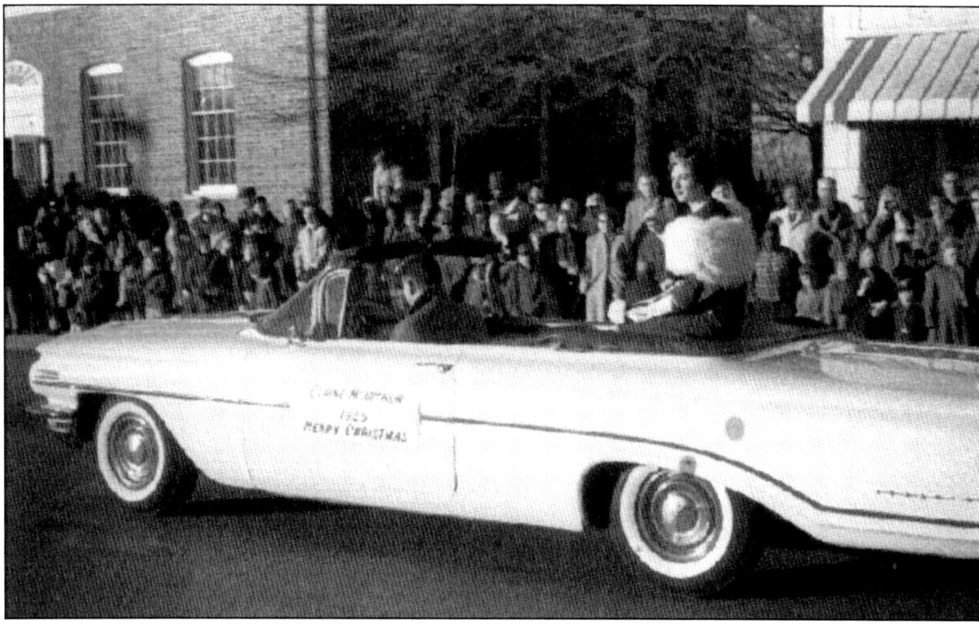

Parades remain important events. In front of the former Davis Sisters and the West Main Post Office is Elaine McArthur (Hill). With stole and tiara, the queen demonstrates the height of fashion. Tommy McBrayer (of McBrayer Motors on South Broadway and member of city council for eight years) drives her chariot, a white Chevrolet Impala convertible with red interior, owned by Bill Smith, a Grindstaff's employee since 1960. (Courtesy of Bill McArthur.)

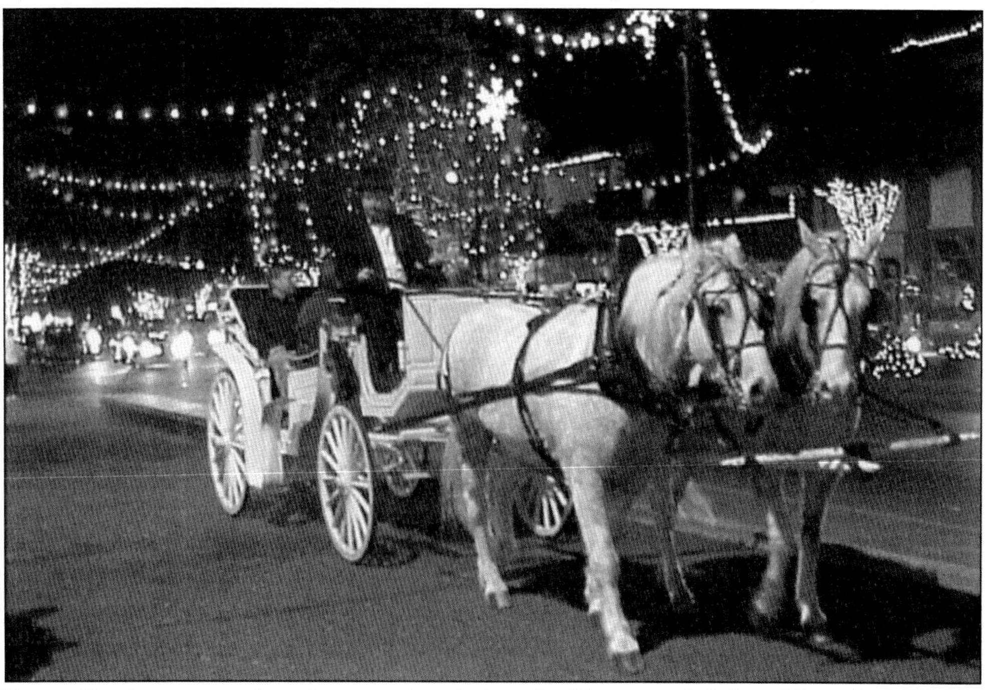

Forest City is an annual tourist attraction during the Christmas holidays. More than 500,000 lights transform the city into a winter wonderland. Horse-drawn carriage rides give the visitor an opportunity to observe the historical business district of Forest City. (Courtesy of Bob Morgan.)

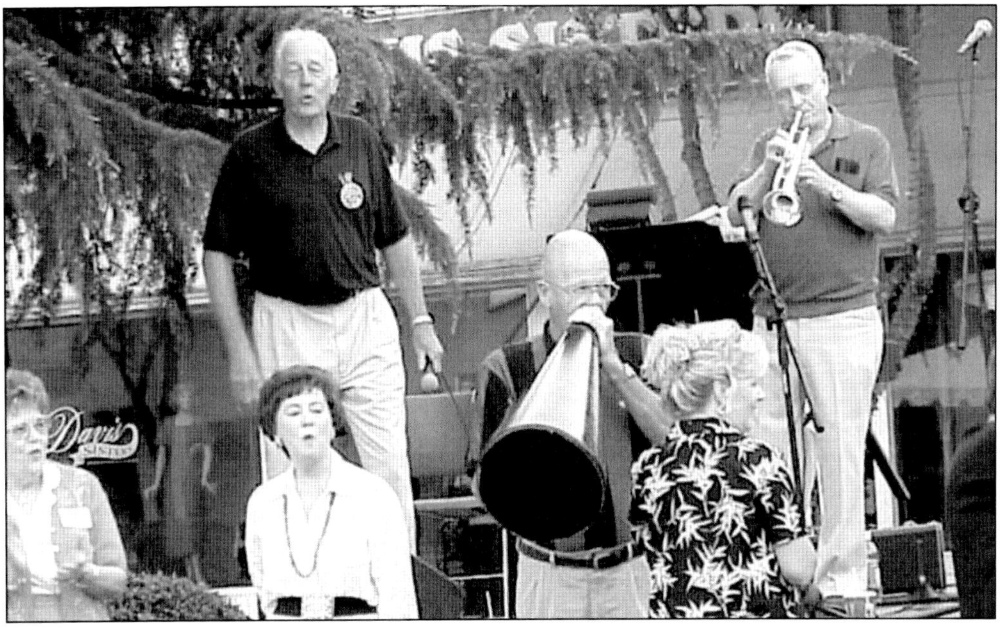

All-class reunions bring former students to town at the same time. Events on the square and in the Isothermal Community College Foundation Building provide opportunities for "catching up," eating, and enjoying the entertainment planned. Here Keith Price (back row on left) and Eddie Parker (with megaphone) emcee the show in Central Plaza. The former cheerleaders include Faye McCurry Thompson and Janine Collins. Can you identify the other faces? (Courtesy of Bob Morgan.)

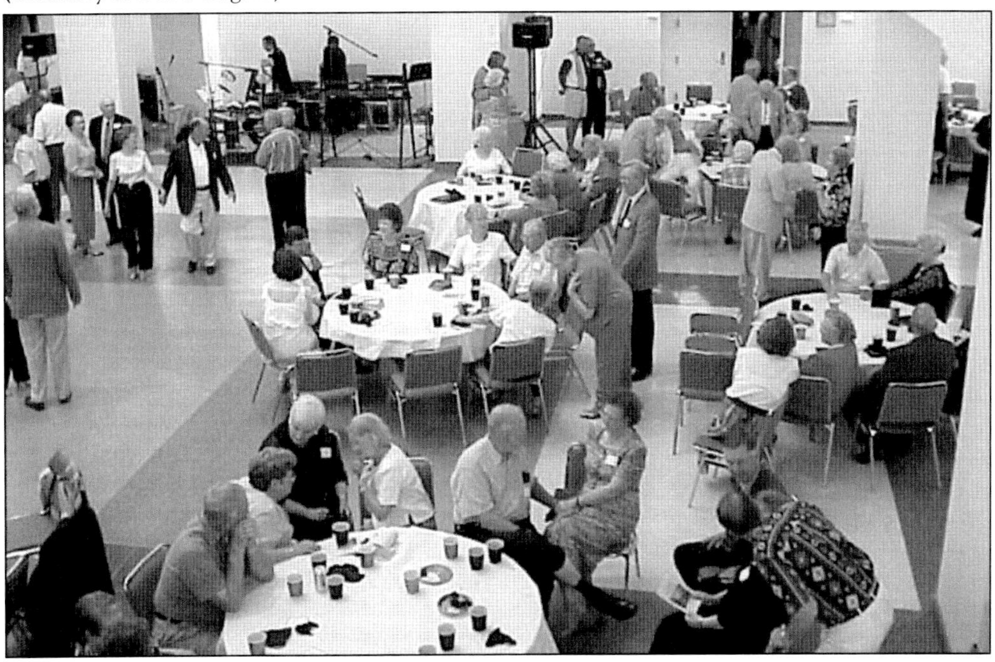

A live band, fine food, and much chitchat characterize an evening affair at an all-class reunion. Included are Robert M. Watkins, Evelyn Watkins, Bill McArthur, and Mary McArthur. (Courtesy of Bob Morgan.)

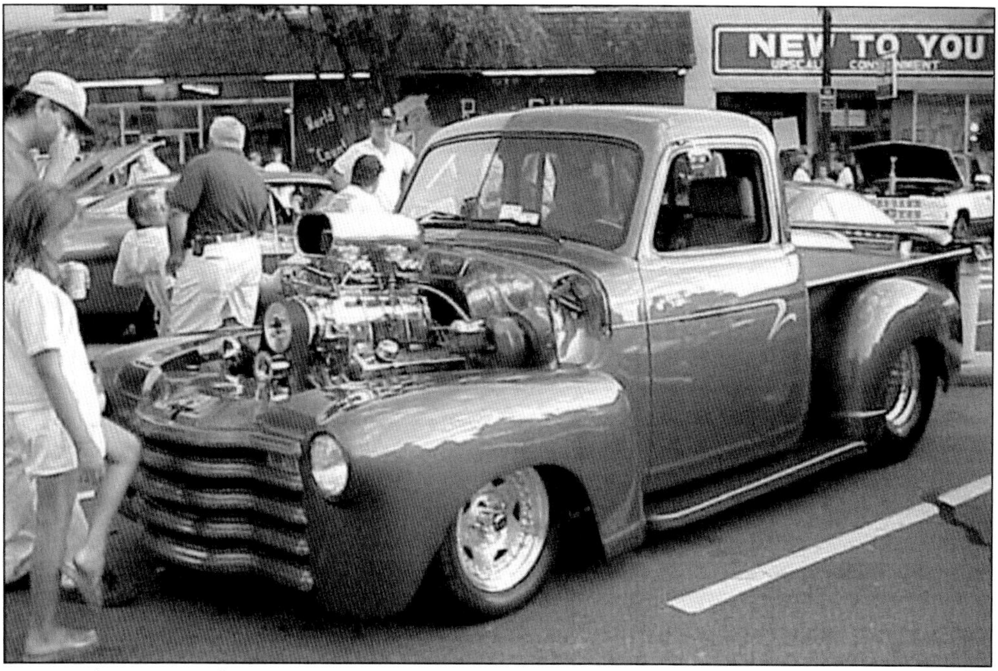

Many other events draw visitors to Main Street. Antique car shows and the annual August "Hot Nights and Cool Rides" attract car enthusiasts from all over. This modified pick-up brings examination from young and old alike. (Courtesy of Bob Morgan.)

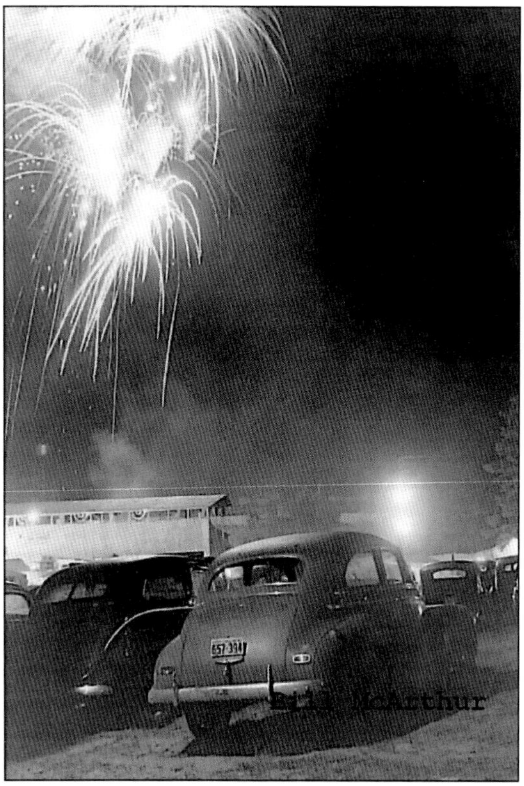

Fireworks attest to the fun and frolic available in Forest City, along with the hard work and dedication of the residents. (Courtesy of Bill McArthur.)

All entertainment does not have to be expensive. This photograph shows Charlie Johnson Goforth Sr. (left) and an unidentified friend enjoying a juicy watermelon where Graham Cash currently stands. Goforth was the owner of Goforth's Cafe (page 57). In the background, a peddler's covered wagon boasts a sign declaring his produce "Sweet." (Courtesy of Frances Goforth Pilgrim.)

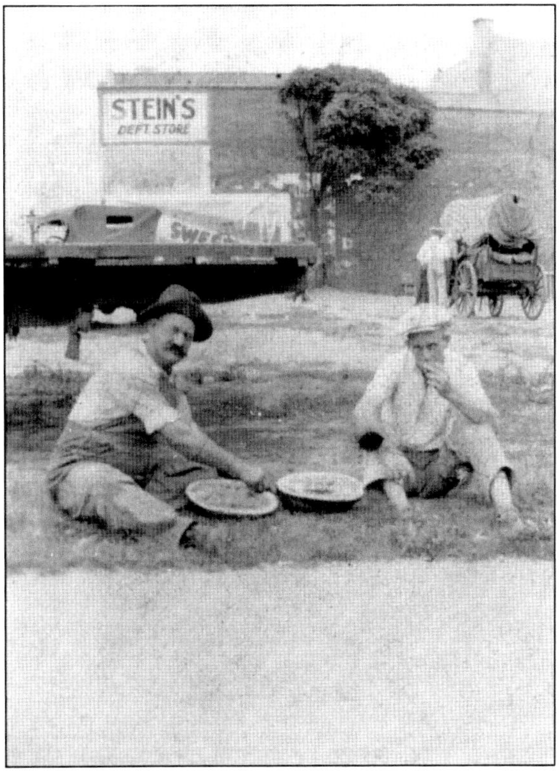

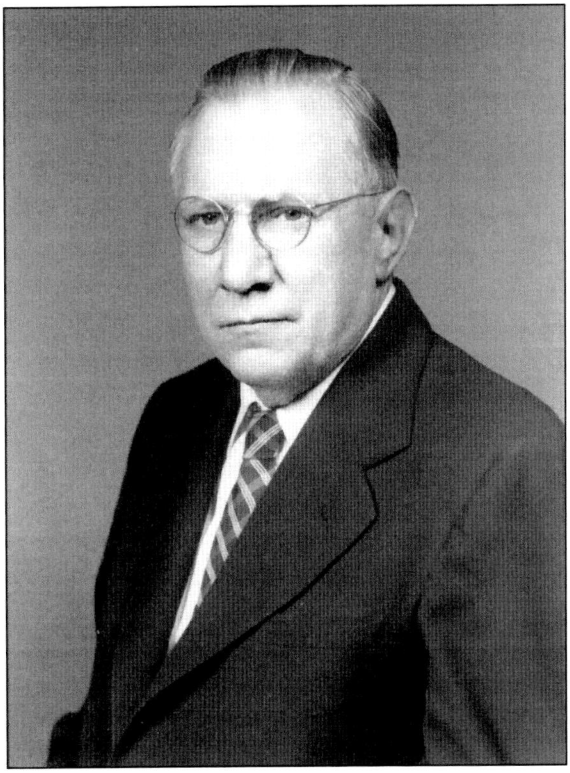

Preston Lynhardt Marks opened Marks Shoe and Harness Shop in 1916 on the south side of the square. Marks was director of the First Federal Savings and Loan, an active member of the Masonic Lodge, and controlling partner in the family shoe business. Griffin wrote: "But despite his success as one of the city's oldest businessmen, he still reserves the rights to go fishing any time he desires." (*Courier*, September 30, 1954). (Courtesy of Mary Lee Curtis.)

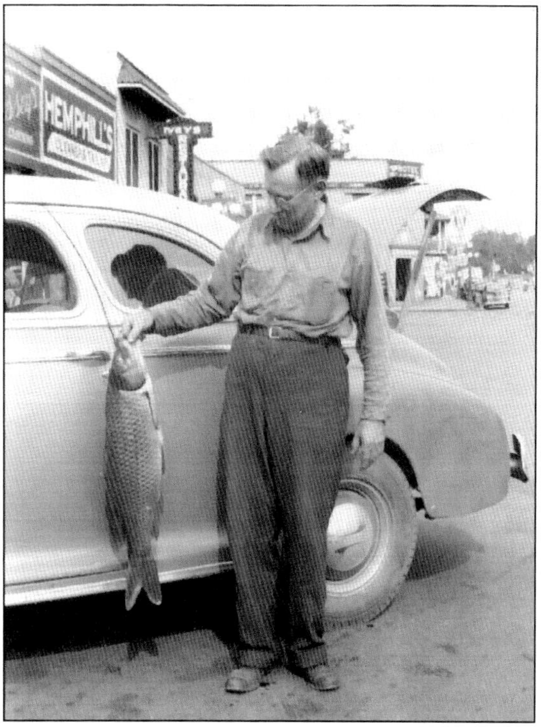

Area lakes, ponds, and rivers furnished endless hours of relaxation and contentment. Preston Lynhardt Marks—the local cobbler and business leader—had a thriving business at the corner of East Main and Mill. A dedicated civic worker and fishing enthusiast, Marks proudly displays his catch, perhaps a carp. (Courtesy of Mary Lee Curtis.)

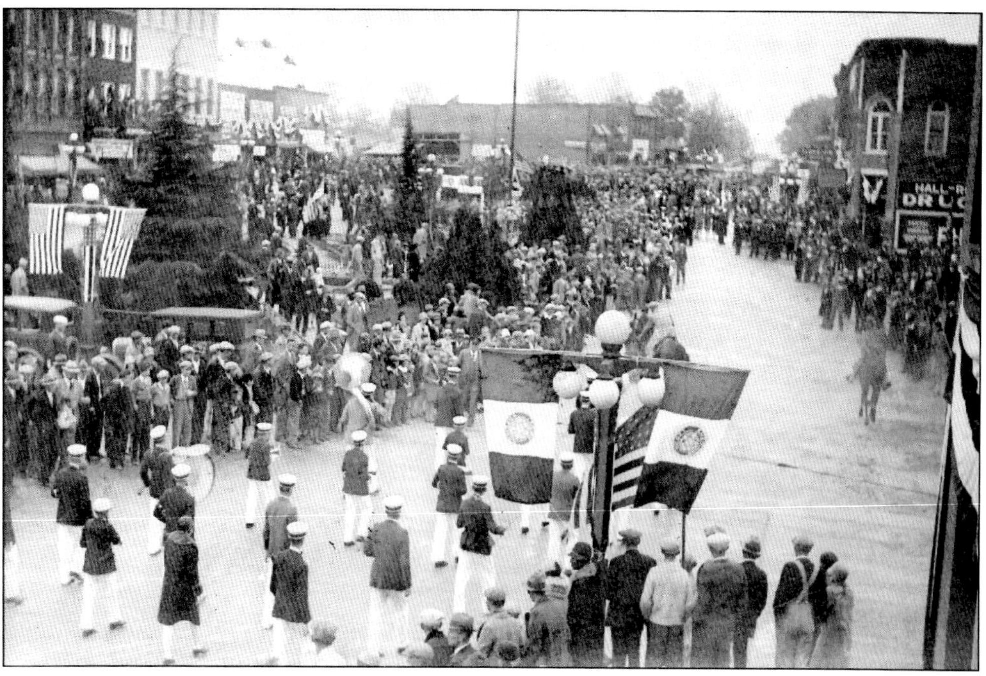

The public often turned out in large numbers to socialize, to hear the music, and to view the floats in local parades. Storefronts draped with bunting and streets lined with flags indicated the preparation that the town made for this American Legion Parade of 1939. The image is a history lesson: old storefronts, an old-time carnival, antique streetlights, early automobiles, vintage clothing, Hall-Reinhardt Drugs, and other sights. (Courtesy of Charles Vess.)

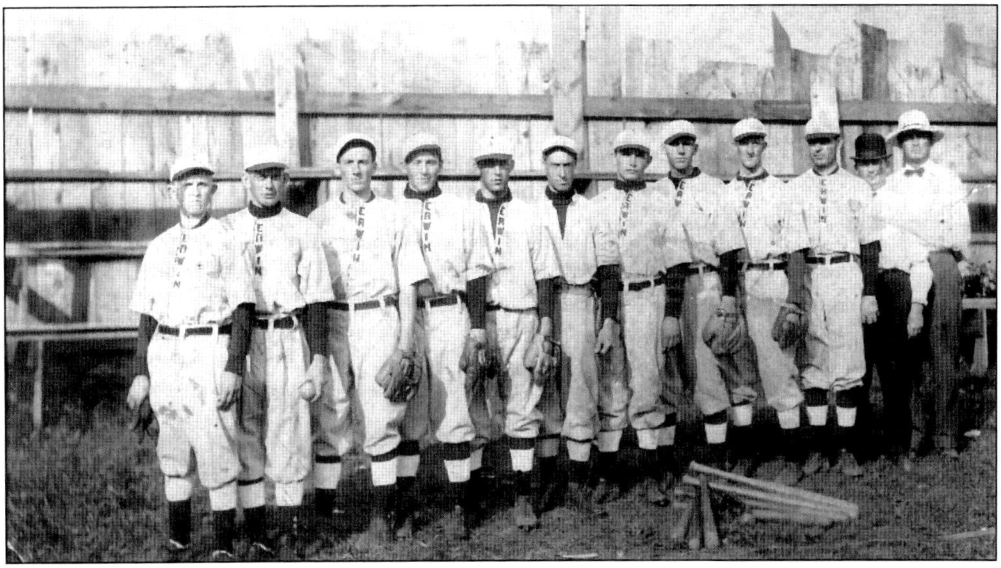

A popular pastime in Forest City has always been baseball—little league, high school, mill teams, American Legion, and semi-pro. In 2002, 2003, and 2004, the East Rutherford High School Cavaliers won the North Carolina High School Athletics Association 2-A State Baseball Championship. This picture shows an early Forest City area, semi-pro team in hand-me-down uniforms. (Courtesy of Jim Hemphill.)

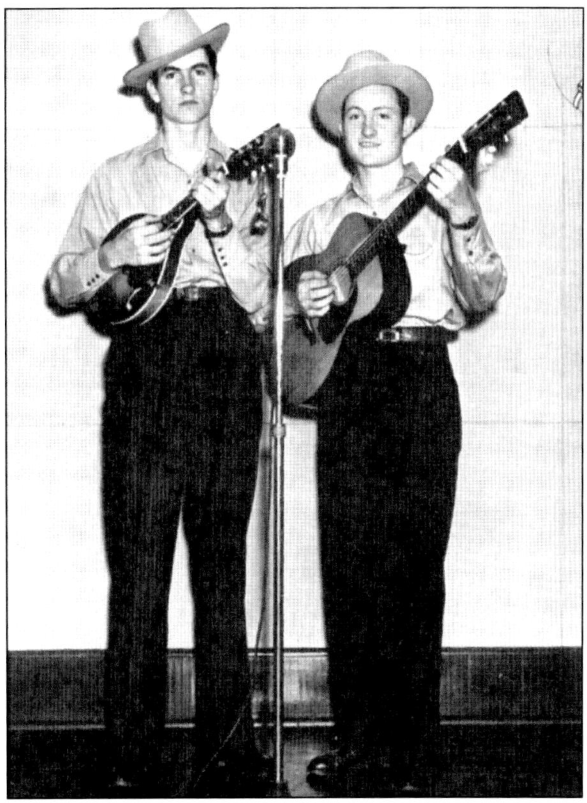

Two entertainers who knew Forest City well were Jesse and Jim McReynolds. These bluegrass musicians earned a place on the *Grand Ol' Opry* stage. Hired by WBBO and frequently a guest of Jerrell S. Bedford on WAGY, Jesse McReynolds will be a part of the 80th anniversary celebration of the *Grand Ole Opry*. (Courtesy of Jerrell S. Bedford.)

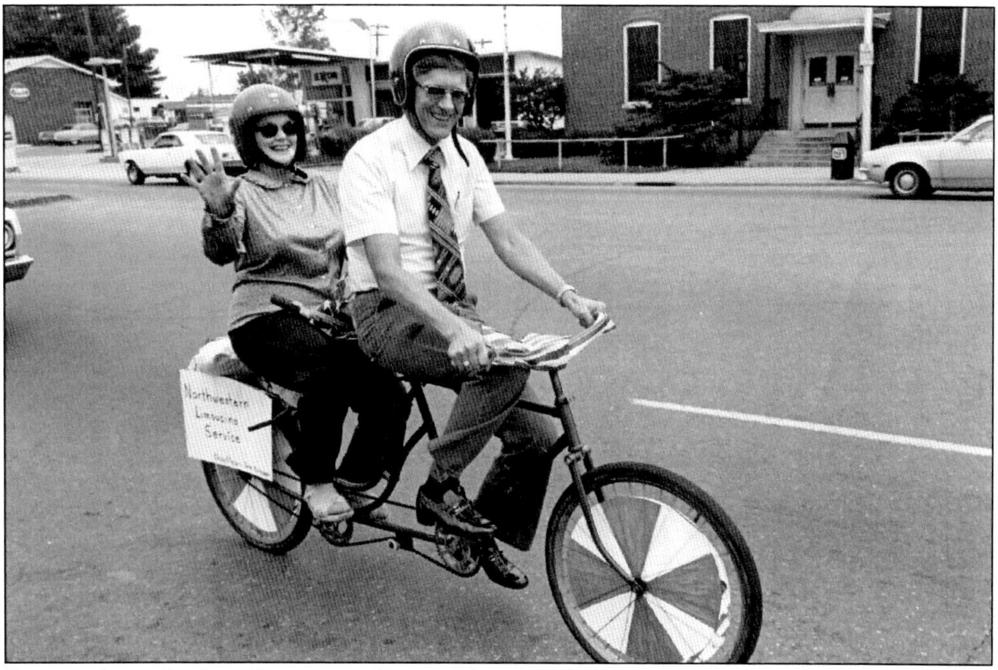

Even work can be fun. Contests within and between businesses can increase employee efforts. This photograph shows the results of losing a competition: Colleen Biggerstaff and Jack Buchanan (chauffeur and CEO of Northwestern Bank) had to operate a limousine service. Their bike "limousine" is cruising by the post office at its old West Main location. (Courtesy of Colleen Jenkins Biggerstaff.)

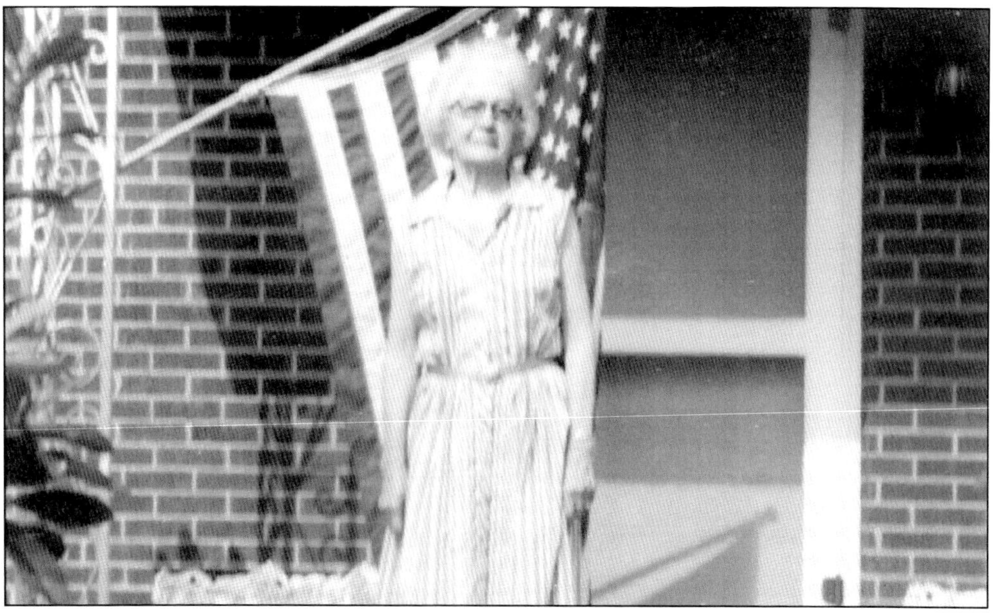

Another contest, this one sponsored by WLOS-TV, produced Selma Jane Price Harrill as winner. Here she shows her prize: a U.S. flag. Her poem titled "This Is America" brought public recognition. Mrs. Harrill, an accomplished painter, wrote of discovering America at age four and a half when she saw the lamplighters at dusk. (Courtesy of Jane Thompson Gurley.)

Seven

Transportation and Communication
Linking to the World

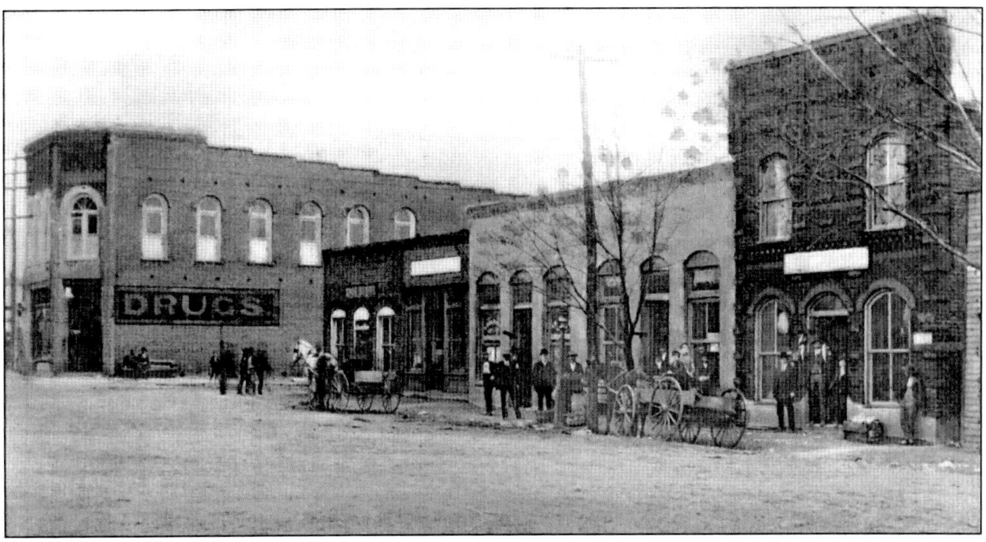

Forest City/Burnt Chimney grew up at the crossroads of the Lincolnton, the Shelby, the Rutherfordton, and the Spartanburg Roads. The roads encouraged contact and trade. This postcard demonstrates both the permanence of some parts of downtown Forest City and the progress that has occurred. Any person who has seen the south side of the streets today will recognize on this card some of the storefronts: a drug store (far left), a shoe store, and a grocery store (fourth from the left). No cars or paved streets appear in this early street scene, but there is evidence of the first types of traffic: travel by foot, horseback, wagons, and buggies. (Courtesy of Sara Jolley.)

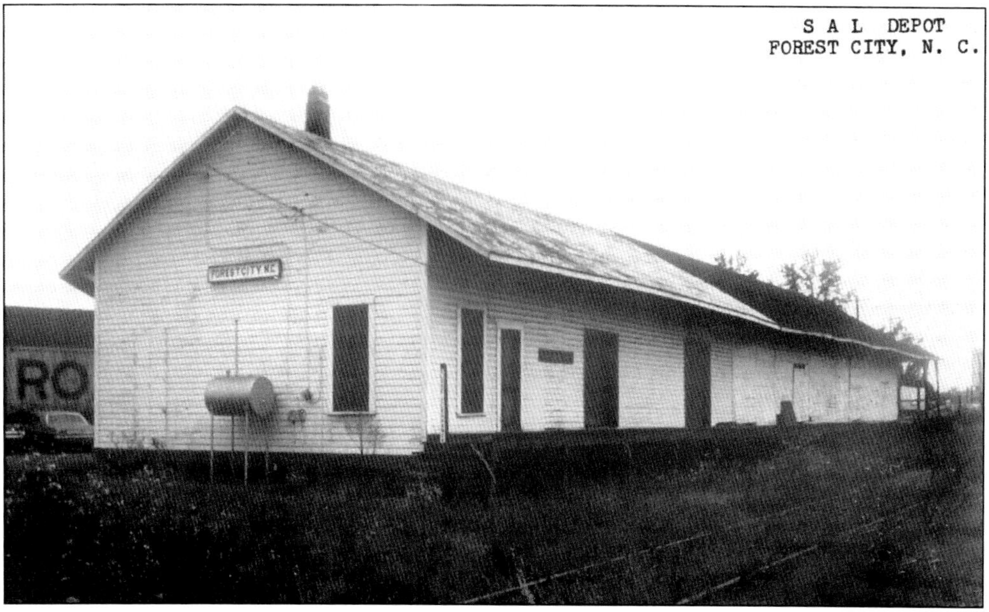

The North Carolina Legislature granted a charter in November 1855 to the Wilmington, Charlotte, & Rutherfordton Railroad. The western portion of the line reached Lincolnton (1861); the Civil War halted construction. Building resumed in the 1870s under the name Carolina Central; the railroad came through Forest City and on to Rutherfordton (1887). The Carolina Central and the Seaboard Air Line Railway merged in 1901. The depot was in west Forest City. (Courtesy of Paul Tim Jones Jr.)

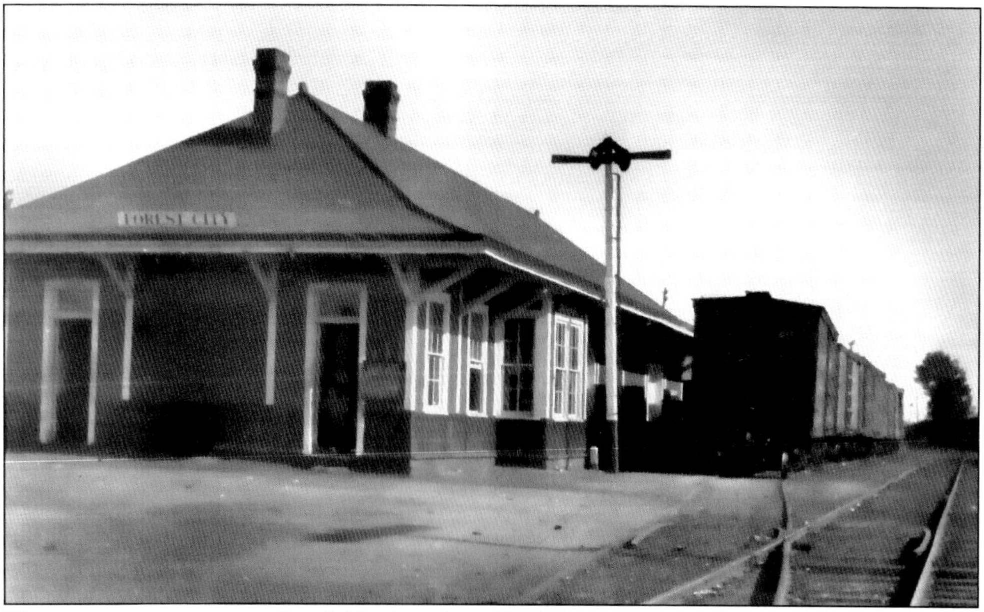

The next major county railroad (the line from Blacksburg to Marion) was the Georgetown & North Carolina Narrow Gauge Railway Company. In 1885, it became the Charleston, Cincinnati, & Chicago Railroad, commonly called the Three Cs. In 1890, the line was complete. After bankruptcy, the line became part of the Southern Railway. This Forest City Southern Railway Depot photograph includes the semaphore train order signals. (Courtesy of Bill McArthur.)

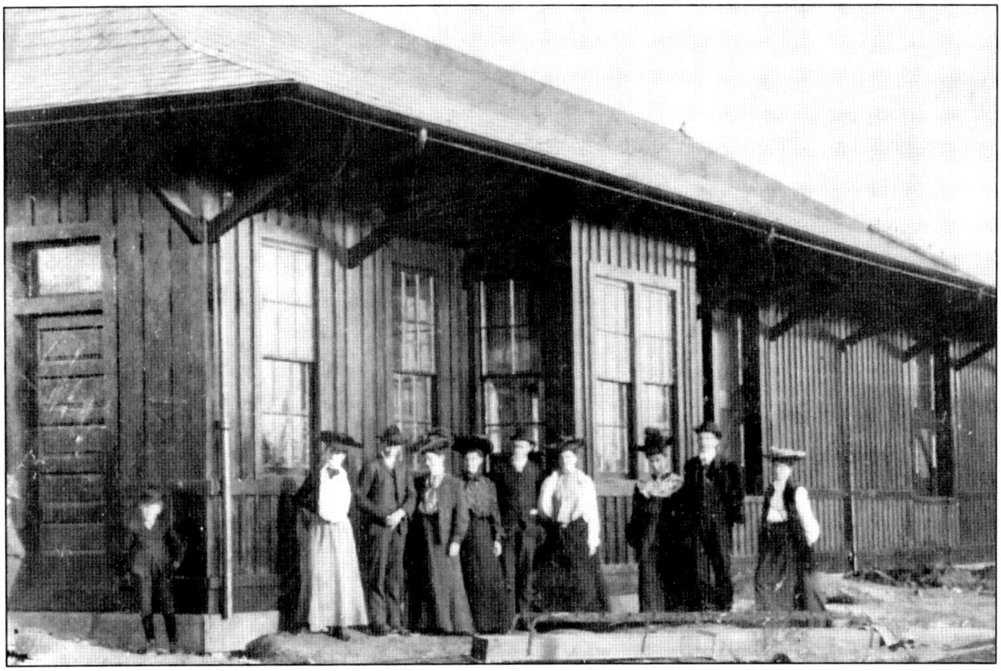

A trip to the train station to observe the trains was a popular and inexpensive activity. This 1906 view shows local residents at the Southern Railway Depot on Depot Street. From left to right are unidentified child, Minnie Fortune Blanton, unidentified, Edna Long Burkholder, Emma Harrill Flack, Lane McDaniel, Fannie Fortune Lowe, Chinara Flack Wilson, unidentified, and Nora Flack Elliott. (Courtesy of the First Baptist Church and Betty Jo Carpenter.)

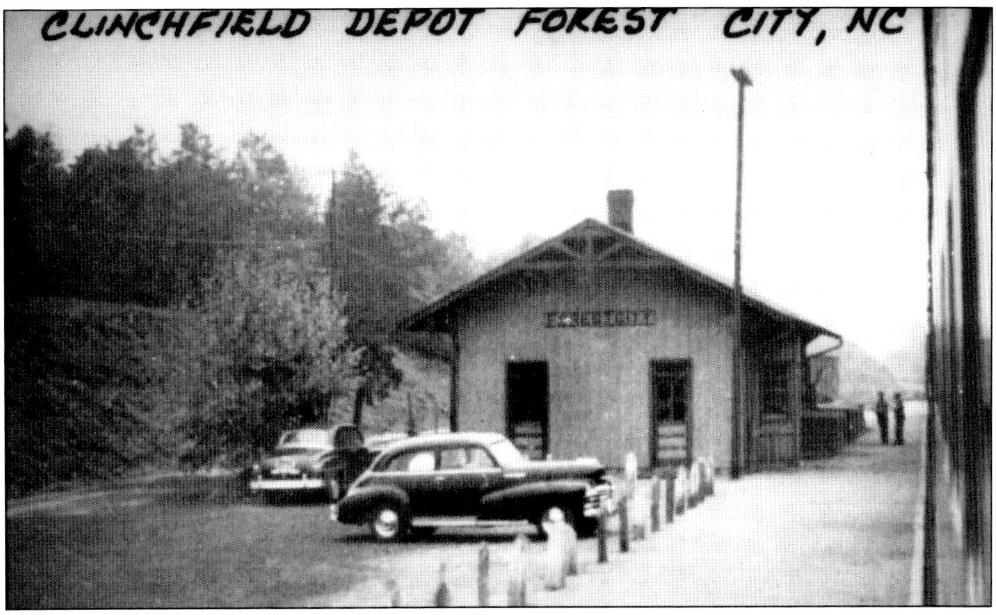

The Carolina Clinchfield & Ohio, or the CC&O, was the final railroad constructed in Forest City. Constructed in 1909, the CC&O ran between Spartanburg, South Carolina, and Elkhorn City, Kentucky. This is a photograph of train #37, Clinchfield's northbound passenger train, stopped at Forest City. (Courtesy of A. R. Poteat.)

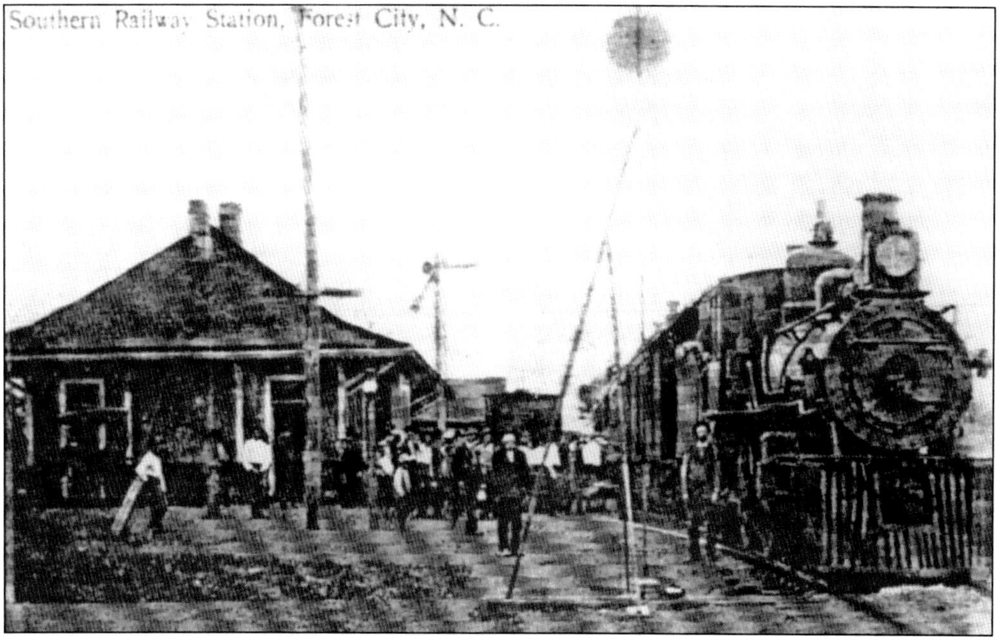

Much has changed in 118 years of railroading. Southern Railway is gone; there are no tracks or depot. The Seaboard Air Line Depot is gone. The short line Thermal Belt Railroad Company uses the tracks between Forest City and Bostic. The Clinchfield—now part of CSX Transportation—operates up to 25 trains a day and hauls coal and merchandise. This is the Southern Railway Station in Forest City. (Courtesy of A. R. Poteat.)

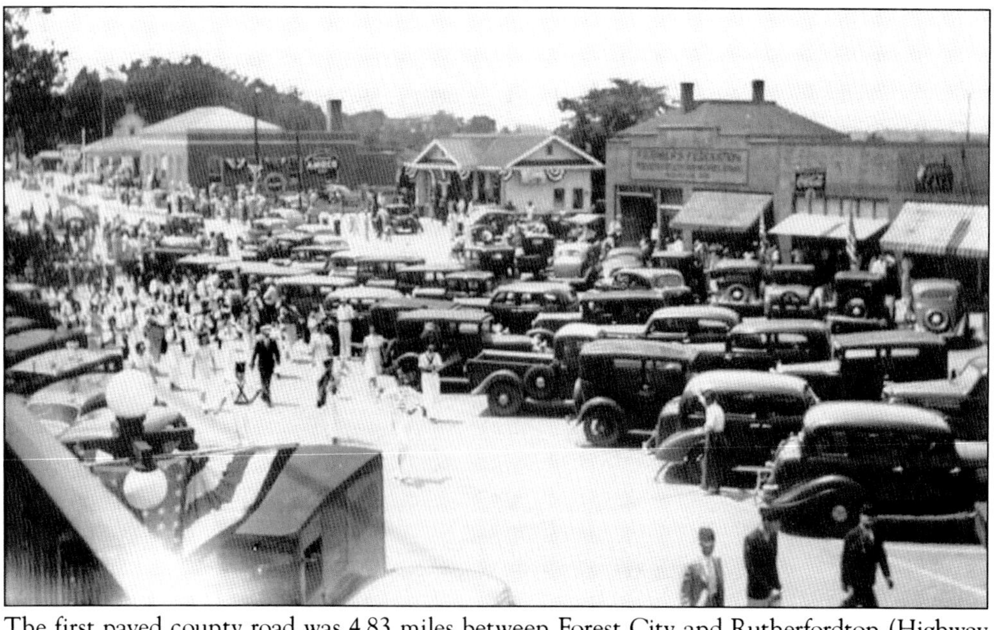

The first paved county road was 4.83 miles between Forest City and Rutherfordton (Highway 20/74) for $132,968 in 1922. Here American Legion Parade marchers perform on a paved West Main Street in the 1930s before Stallings, A&P, or Davis Shop. Houses come all the way to the old brick post office. The Amoco and ESSO Stations at Yarboro are now gone. (Courtesy of Dr. W. L. Stallings and Betty Jo Carpenter.)

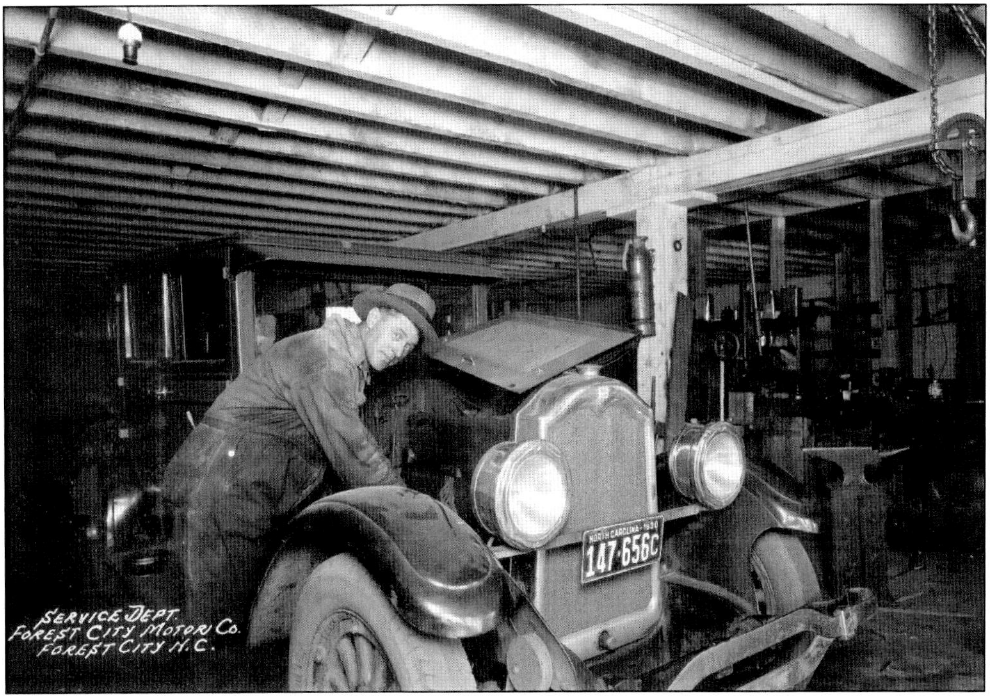

Albert Mauney considered keeping his car in good condition a top priority. Here Mauney works on the engine of a 1930 Buick in the service department of Forest City Motor Company on Main Street. During World War I, Albert served in France with Willis Towery, for whom the American Legion Post #74 received its name. (Courtesy of William "Bill" Brown.)

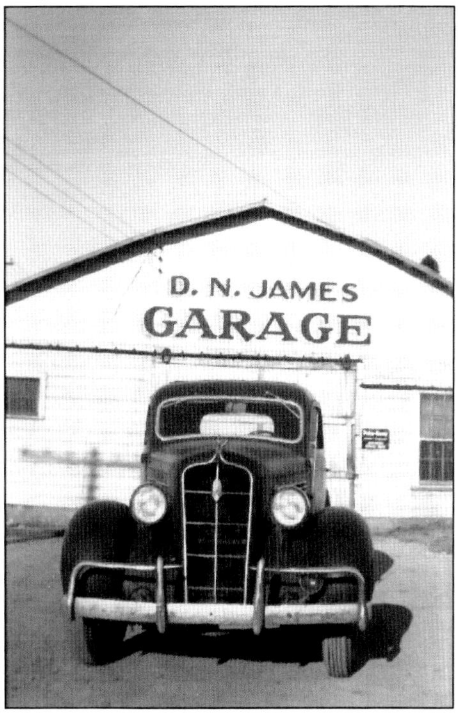

Forest City has maintained a large number of automobile garages and tune-up shops. One of the early establishments was D. N. James's Garage. New and used automobile dealers continue to thrive in the area. In fact, Forest City has the title of "Little Detroit in Western North Carolina." (Courtesy of Frances Goforth Pilgrim.)

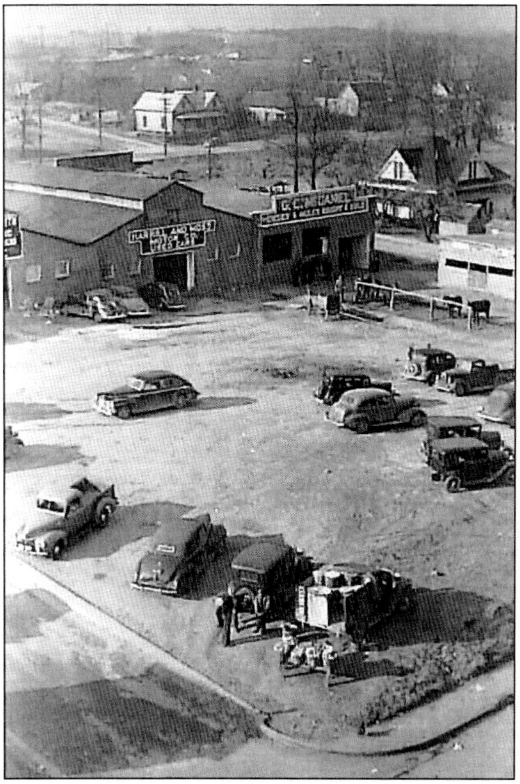

Not everyone owned cars. Grover C. McDaniel maintained a livery stable on Trade Street where one could purchase an animal. Grover was a blacksmith and farrier who helped maintain healthy hooves on local animals. His work near the fire was hot in summer; adequate ventilation in winter meant a cold workplace. (Courtesy of W. H. McArthur.)

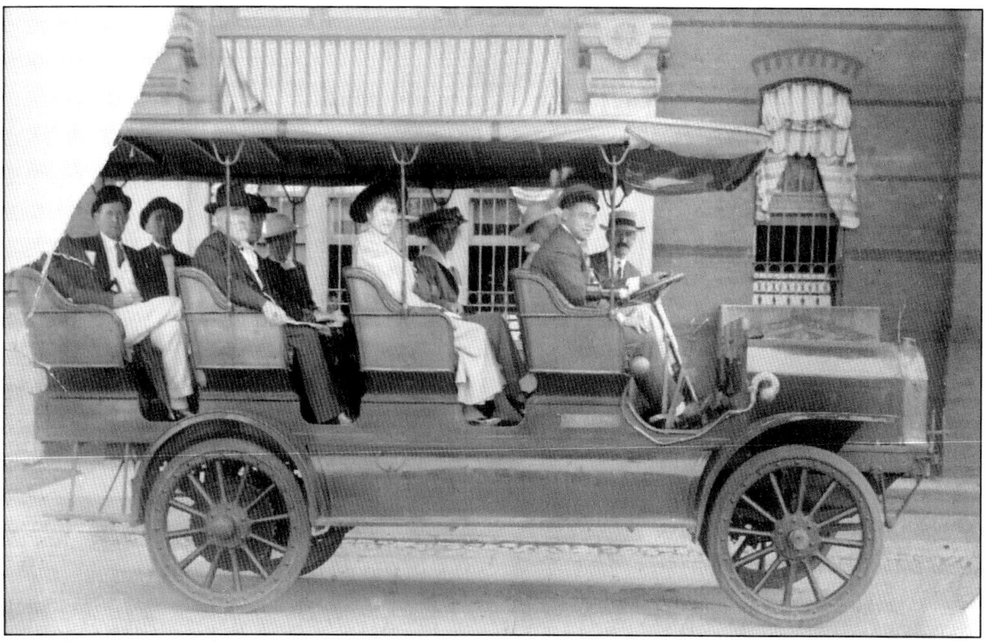

Not all vehicles of the era were single-passenger conveyances. This photograph includes, from left to right, (back seat) Burt Bridges and C. S. Hemphill, T. R. Padgett, Newt Biggerstaff and wife, Mrs. T. R. Padgett, and other unidentified passengers. This sightseeing bus was in Baltimore, Maryland; the business managers were on a buying trip. (Courtesy of Jim Hemphill.)

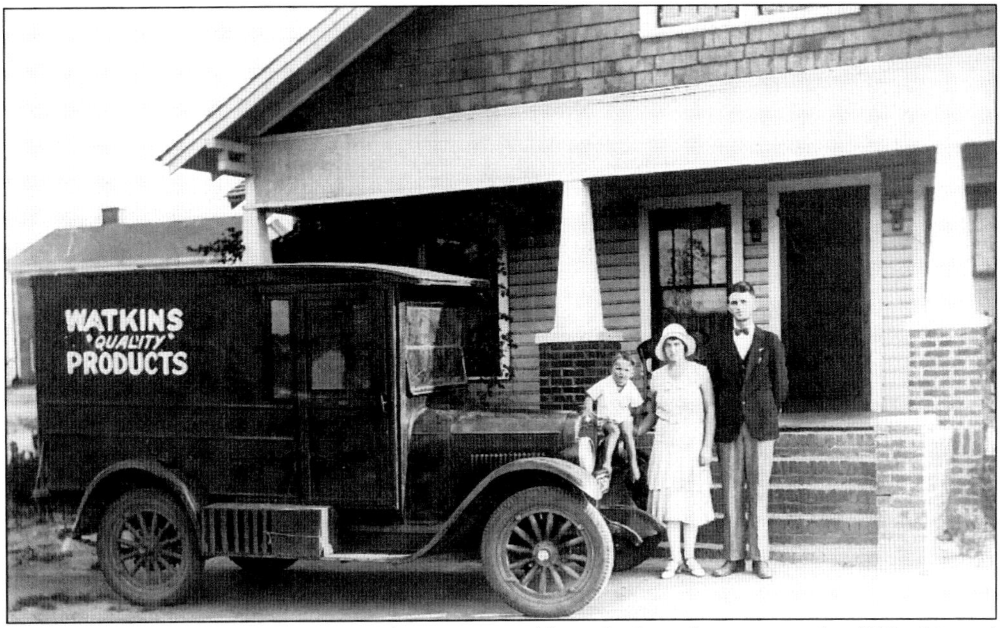

Dewey Carpenter, a Wake Forest graduate, was unable to find employment in the 1930s. He and his young wife, Walda Morris Carpenter, purchased a Chevrolet panel truck to sell Watkins Products (tooth powder, flavoring, household products) house-to-house. Perched proudly on the hood is Dewey Carpenter Jr. Walda was a former teacher and Welfare Department employee. (Courtesy of Walda Morris Carpenter and Evelyn Morris Ferree.)

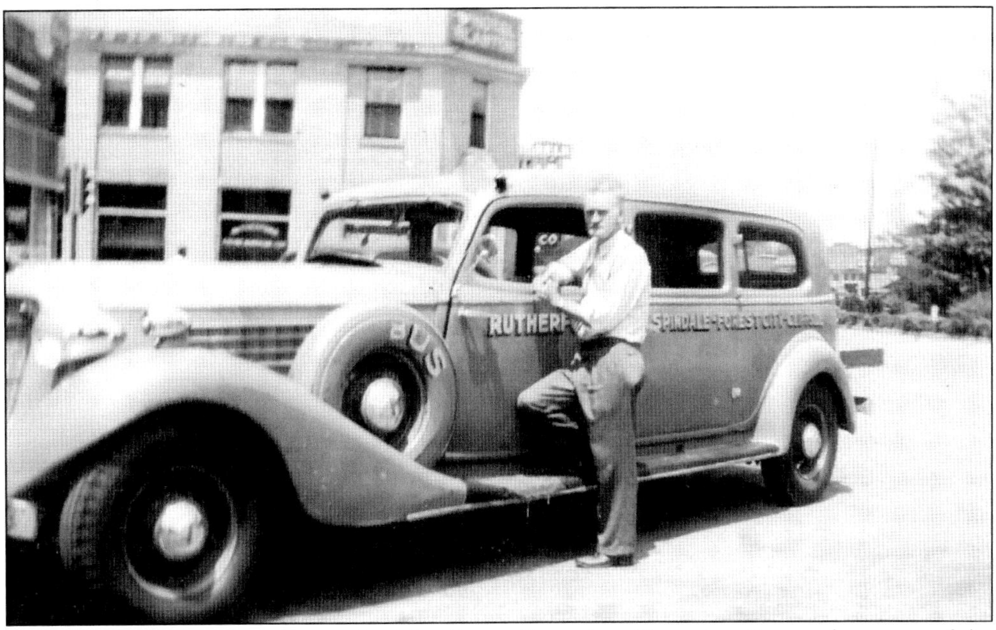

Serving the Forest City area was the Blue Goose limousine. Here, Ivey Drum, the owner of the car, park in front of Ivey's Restaurant (on the south side of the square). George Ivey Drum and his wife (Grace Hendrick Drum) managed Ivey's. They advertised "Where Friends Meet, to Relax and Eat." Two lamb chops (broiled) with bread, butter, and potatoes was 65¢. Lyles Mason sometimes drove the Blue Goose. (Courtesy of Geneva Drum Jenkins.)

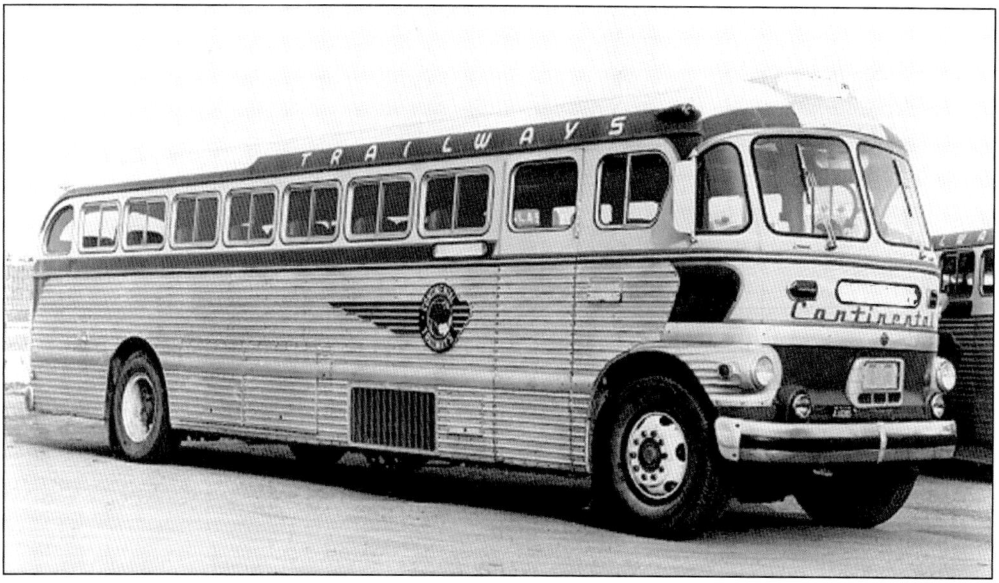

This stock photograph of a Trailways bus illustrates the means by which many residents could travel in comfort both short or long distances to visit friends, to vacation, to complete business, or to serve Uncle Sam. In the 1950s, the Trailways Bus Station in Forest City was on Cherry Mountain Street. (Courtesy of the authors.)

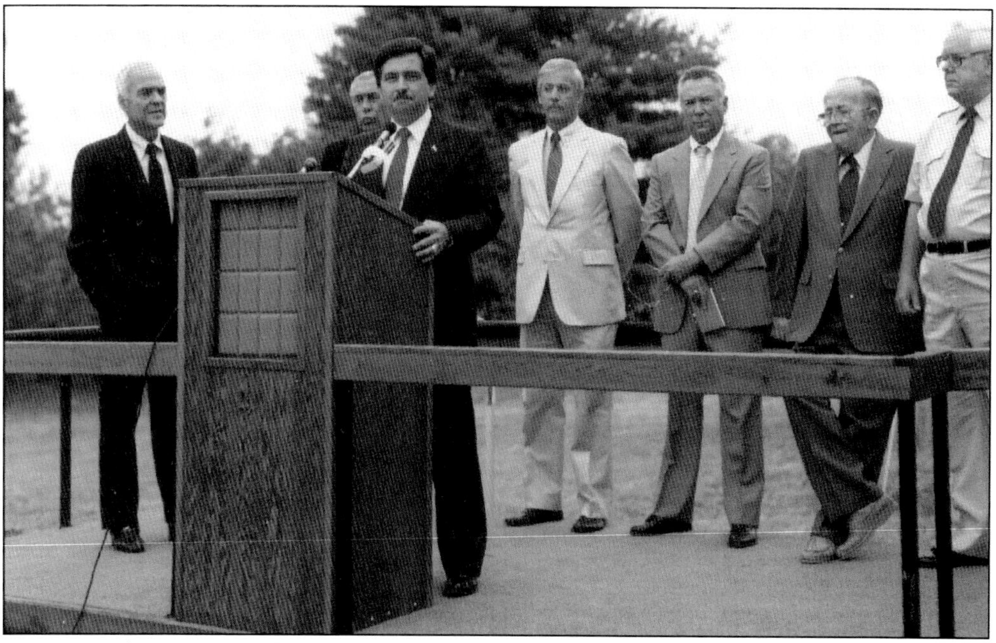

On September 1, 1987, officials broke ground for U.S. 74 Bypass to I-26; work for this link had begun in the 1960s. Dignitaries pictured here are, from left to right, North Carolina representative Charles ("Babe") Owens, Russell Duncan, Jim Bishop (Gov. Jim Martin's Western North Carolina representative), Jack Metcalf (Spindale mayor), North Carolina Department of Transportation chief engineer Earl McEntire, county commissioner chair Fred Crowe, and Rutherfordton mayor Fred Williams. Not pictured is Forest City mayor Ron Guy. (Courtesy of Jim Bishop.)

J. Worth Morgan, a prominent Forest City banker with distinguished careers at both Farmers Bank and Trust and Union Trust Company, made the first direct-dialed telephone call between Forest City and Rutherfordton. Here he places that first call to the mayor of Rutherfordton. (Courtesy of Bob Morgan, J. Worth Morgan's son.)

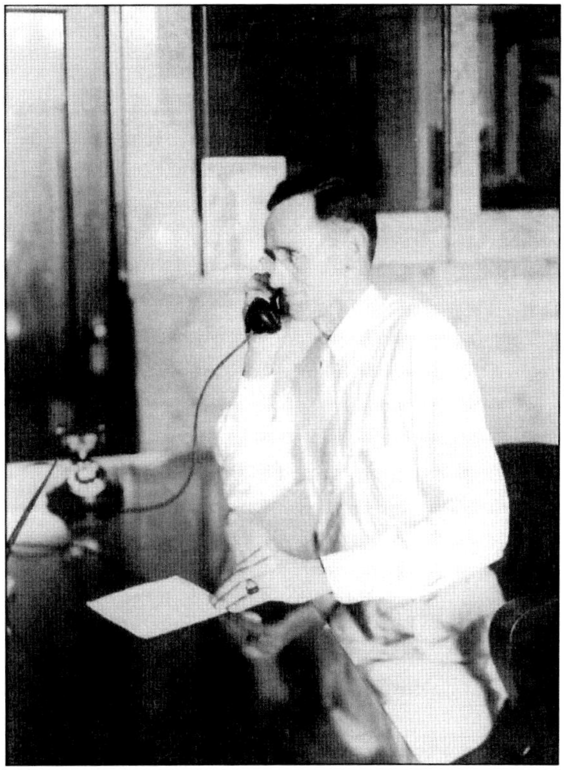

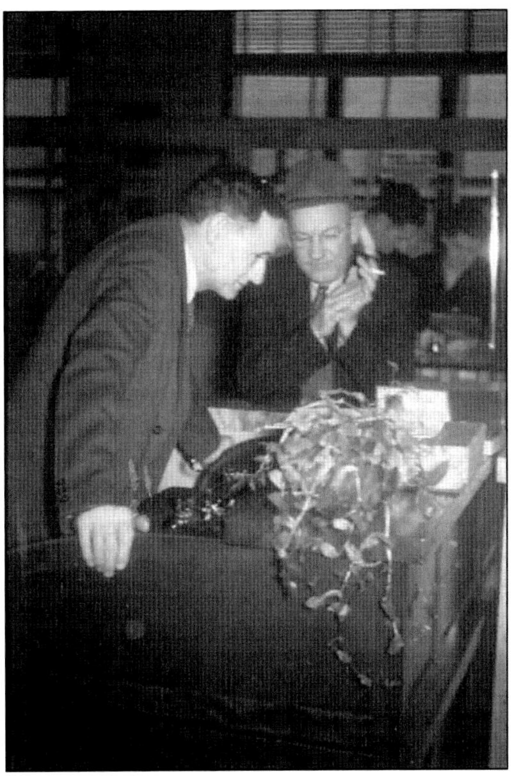

Here J. Worth Morgan (left) and Clarence Griffin, county historian and newspaper editor, examine the telephone equipment on the desk and comment on the impact that the telephone may have. Other local publications have included *The Ledger*, *Progress*, *Free Press*, *Daily Bulletin*, *This Week*, and *The Harris Herald* (published by Rev. Milton Robinson). (Courtesy of Bob Morgan.)

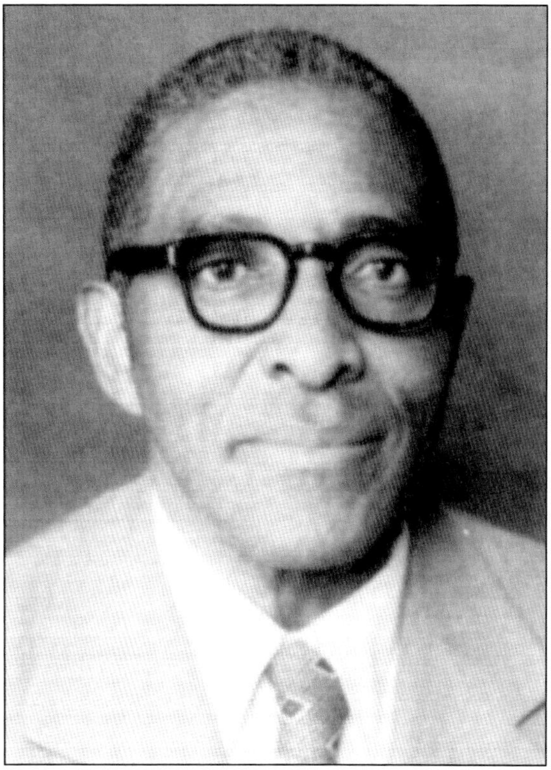

Rev. Milton Robinson earned an A.B. (Johnson C. Smith University), an M.S. in educational administration (North Carolina Agricultural and Technological University), and a doctor of divinity (Livingstone College). He was a Pullman porter, brickmason, past-presiding elder for the A.M.E. Zion Church, teacher, newspaper editor, and father of 11. His newspapers (*Harris Herald* and *Star of Zion*) sold throughout the county and even in other states. (Courtesy of Milton B. Robinson Jr.)

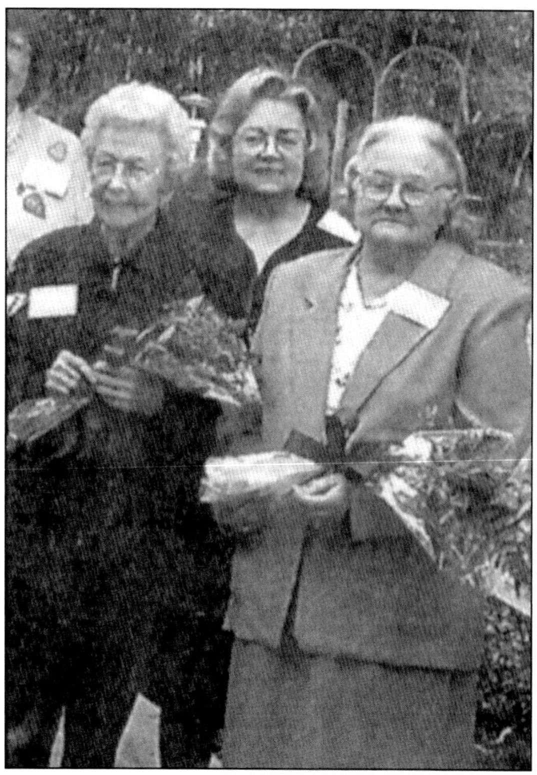

Virginia Biggerstaff Rucker, journalist since 1946, served as president of the North Carolina Press Women and was the first woman to receive the Kiwanis Club Special Cup Award. Virginia (left) and Nancy Ferguson (far right)—county historian since 1988 and author of *Rutherford County 1979: A People's Bicentennial History*—received the DAR's "Women in History" Recognition. Anita Davis (center) received recognition also. (Courtesy of *Daily Courier*.)

Publisher James R. Brown has served the *Courier* since 1998 and brings experiences from Ohio, California, and Florida. Brown currently serves as chair of the Realize Rutherford Steering Committee and is a board member of Rutherford County Senior Center, Life Services, and Foothills Connect; he has been president of the Leadership Rutherford Board and active in the Chamber of Commerce, the Lions Club, and St. Francis Episcopal Church. (Courtesy of James R. Brown.)

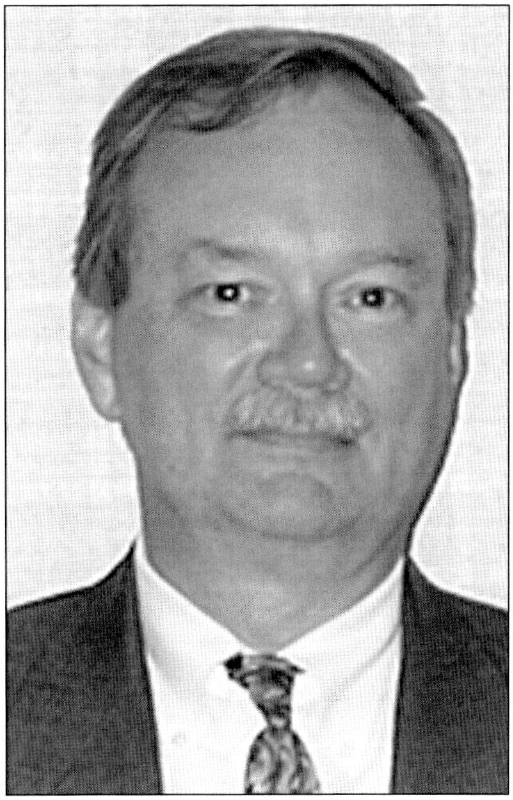

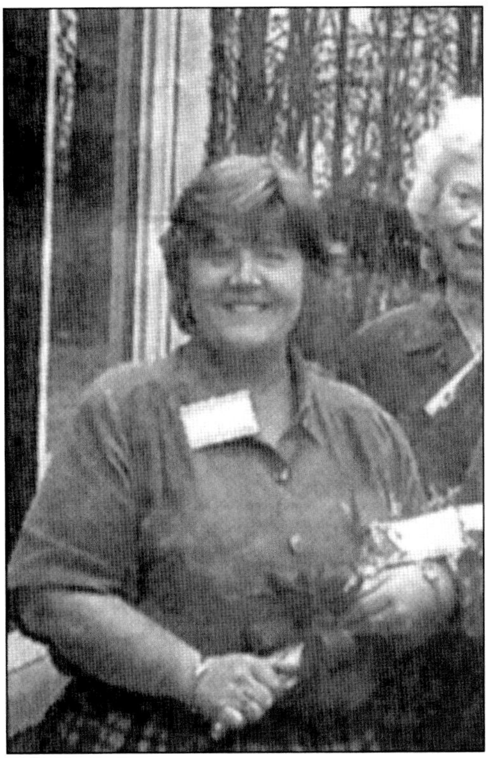

Features editor Jean Gordon is the daughter of the late Irene Crawford Gordon and Edgar Gordon; she began her newspaper work 35 years ago as typesetter at the *Rutherford County News* in 1970. She became news editor (in 1972) and editor (in 1986); when Forest City Publishing bought *The News* in 1994, she went to the *Daily Courier*. Here she receives the DAR's "Women in History" Award. (Courtesy of *Daily Courier*.)

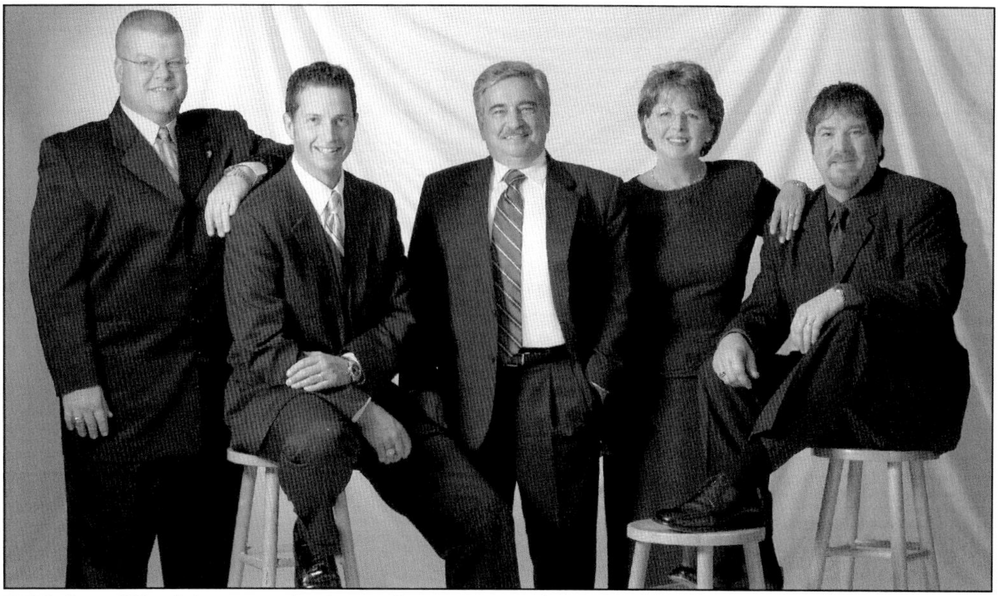

WBBO on West Main was the first radio station in the county in 1946. Charles Melton and Jim Bishop worked at the West Main WBBO (now WWOL). Jim Bishop is at WCAB on Whitesides Road in 2005. WCAB, started in 1966, is a 24-hour, 1,000-watt powerhouse. Jim also performs with the gospel group "In His Glory." From left to right are Howard Gordon, Thad Harrill, Jim Bishop, Diane Harrill, and David Roach. (Courtesy of Jim Bishop.)

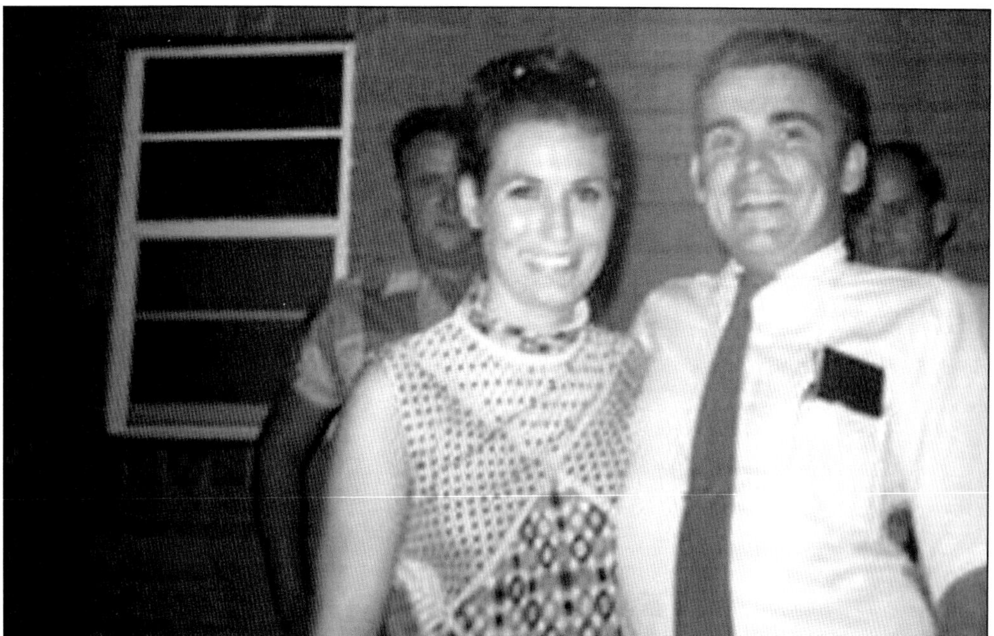

Jerrell S. Bedford, husband of Pat Bailey Bedford, broadcast for WAGY from 1962–1981. Here he stands with Loretta Lynn. Brothers-in-law Hoyle Lovelace and "Uncle Bud" Becknell founded in 1957–1958 the county's second station (off Hudlow Road) and also City Radio and Jewelry Company, the fifth store from the corner of Main and Thomas; Nell Price Burns, author Anita Price's mother, worked there until it closed. (Courtesy of Jerrell Bedford.)

Eight

BUSINESSES AND ORGANIZATIONS
Meeting Needs

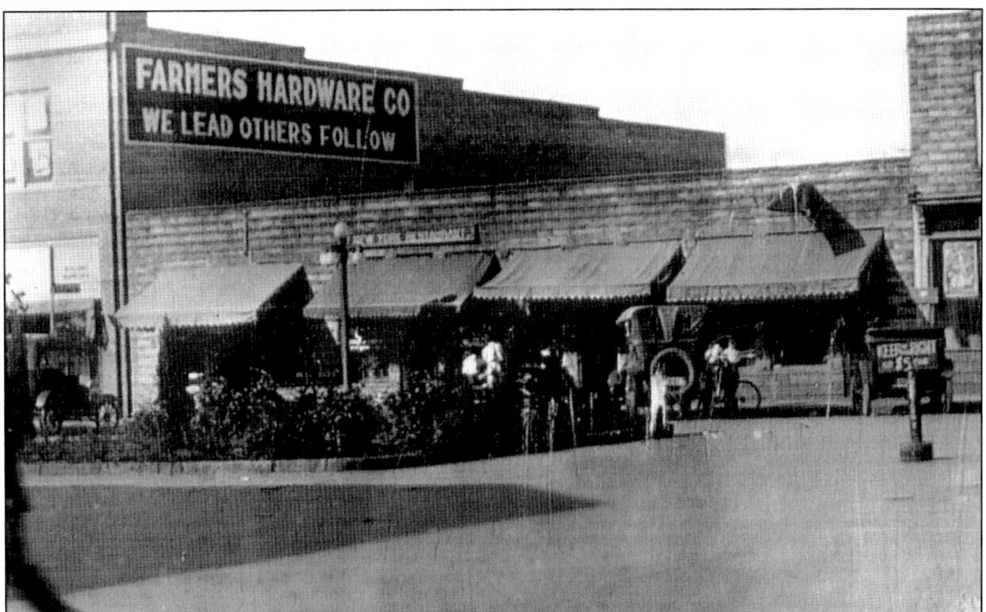

"We lead, others follow" is the business slogan of the Farmers Hardware Company, founded by J. F. Weathers and operating at the same location since 1916. This photograph shows no sidewalks at the time. The Ford T Models at the storefronts help to date this image; the vehicles are, of course, all the same color: black. The New York Restaurant behind the gas streetlight did not survive the Southern hospitality. (Courtesy of Frances Goforth Pilgrim.)

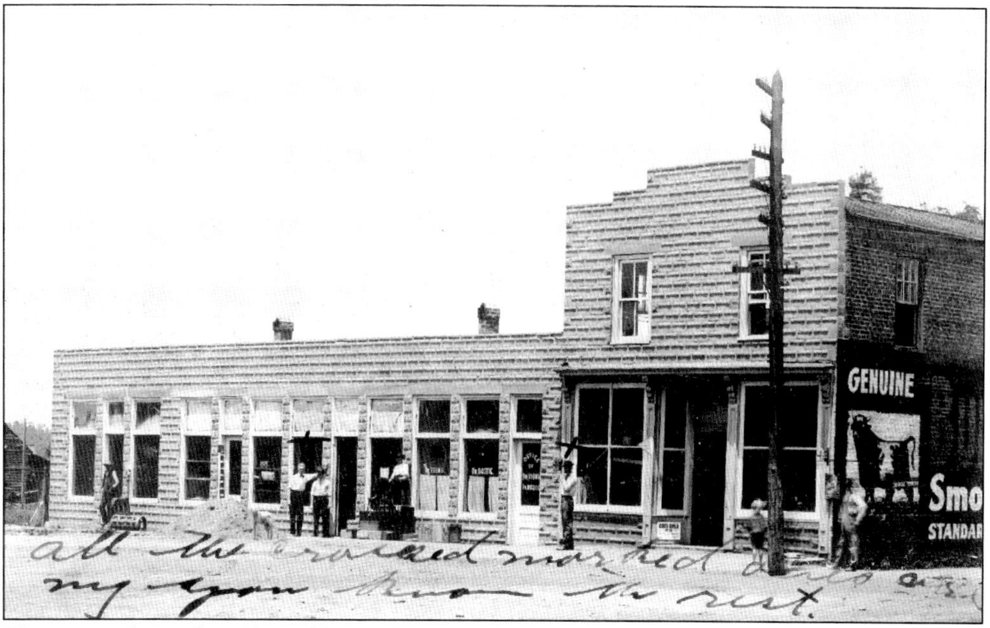

This scene shows the office of Dr. G. E. Young (physician and the "first mayor, being named in Legislative action that incorporated Burnt Chimney" [Griffin, 556]). Dr. W. C. Bostic's name is visible on this postcard showing West Main. Messages were written on the front of these early postcards. A small sign at the bottom of the door invites shoppers to come in for "Coca-Cola on ice." This scene predates Farmers Hardware, which opened in 1916 and would have would have been in the far left corner. (Courtesy of First Baptist Church and Betty Jo Carpenter.)

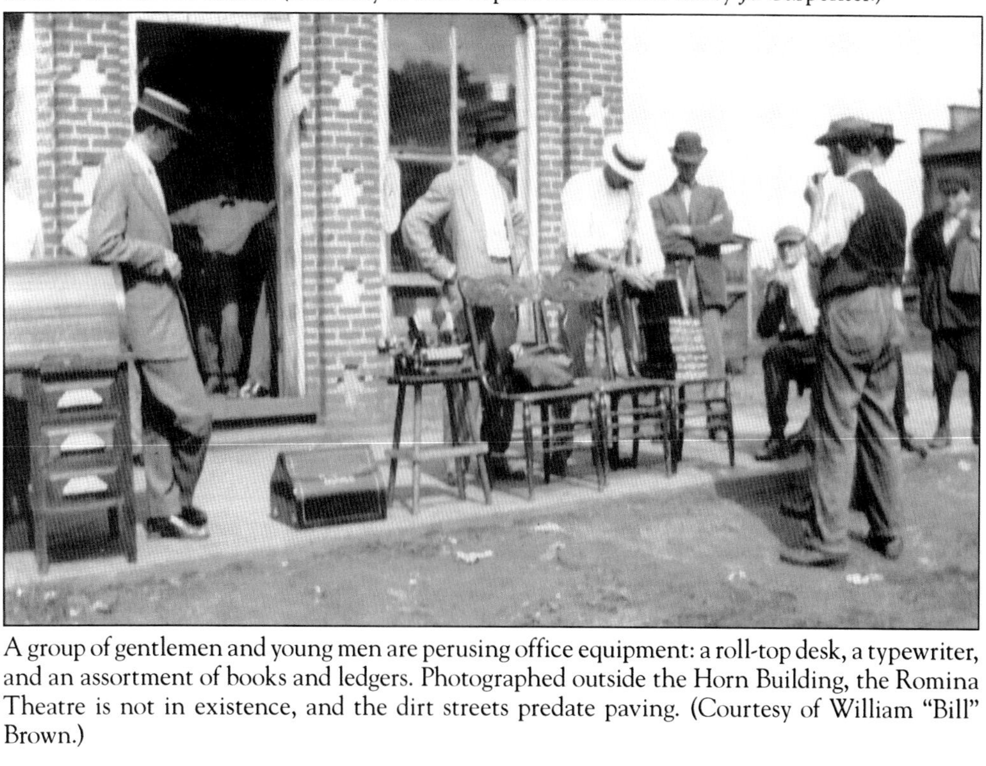

A group of gentlemen and young men are perusing office equipment: a roll-top desk, a typewriter, and an assortment of books and ledgers. Photographed outside the Horn Building, the Romina Theatre is not in existence, and the dirt streets predate paving. (Courtesy of William "Bill" Brown.)

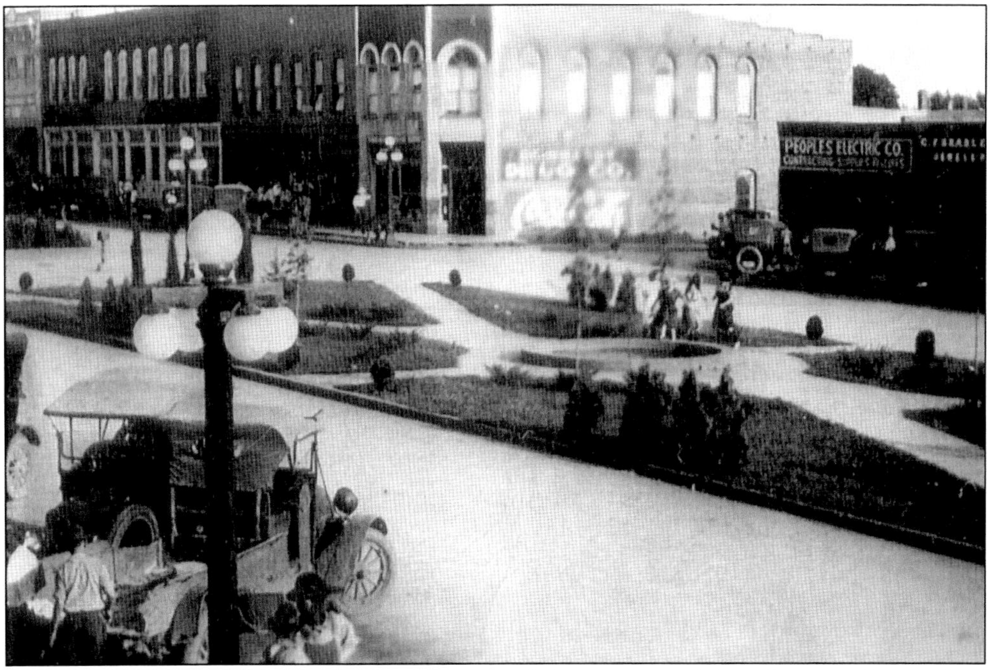

The above photograph shows a very early view of the square on Main Street in Forest City. Reinhardt Drug Company, People's Electric Company, and C. F. Bradley Jewelers are visible here from left to right. In the center of the photograph are four young women playing around the pool. In the foreground some young men are loading the delivery truck for Jones's Grocery Store. The streetlights are gas-fueled. (Courtesy of Frances Goforth Pilgrim.)

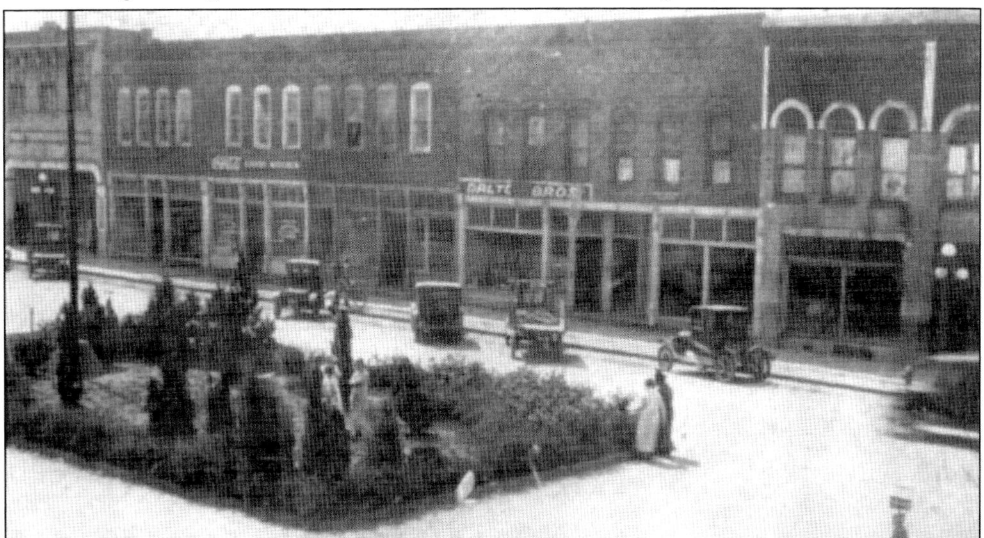

The different angle from the photographer's camera (possibly from the Horn Building) shows the south side of Main Street. Captured by the camera lens are (left to right) a theater, the Candy Kitchen, a barber shop, Dalton Brothers and Lewis's Dentistry. This photograph dates to the early 1920s. (Courtesy of Mary Lee Curtis.)

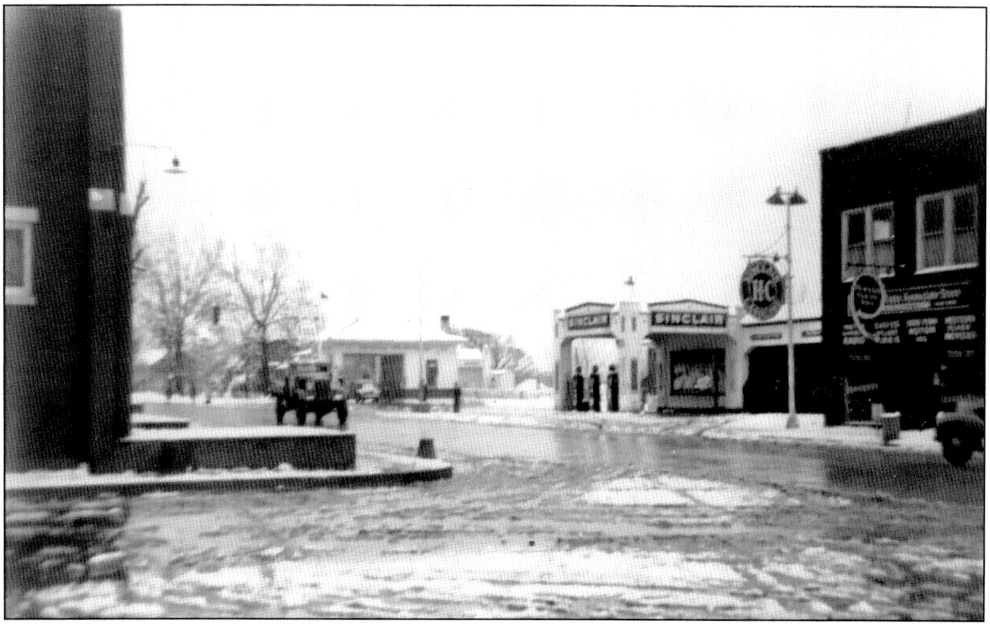

It does not matter about the weather or seasons; Forest City businesses remain in operation to serve the community. At the left of the photograph is the old Methodist church on the corner of East Main and North Broadway. Opposite the church is Western Auto, which has remained open in the same location more than 50 years. The Sinclair and ESSO Stations have long ceased to exist. (Courtesy of Geneva Drum Jenkins.)

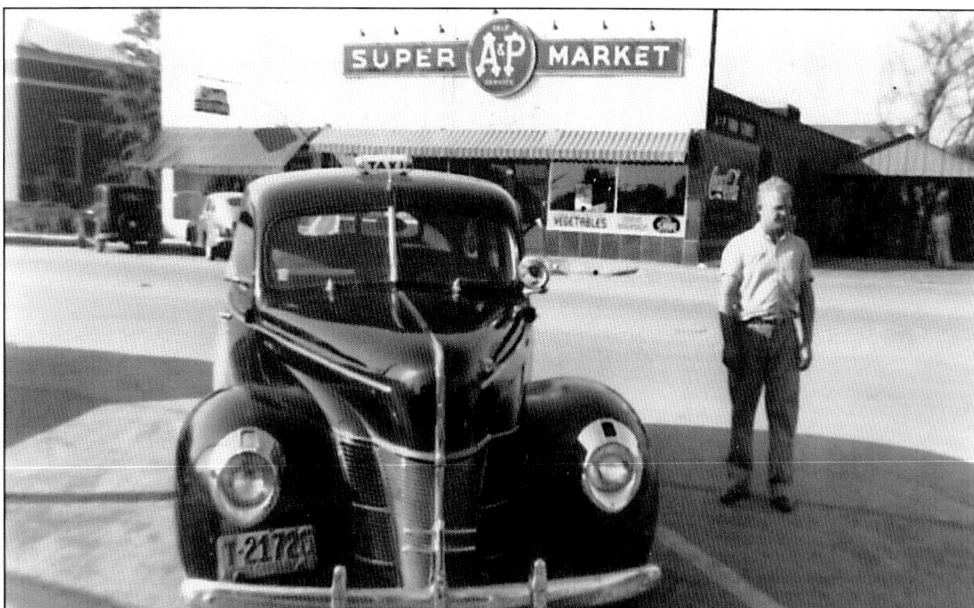

At the opposite end of the street from the Western Auto were the A&P and the Davis Sisters. Located beside the old brick post office on Main Street, these shops were a popular place for local women to purchase clothing and the family groceries at one stop. Parked on the street is a taxi bearing a 1943 North Carolina license plate. The cabbie is Red Hawkins. (Courtesy of Geneva Drum Jenkins.)

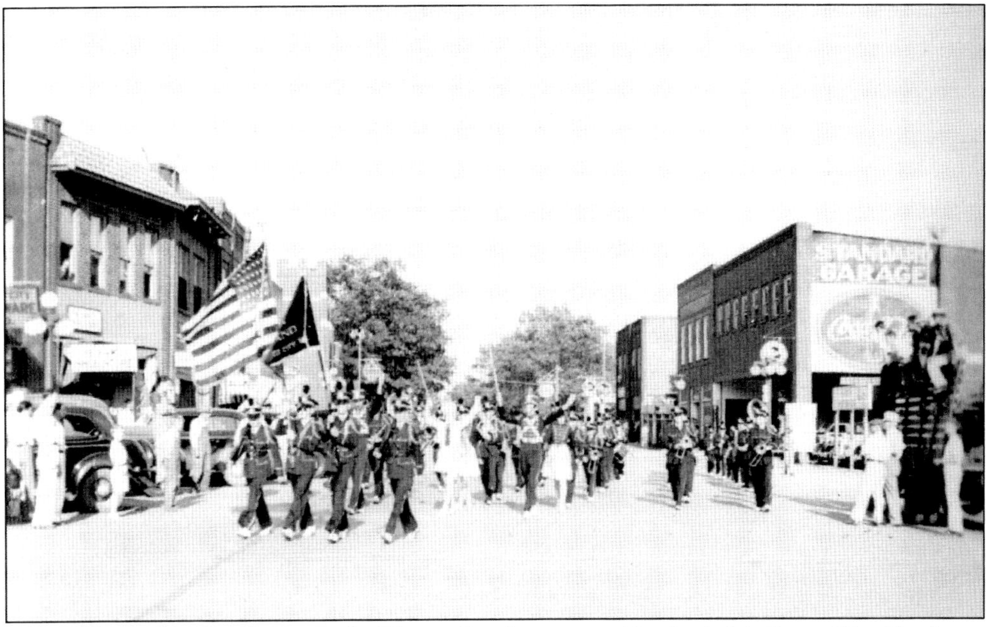

Images of parades provide a record of Forest City businesses. On the left is Forest City Hardware Company and Family Shoe Store. The Methodist church is at the corner of North Broadway and Main; across the street is the Standard Garage. Moving eastward, one sees the Western Auto, the Sinclair, and the ESSO. (Courtesy of Dr. W. L. Stallings and Betty Jo Carpenter.)

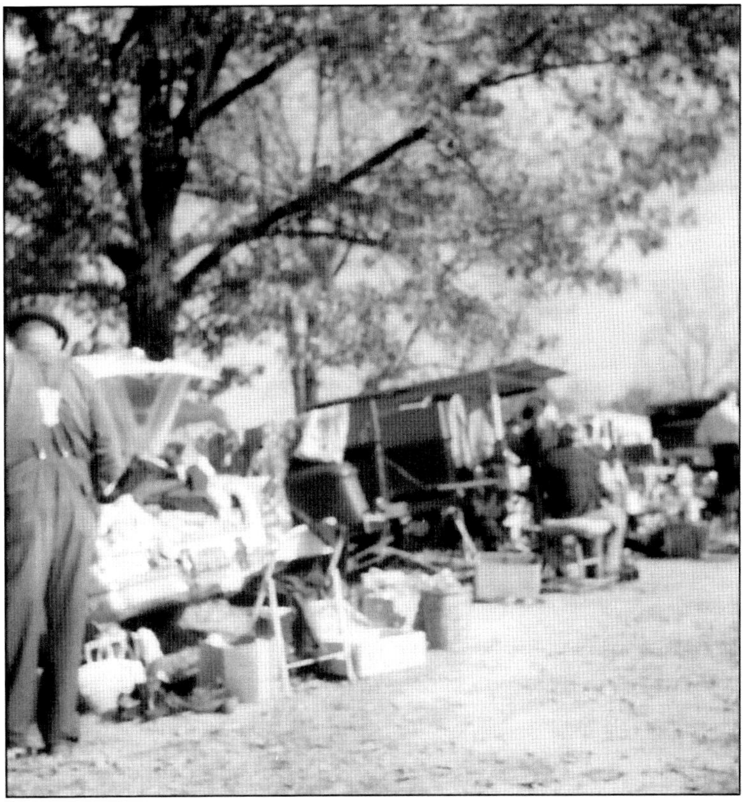

Enterprising citizens set up merchandise displays at the Bone Yards or Trade Lots. Locals can obtain everything from a pocketknife to a hunting dog. Edward Rollins Price offered this advice: "Mark it so you make a profit, but low enough that the buyer is happy. Don't mark it so high you have to take it back home." (Courtesy of Rebecca Jane Harrill Thompson and Jane Thompson Gurley.)

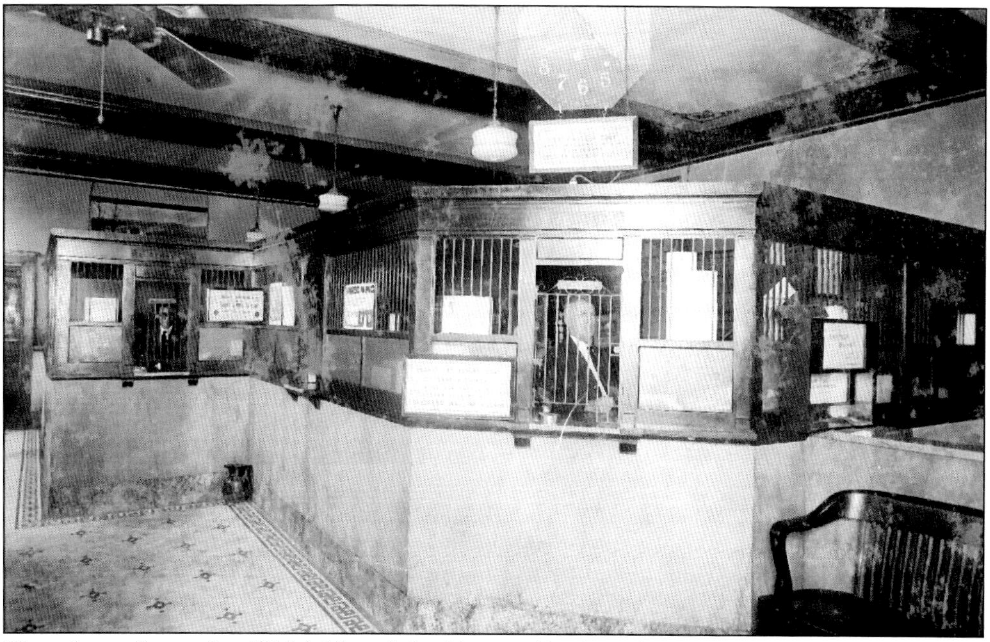

This photo shows the 1925 lobby of the Farmers Bank and Trust Company, a yellow brick building still in existence on Main Street. At the front teller window is Robert Biggerstaff, bank manager. At the rear window is J. Worth Morgan, a loan and discount teller at the time. (Courtesy of Bob Morgan.)

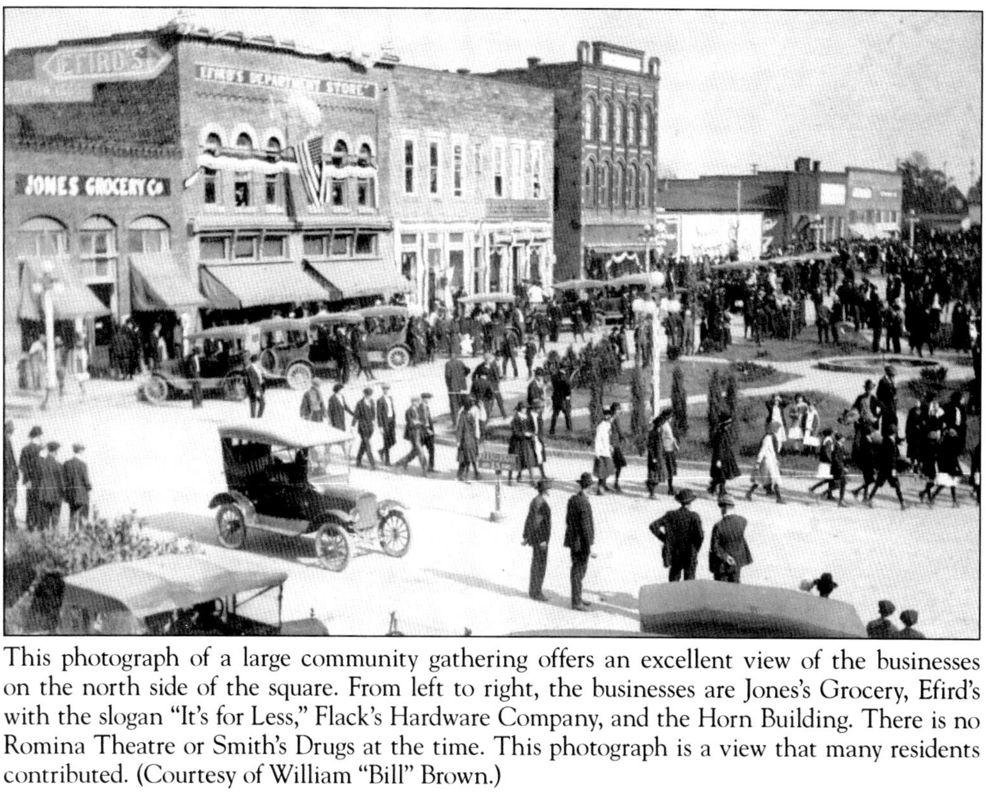

This photograph of a large community gathering offers an excellent view of the businesses on the north side of the square. From left to right, the businesses are Jones's Grocery, Efird's with the slogan "It's for Less," Flack's Hardware Company, and the Horn Building. There is no Romina Theatre or Smith's Drugs at the time. This photograph is a view that many residents contributed. (Courtesy of William "Bill" Brown.)

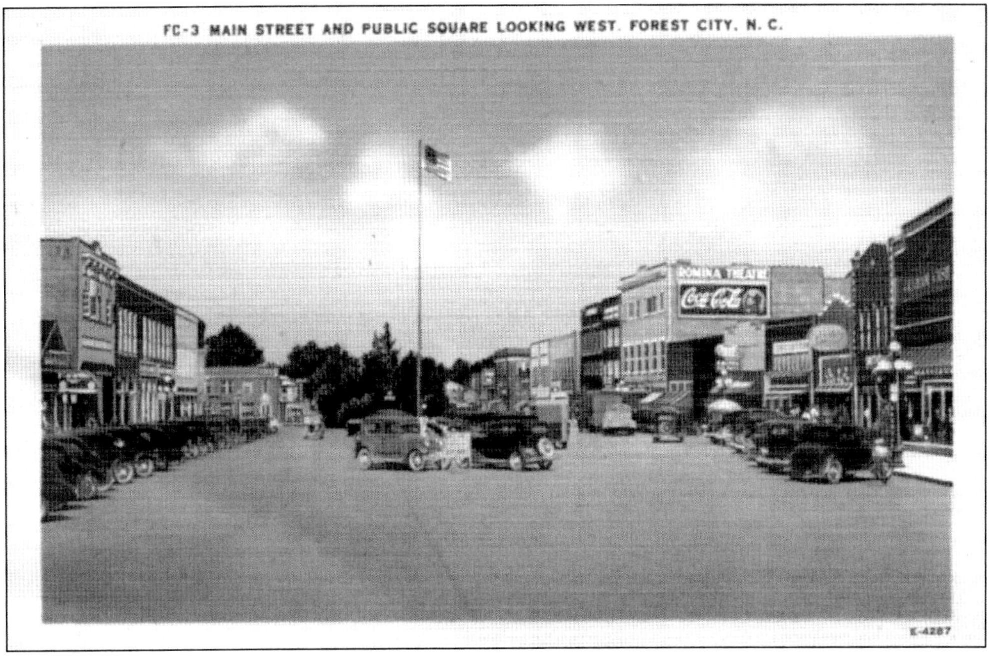

This postcard shows the historic downtown district of Forest City. This view (looking west) should bring back pleasant memories to many readers. (From the author's collection.)

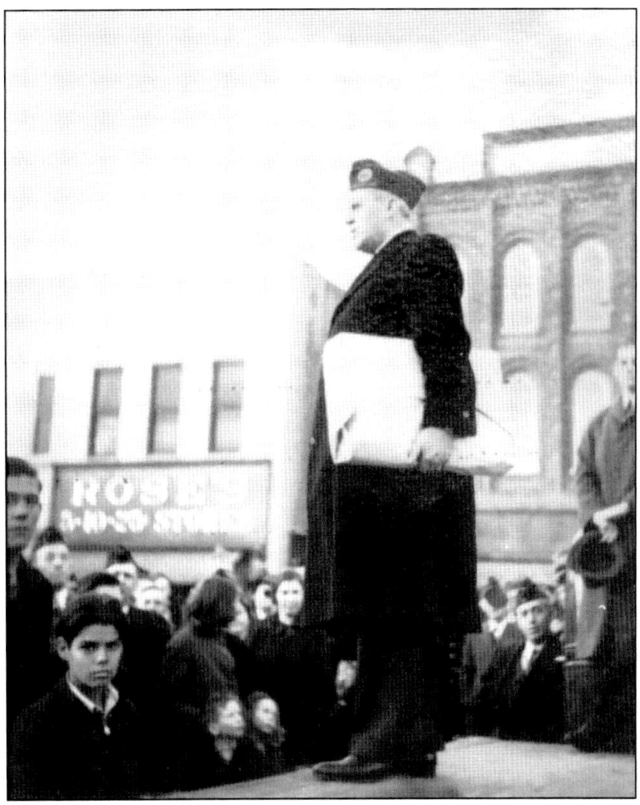

Behind the national commander of the American Legion, one can see on the north side of the street Rose's 5-10-25¢ Stores; Dr. Jack A. Wofford later operated his optometry office above the "Dime Store." Also visible is Charles Erwin (right) and the Horn Building with corbel brickwork, recessed panels, and arched windows. (Courtesy of Dr. W. L. Stallings and Betty Jo Carpenter.)

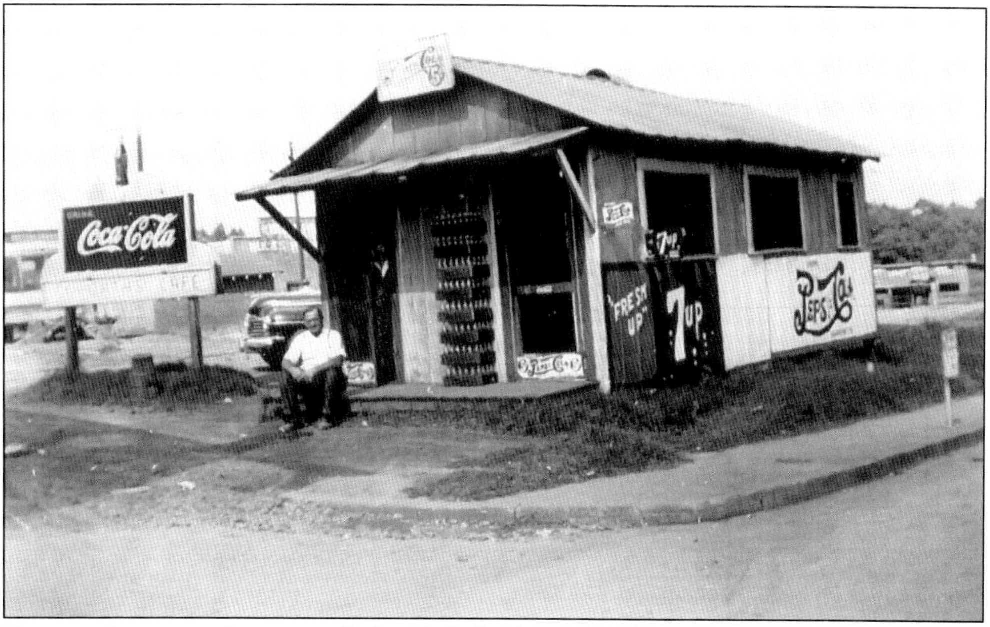

Two popular eating places were Goforth's Cafe (the tin building still in use in 2005 on Powell Street) and Ivey's Restaurant on Main. Charles Johnson Goforth is enjoying a brief respite from the kitchen; his sign advertises his soft drinks for 5¢. In the background is McDaniel's Livery with the slogan "Mules Bought and Sold." (Courtesy of Dr. W. L. Stallings and Betty Jo Carpenter.)

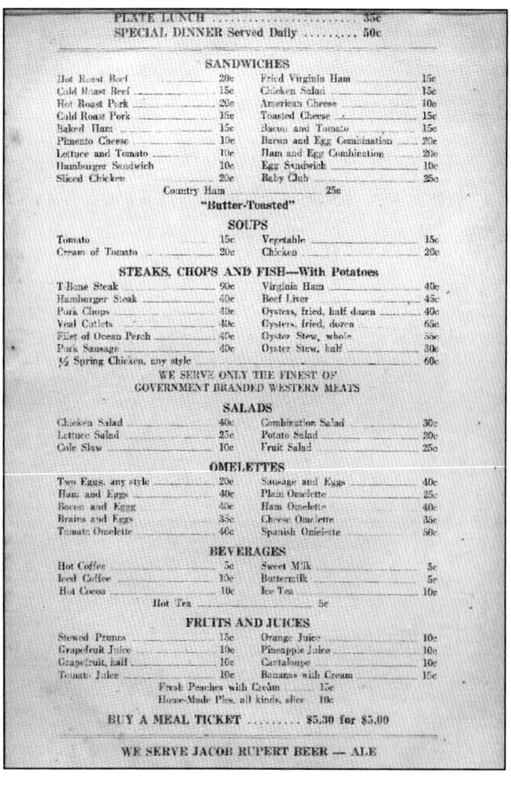

PLATE LUNCH 35c
SPECIAL DINNER Served Daily 50c

SANDWICHES

Hot Roast Beef	20c	Fried Virginia Ham	15c
Cold Roast Beef	15c	Chicken Salad	15c
Hot Roast Pork	20c	American Cheese	10c
Cold Roast Pork	15c	Toasted Cheese	15c
Baked Ham	15c	Bacon and Tomato	15c
Pimento Cheese	10c	Bacon and Egg Combination	20c
Lettuce and Tomato	10c	Ham and Egg Combination	20c
Hamburger Sandwich	10c	Egg Sandwich	10c
Sliced Chicken	20c	Baby Club	25c

Country Ham ______ 25c
"Butter-Toasted"

SOUPS

Tomato	15c	Vegetable	15c
Cream of Tomato	20c	Chicken	20c

STEAKS, CHOPS AND FISH—With Potatoes

T-Bone Steak	90c	Virginia Ham	40c
Hamburger Steak	40c	Beef Liver	45c
Pork Chops	40c	Oysters, fried, half dozen	40c
Veal Cutlets	40c	Oysters, fried, dozen	65c
Filet of Ocean Perch	40c	Oyster Stew, whole	55c
Pork Sausage	40c	Oyster Stew, half	30c

½ Spring Chicken, any style ______ 60c

WE SERVE ONLY THE FINEST OF
GOVERNMENT BRANDED WESTERN MEATS

SALADS

Chicken Salad	40c	Combination Salad	30c
Lettuce Salad	25c	Potato Salad	20c
Cole Slaw	10c	Fruit Salad	25c

OMELETTES

Two Eggs, any style	20c	Sausage and Eggs	40c
Ham and Eggs	40c	Plain Omelette	25c
Bacon and Eggs	40c	Ham Omelette	40c
Brains and Eggs	35c	Cheese Omelette	35c
Tomato Omelette	40c	Spanish Omelette	50c

BEVERAGES

Hot Coffee	5c	Sweet Milk	5c
Iced Coffee	10c	Buttermilk	5c
Hot Cocoa	10c	Ice Tea	10c

Hot Tea ______ 5c

FRUITS AND JUICES

Stewed Prunes	15c	Orange Juice	10c
Grapefruit Juice	10c	Pineapple Juice	10c
Grapefruit, half	10c	Cantaloupe	10c
Tomato Juice	10c	Bananas with Cream	15c

Fresh Peaches with Cream ______ 15c
Home-Made Pies, all kinds, slice 10c

BUY A MEAL TICKET .... $5.30 for $5.00

WE SERVE JACOB RUPERT BEER — ALE

Many diners frequented Ivey's Restaurant on the south side of the square. Lyles Mason sometimes helped—doing whatever was needed—in the restaurant. This menu gives a choice of coffee, milk, tea, buttermilk (5¢), or Jacob Rupert Beer/Ale. The 1948–1949 beer license indicates the county was "wet" at the time. Over the restaurant was Gilbert's Studio, later purchased by Robert M. Watkins. (Courtesy of Geneva Drum Jenkins.)

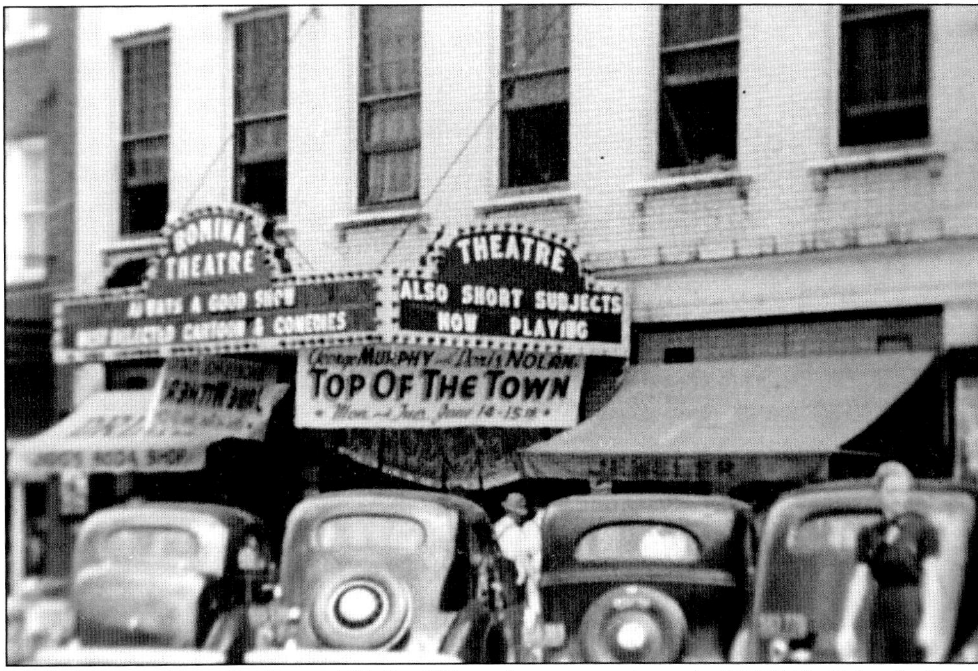

Cliffside native Reno Bailey and Phillip White (longtime principal of Cliffside School) shared this view of the Romina Theatre on the Web site http://RememberCliffside.com/. The marquee advertises the movie *Top of the Town* with the ever-popular Short Subjects, which often included newsreels during World War II. (Courtesy of Reno Bailey and Phillip White.)

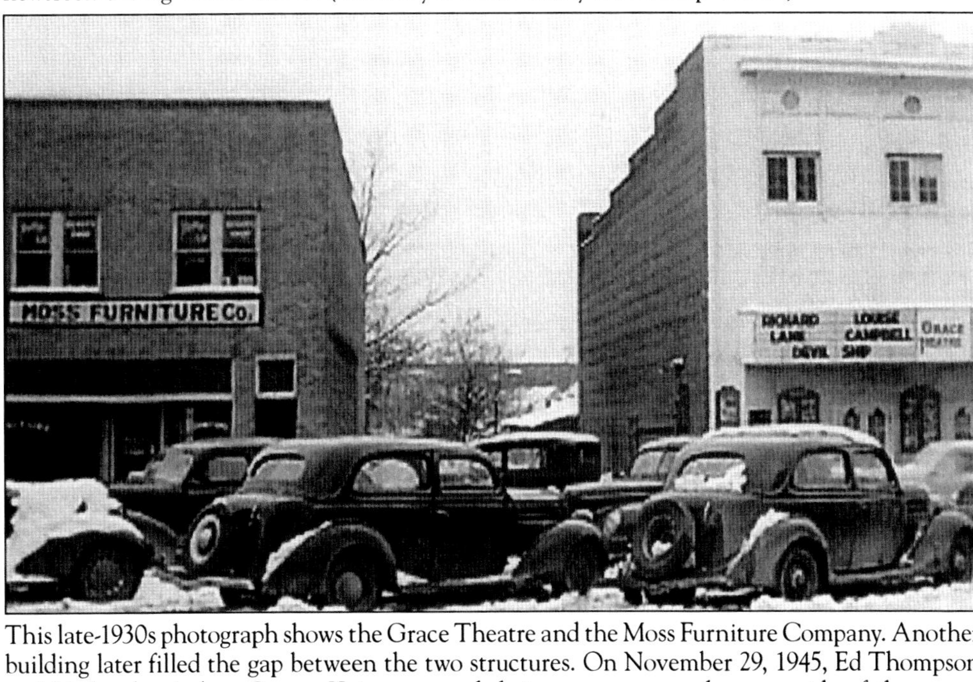

This late-1930s photograph shows the Grace Theatre and the Moss Furniture Company. Another building later filled the gap between the two structures. On November 29, 1945, Ed Thompson and his brother-in-law, Grover Kaiser, opened their restaurant on the same side of the street; they named the establishment after their sons: Ron and Eddy. Ron and Eddy's operated until February 11, 2003. (Courtesy of Nell Jenkins Moss.)

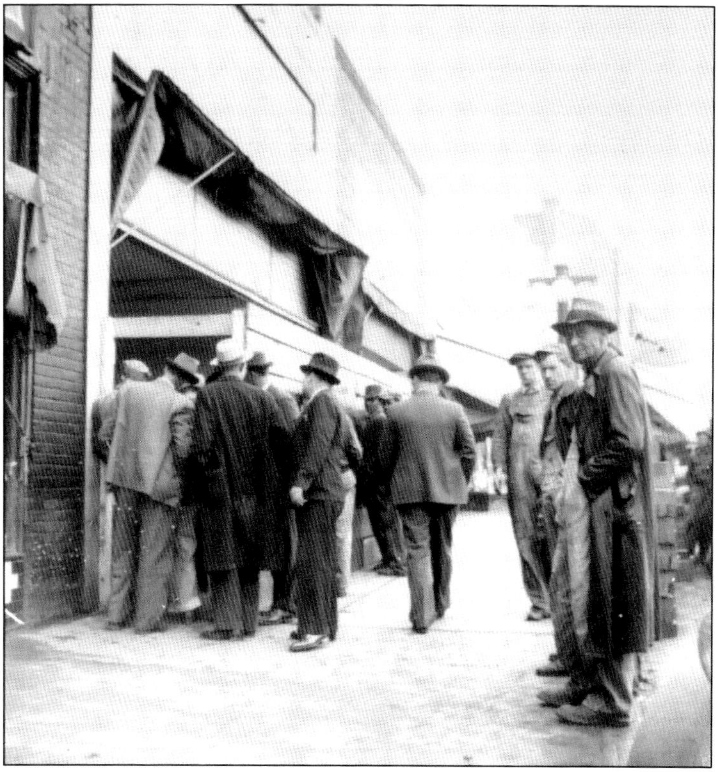

In 1939–1940, bystanders observe and supervise construction of Smith's Drug Store. Smith's pharmacists/managers/owners have included Lloyd Shuford, Grady Shuford (Lloyd's son), and Ernest Holt. Pharmacist Milton Higdon, husband of Helen Dobbins, came to Smith's in 1955 and worked there for more than 40 years. Hugh Moore is a professional pharmacist now at Smith's. John Higgins has served in several capacities—owner, manager, and pharmacist—since 1991. (Courtesy of Dr. W. L. Stallings and Betty Jo Carpenter.)

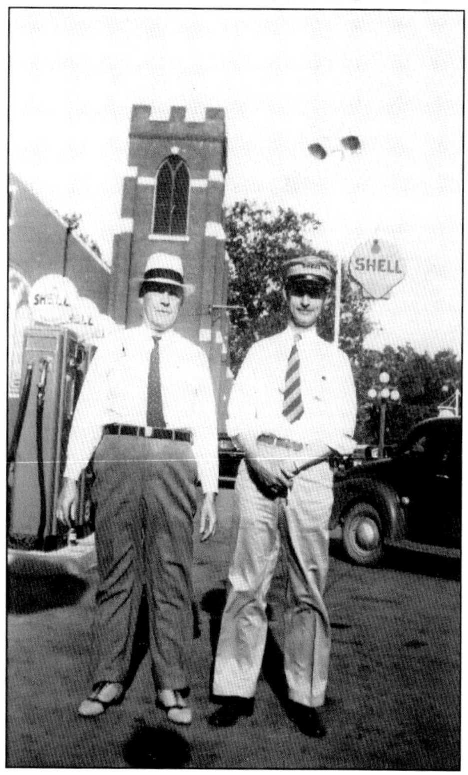

On East Main was the Shell Service Station beside the Methodist church. Here is B. B. Doggett (left), the first automobile dealer in Forest City. Doggett's dealership opened in 1917, and he sold Ford T Models. By 1922, he was offering Fords for $319 F.O.B. (free on board). Wearing the Shell Service cap is Clarence Lloyd Morris Sr., father of Martha Grace Morris Estes. (Courtesy of Martha Grace Morris Estes.)

Faithful Ford customers Lola Burns Hamrick and her brother Robert Ewart Burns pose beside their T Model. The two-seater convertible was a means of recreation and transportation. Lola wears a cloche hat, and Ewart wears a cloth driving cap. (Courtesy of Lucille Hamrick Carpenter, daughter of Lola Burns Hamrick.)

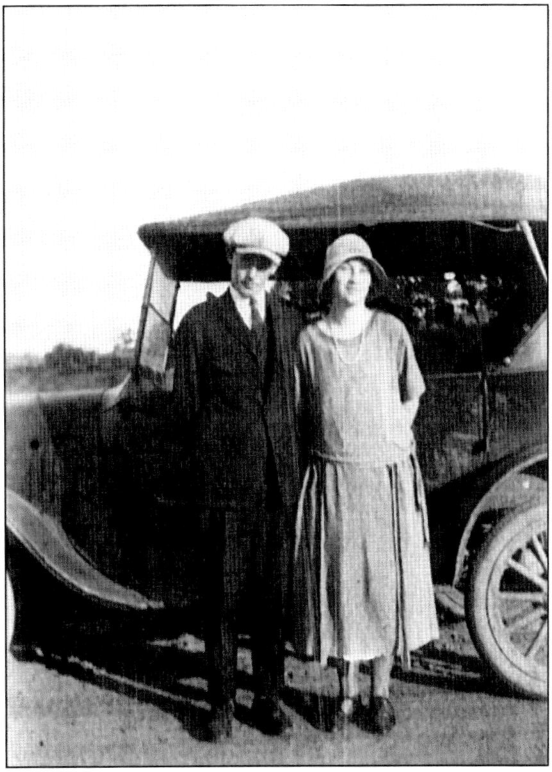

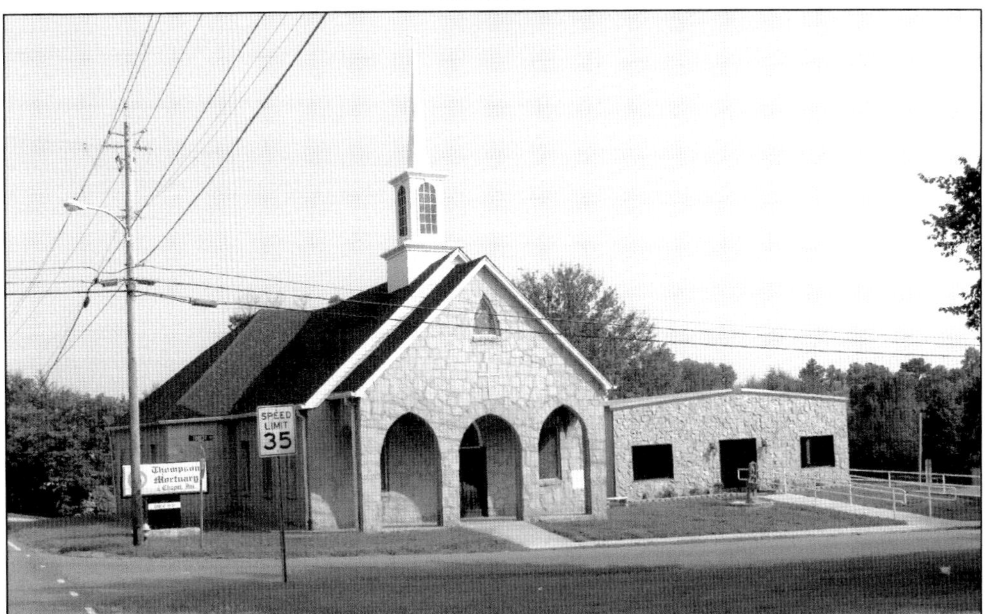

Thompson Mortuary and Chapel, Inc. (at the corner of Hardin Road and Forest Street) has been in service since 1935. The late Thomas C. Thompson and his wife, Mary Fredrick Thompson, took over the management for many years. The couple also helped in the management of Thompson's Rest Home, the first rest home for African Americans in the county. (Courtesy of James M. Walker.)

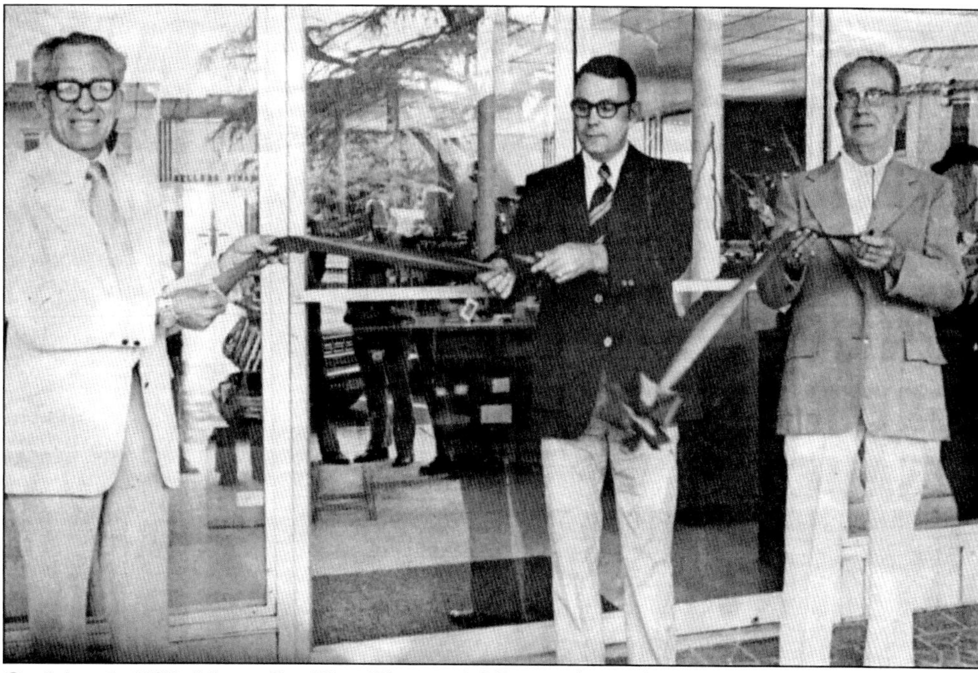

On May 4, 1977, Mayor Pro Tem Blanton McBrayer (center) cut the ribbon for the official opening of Price's Inc., Forest City's newest business at Main and Cherry Mountain. At left is Falls W. Price, World War II veteran of the European Theater. At right is former Seaboard Air Line Railway engineer Edward R. Price, who transported many troops during the war. (Courtesy of *This Week/Courier-Sun* and Carolyn Grindstaff Barbee.)

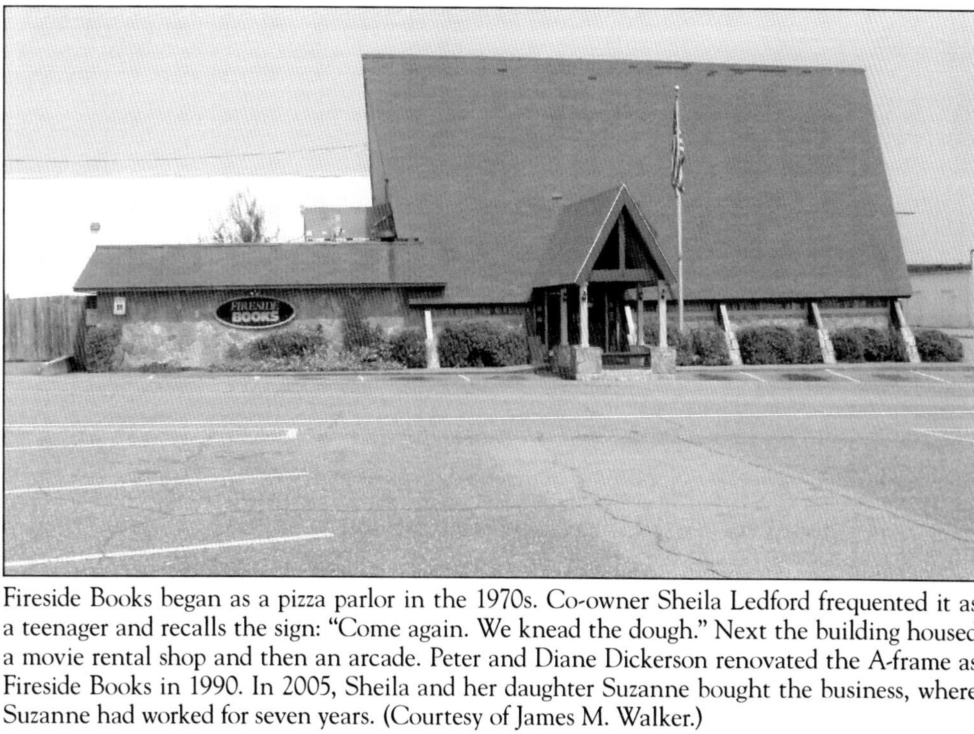

Fireside Books began as a pizza parlor in the 1970s. Co-owner Sheila Ledford frequented it as a teenager and recalls the sign: "Come again. We knead the dough." Next the building housed a movie rental shop and then an arcade. Peter and Diane Dickerson renovated the A-frame as Fireside Books in 1990. In 2005, Sheila and her daughter Suzanne bought the business, where Suzanne had worked for seven years. (Courtesy of James M. Walker.)

Many types of businesses have flourished in Forest City. There were, for instance, at least three dairies in the city. The milkman (or woman) delivered to your front door milk fresh from the dairy. These milk bottles from the W. S. Bridges Dairy illustrate both the quart- and pint-sized glass containers. The bottles are from the collection of Daniel and Beth King. (Courtesy of James M. Walker.)

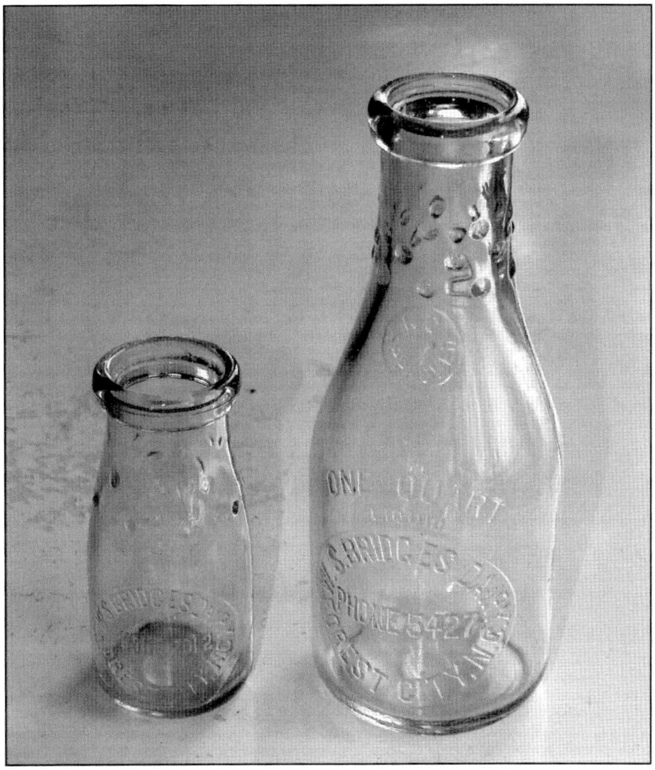

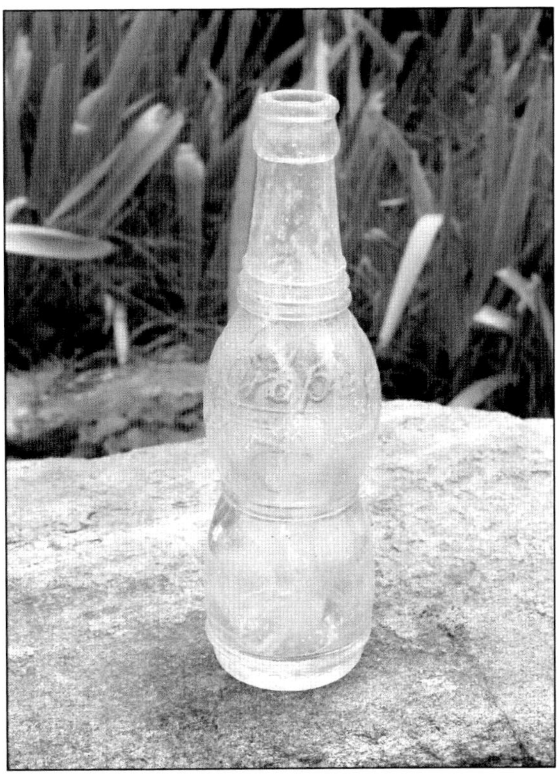

The Coca-Cola Bottling Company in Forest City dates from 1908. The building still stands on Depot Street. Other bottling companies also flourished in Forest City. The second bottler to open (in 1921) was the Nu-Grape Bottling Company at Beaver and Florence. Pepsi-Cola opened its bottling company on Mill Street beside the Wesleyan Church. The Nu-Grape bottle is from the collection of Daniel and Beth King. (Courtesy of James M. Walker.)

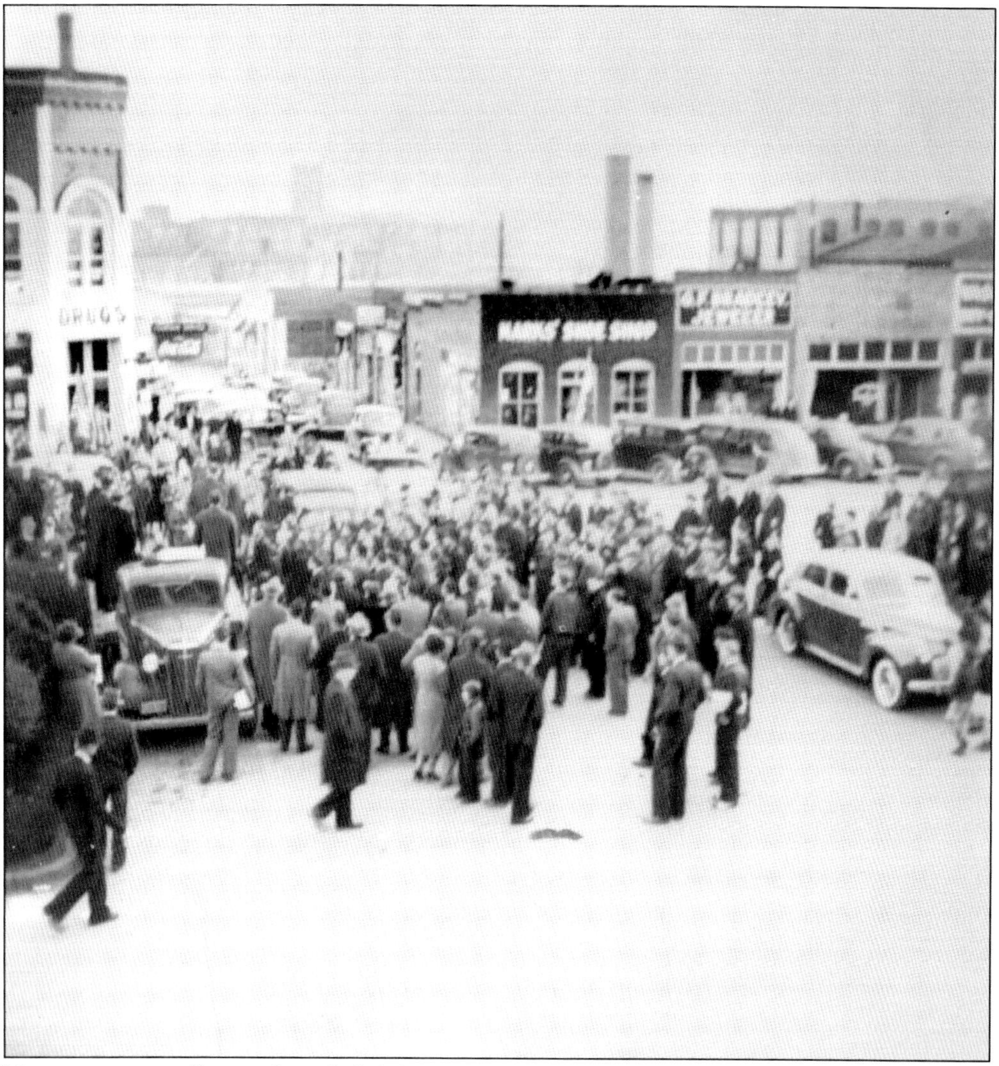

Visitors come to Forest City. Bob Morgan saw Pres. Franklin D. Roosevelt on September, 10, 1936, from a pecan tree near Carolina and East Main. The national commander of the American Legion in 1939 visited also. A grocery sign—possibly for Watkins Grocery—extends from the corner of the drug store. Florence Mills, Marks' Shoe Shop, and C. F. Bradley Jewelers are evident. (Courtesy of Dr. W. L. Stallings and Betty Jo Carpenter.)

Nine

Florence Mills
Manufacturing for the World

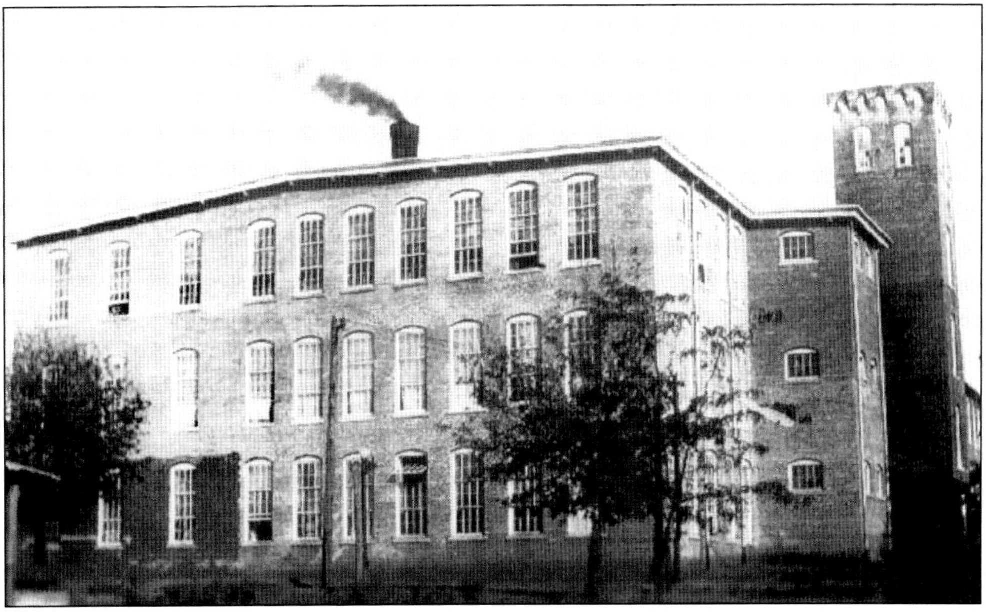

Textiles were vital to the development and life of Forest City. In 1885, the Forest City Cotton Mill, located on Depot Street, began to manufacture yarn. Sometime later, the mill closed. Raleigh Rutherford Haynes—with his associates—purchased the Forest City Cotton Mills in 1892, according to the Register of Deeds. The same year, they formed the corporation of the Florence Mills to manufacture cotton, wool, and flax thread and cloth in Forest City. After demolishing the old mill, construction of a new plant began. In 1897, the new Depot Street facility opened with its 12,0000 spinning spindles, 200 Draper looms, and 200 Lowell looms. Raleigh Rutherford Haynes named the plant "Florence" after his daughter Florence Haynes (Jenkins). (Mrs. Grover C. Haynes Sr., *Raleigh Rutherford Haynes*, Cliffside, North Carolina, 14ff)

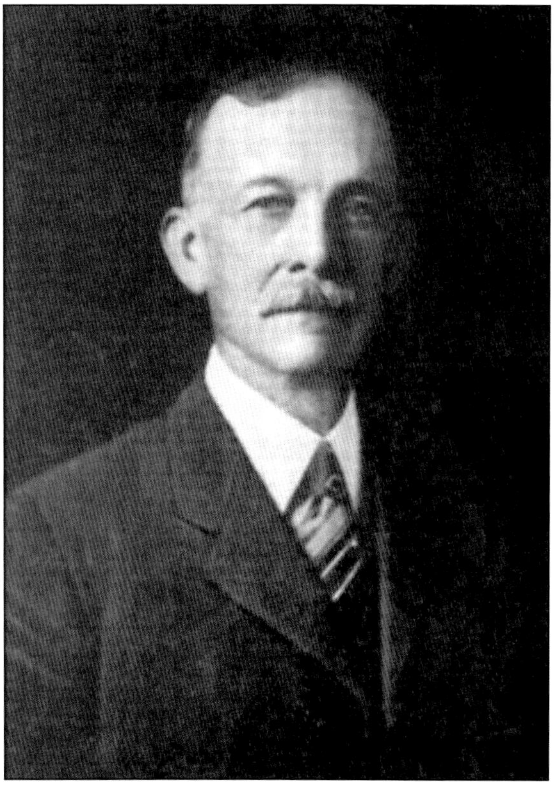

Raleigh Rutherford Haynes (1851–1917) was oldest of the eight children of Charles H. and Sarah Walker Haynes. C. H. Haynes died when Raleigh was eight. Sarah "trained her children with wisdom and foresight . . . [and] counseled him, 'never to go security, never act as guardian, nor hold office' " (Griffin, 596–597). Raleigh married Amanda Loretta Carpenter; they had eight children before her 1890 death. (Courtesy of Hollis Owens Jr.)

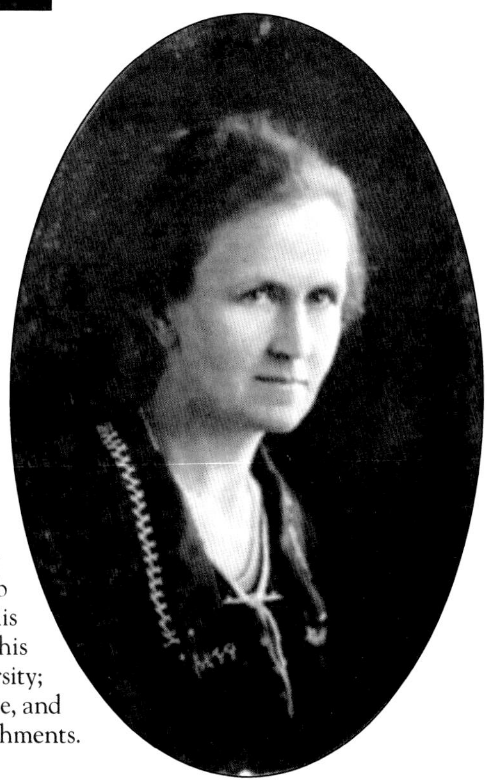

Raleigh Rutherford Haynes named the new Forest City thread and cloth mill for his daughter Florence, pictured here. Florence married Zeb Jenkins; their daughter Jessie married Hollis Owens Sr. Jessie's son Hollis Owens Jr. received his education at Wofford College and Duke University; he became a district judge, a Superior Court judge, and a state representative, among other accomplishments. (Courtesy of Hollis Owens Jr.)

Florence Mills furnished a livelihood to generations of families in the area. Helping in the construction of the original Florence Mills was Columbus Millard ("Bud") Jones. Here he poses with his wife, Fanny Burgin Jones, and son, Paul Tim Jones Sr. (The name of the family dog is unknown.) Paul Tim Jones Sr. worked for 53 years in Florence Mills. (Courtesy of Paul Tim Jones Jr.)

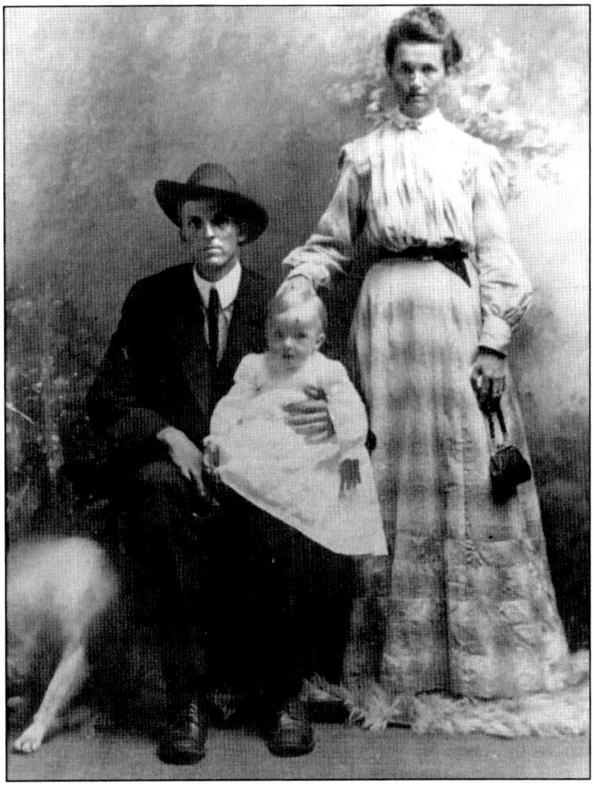

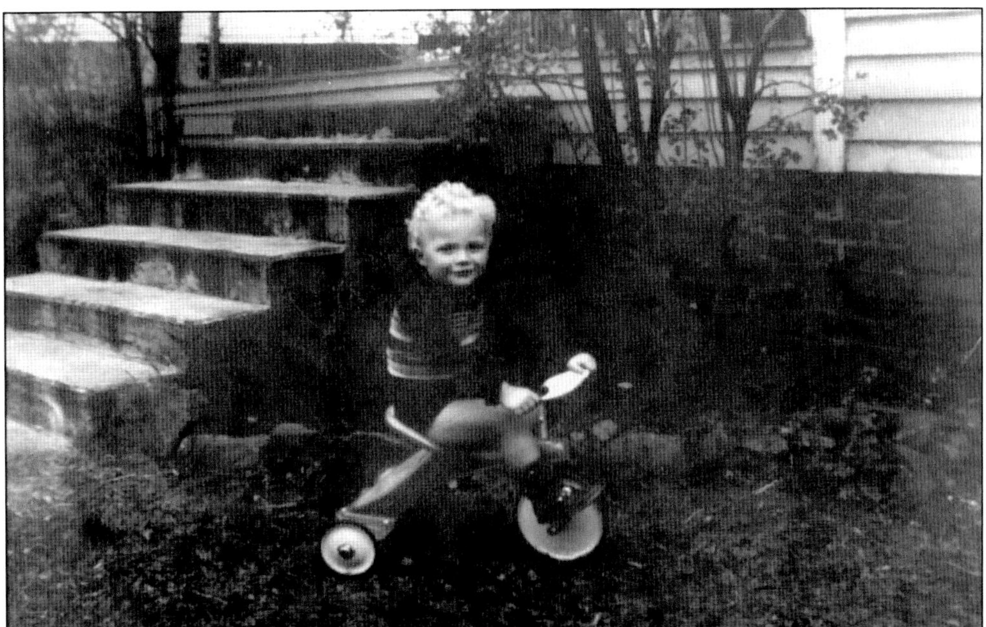

On his red tricycle is Paul Tim Jones Jr.; he grew up in the Florence Mills Village. In the background is his home, typical of most homes "on the hill." (Page 74 has more on the family and their residence.) Paul Tim's Aunt Ruth was at one time the oldest living retiree of Florence Mills; she began work there at the age of 14. (Courtesy of Paul Tim Jones Jr.)

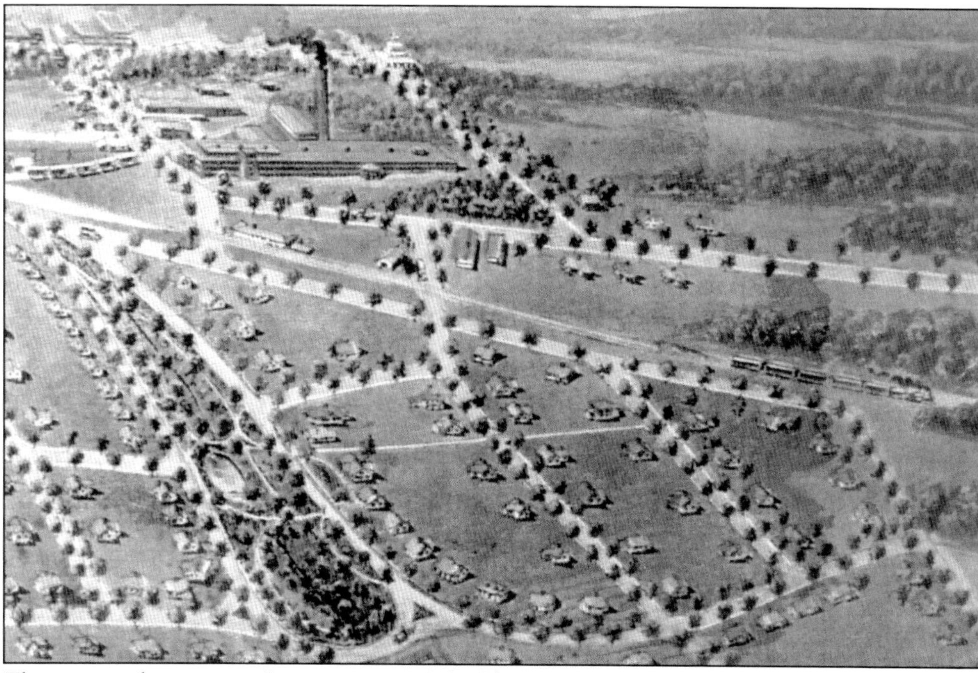

This postcard is an artist's conception of the Florence Mills Village. Visible are the Southern Railway Depot and tracks, the layout of the village, and the Florence Mills plant. The roofline of the Mabry Hotel appears in the distance. (Courtesy of Paul Tim Jones Jr.)

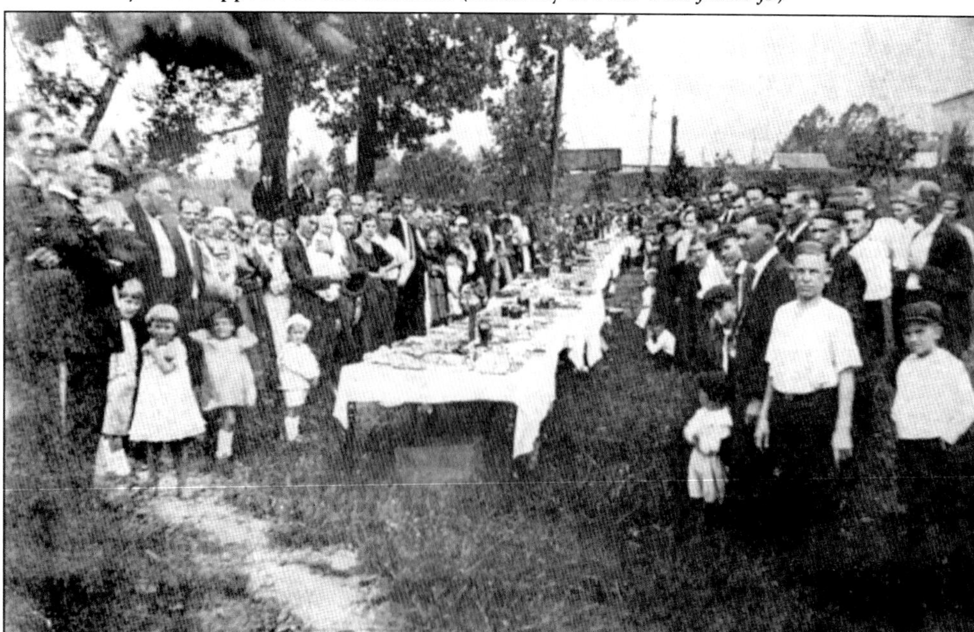

Friendship among workers and their families was a benefit of village life. Here more than 100 share some leisure time; the site of the social is visible at the upper left of the postcard above. Noteworthy is that Florence workers put 10 percent of their wages in war bonds to benefit World War II troops; they received the Minute Man flag because of their participation (Griffin, 78–86). (Courtesy of Mary Lee Curtis.)

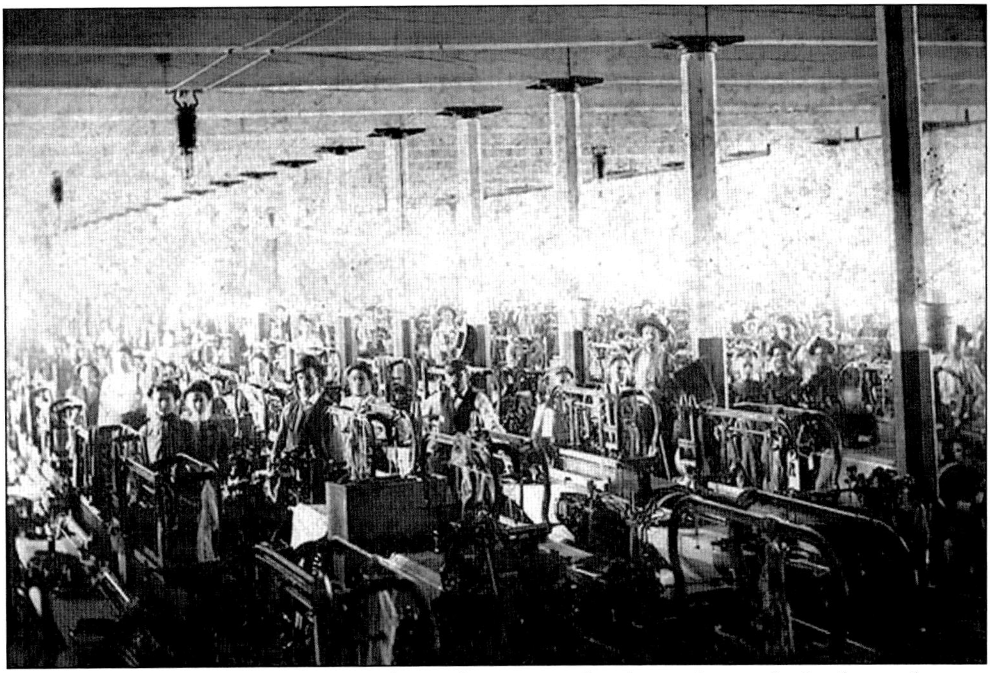

An ever-present part of life for textile employees was the day-to-day work. In this early view inside the mill in Forest City, one can see a variety of workers: men, women, and teenagers. (Courtesy of Danielle Withrow.)

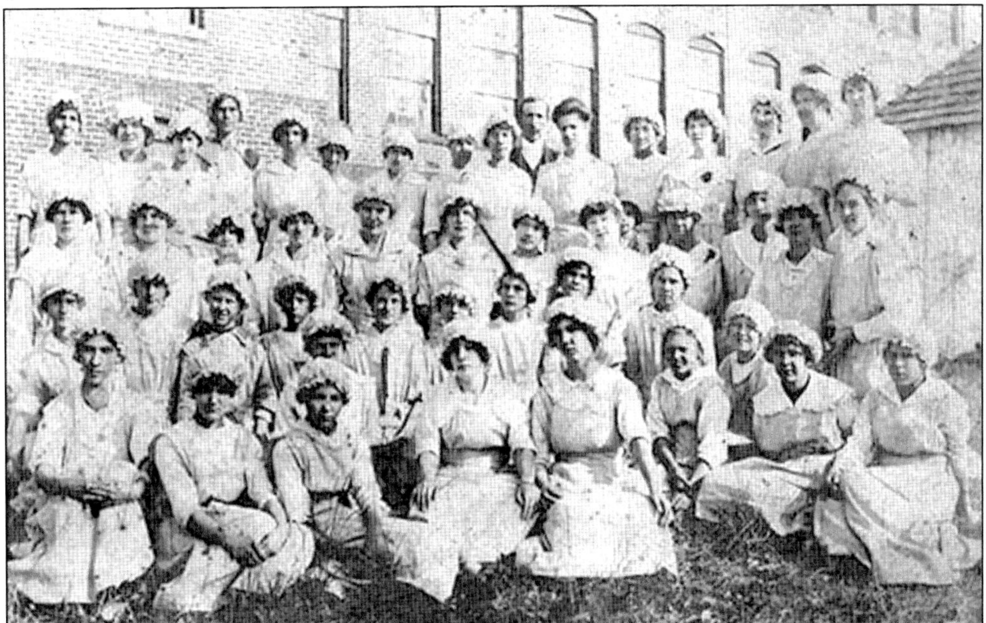

These Florence Mills women workers take a break for a photo shoot. The "mob" hats kept hair protected from lint and dust, prevented hair from becoming entangled in the equipment, and were stylish. (Courtesy of Danielle Withrow.) Later, Emily Post would say, "It is impossible for a hatless woman to be chic." These young women recognized this need long before Emily Post. http://www.themorningnews.org/archives/editorial/womens_fashion_part_iii_hats.php.

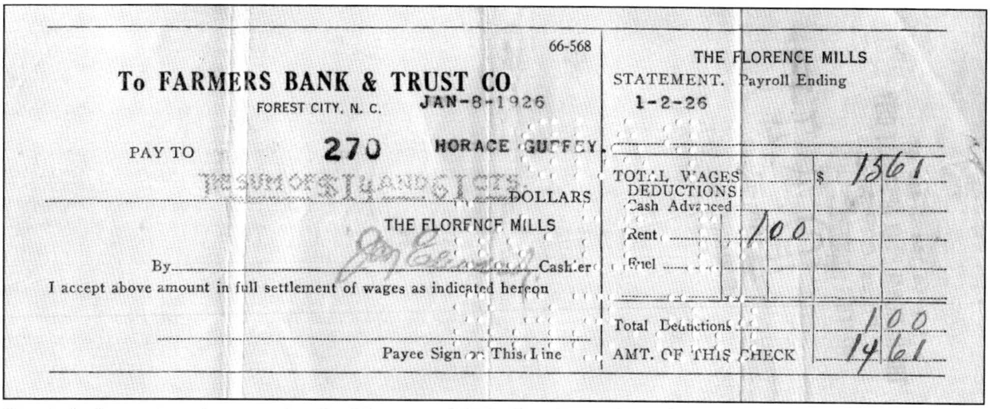

66-568

To FARMERS BANK & TRUST CO

FOREST CITY, N. C. JAN-8-1926

PAY TO 270 HORACE GUFFEY

THE SUM OF $14 AND 61 CTS DOLLARS

THE FLORENCE MILLS

By ________ Cashier

I accept above amount in full settlement of wages as indicated hereon

Payee Sign on This Line

THE FLORENCE MILLS

STATEMENT. Payroll Ending 1-2-26

TOTAL WAGES	$	15 61
DEDUCTIONS Cash Advanced		
Rent	1 00	
Fuel		
Total Deductions		1 00
AMT. OF THIS CHECK		14 61

Copied above is a deposit slip for Florence Mills Employee Number 270, Horace Guffey. Dated January 8, 1926, the slip shows Guffey received $15.61 for his labor. His rent of $1 was deducted from his salary. His wages from the mills went into the Farmers Bank and Trust Company. (Courtesy of Danielle Withrow.)

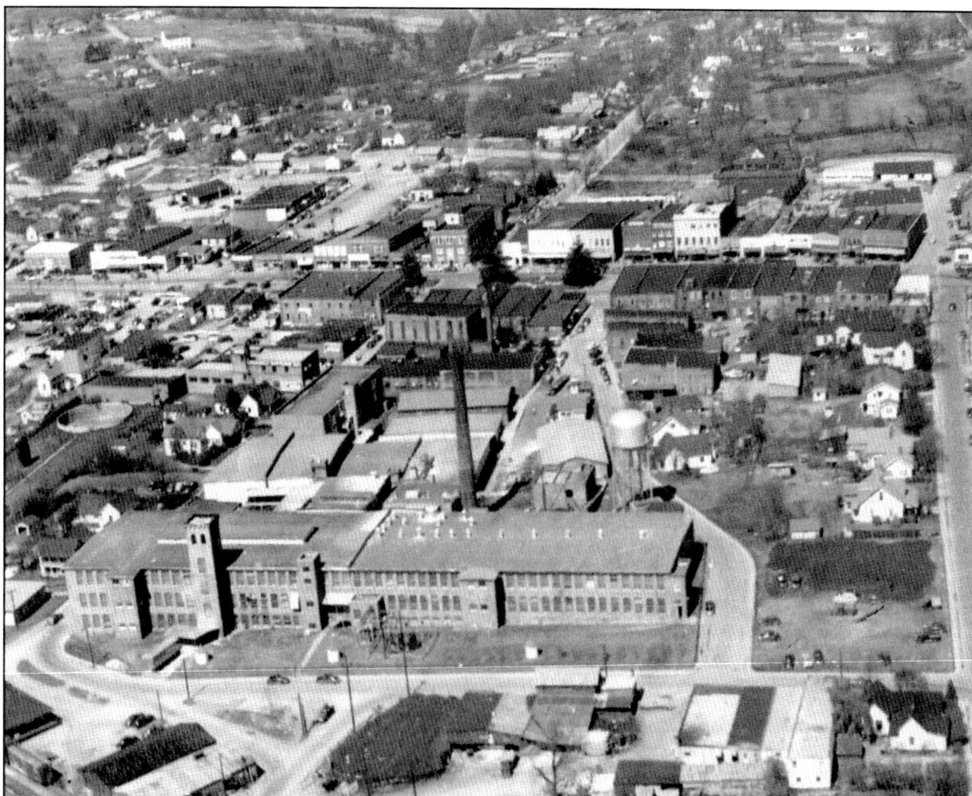

This aerial view of Florence Mills—bounded by Mill Street (east), Depot Street (south and west), and Main Street (north)—shows the smokestack, erected in 1897. Standing 135 feet tall and 16 feet in diameter at its base, it was only 9 feet at the top. Jim Ponder and L. C. and Pose Hardin laid the stack's bricks. Forest City is revitalizing this area and the town. (Courtesy of Danielle Withrow.)

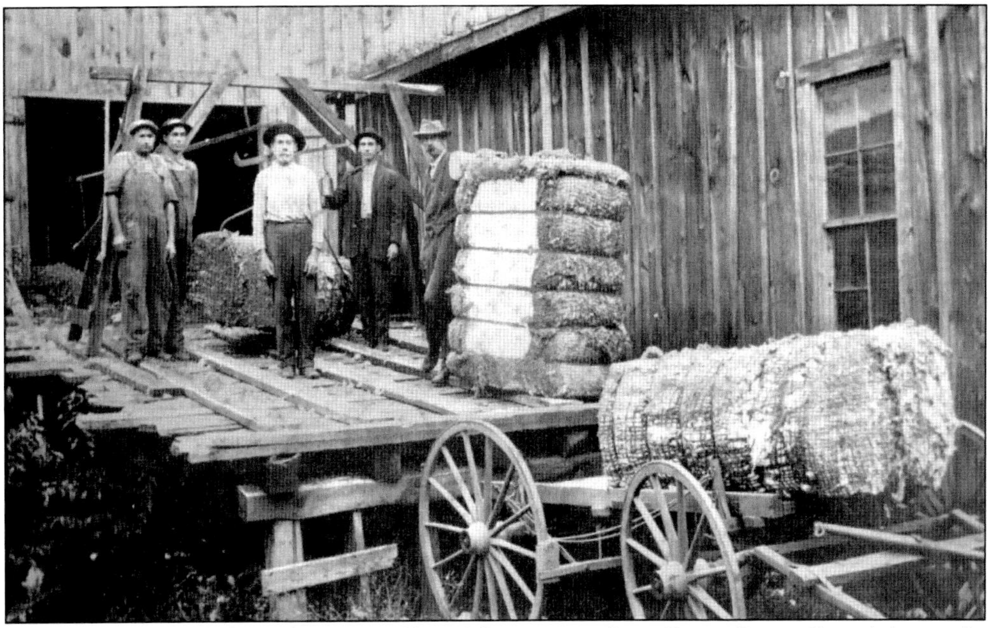

This 1913 gin stood where the County Farm Museum stands on Depot Street. From left to right are unidentified, J. W. Davis, J. W. McDaniel, Robert K. Hollifield, and F. T. Davis. J. W. Davis and son Tom began J. W. Davis Company, Inc. in 1946 with plumbing, heating, building, and electrical service specialties. J. W.'s son, Jack, later joined the firm; son Toliver (local attorney and federal judge) had an office here. (Courtesy of Robert M. Watkins.)

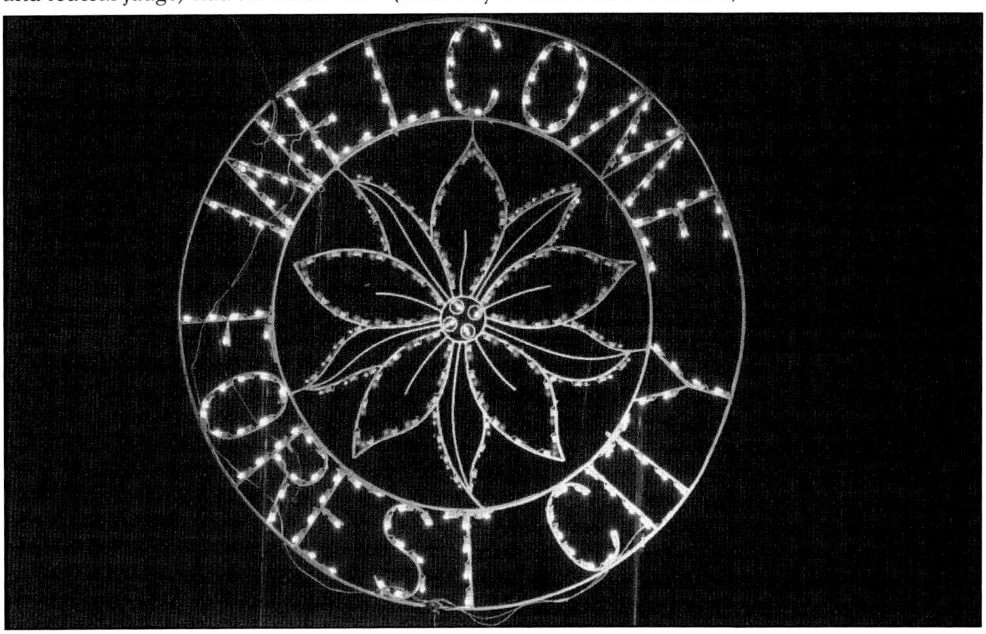

Voted in 1999 as "the most beautiful town in Western North Carolina," the town and its mayor (James W. Gibson in 2005) issued an invitation and a challenge: "come work and grow with us as we strive to take on the challenges of the 21st century, and at the same time retain the simple pleasures and family-friendly atmosphere of small town life" (http://www.TownofForestCity.com/home.html).

INDEX